PC LEARNING LABS TEACHES MICROSOFT WORD FOR WINDOWS 95

PC LEARNING LABS
TEACHES WORD
FOR WINDOWS 95

By Robert Nichols Kulik for

Ziff-Davis Press
Emeryville, California

Curriculum Development	Logical Operations
Copy Editor	Jan Jue
Technical Reviewer	Mark Hall
Project Coordinators	Barbara Dahl and Ami Knox
Proofreaders	Vanessa Miller and Jeff Barash
Production Coordinator, Logical Operations	Gerard D'amico
Cover Illustration	Regan Honda
Cover Design	Regan Honda
Book Design	Laura Lamar/MAX, San Francisco
Screen Graphics Editor	M.D. Barrera
Word Processing	Howard Blechman
Page Layout	M.D. Barrera
Indexer	Valerie Robbins

Ziff-Davis Press, ZD Press, PC Learning Labs, and PC Learning Labs Teaches are licensed to Macmillan Computer Publishing USA by Ziff-Davis Publishing Company, New York, New York.

Ziff-Davis Press imprint books are produced on a Macintosh computer system with the following applications: FrameMaker®, Microsoft® Word, QuarkXPress®, Adobe Illustrator®, Adobe Photoshop®, Adobe Streamline™, MacLink®Plus, Aldus® FreeHand™, Collage Plus™.

If you have comments or questions or would like to receive a free catalog, call or write:
Macmillan Computer Publishing USA
Ziff-Davis Press Line of Books
5903 Christie Avenue
Emeryville, CA 94608
1-800-688-0448

ISBN 1-56276-319-9

Manufactured in the United States of America
10 9 8 7 6 5 4 3 2 1

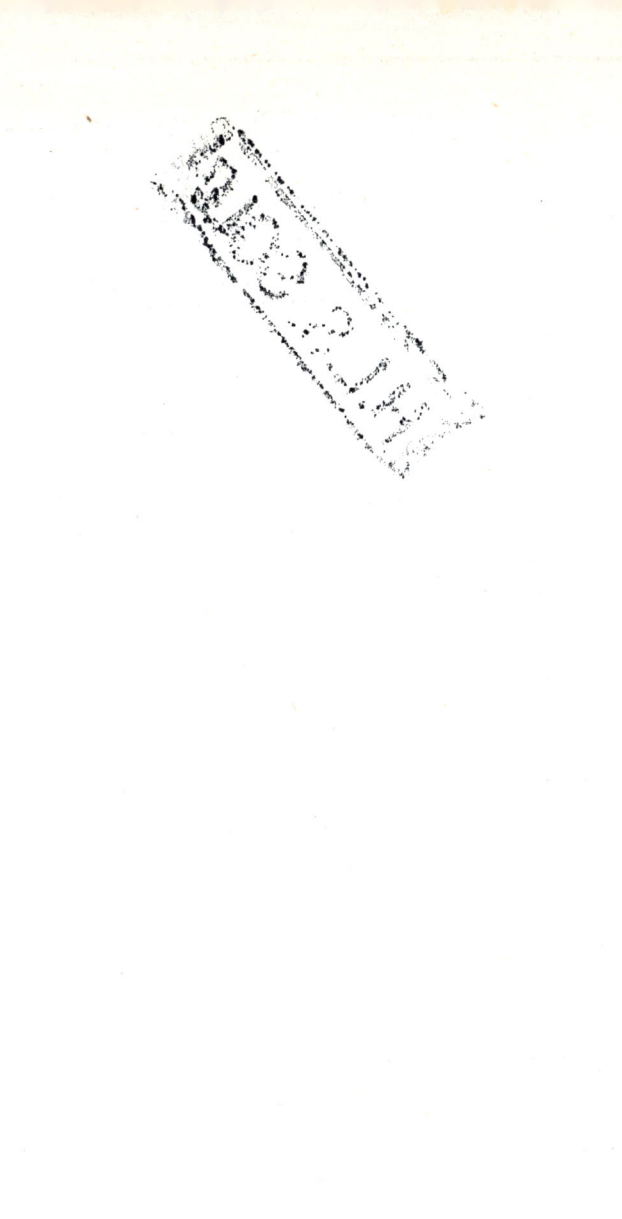

CONTENTS AT A GLANCE

TABLE OF CONTENTS

INTRODUCTION

Welcome to *PC Learning Labs Teaches Microsoft Word for Windows 95*, a hands-on instruction book that will help you attain a high level of Word for Windows fluency in the shortest time possible. And congratulations on choosing Word 7.0 for Windows 95, a powerful and feature-packed program that will greatly enhance your creation and editing of written documents.

We at PC Learning Labs believe this book to be a unique and welcome addition to the ranks of "how to" computer publications. Our instructional approach stems directly from over a decade of successful teaching in a hands-on classroom environment. Throughout the book, we mix theory with practice by presenting new techniques and then applying them in hands-on activities. These activities use specially prepared, sample Word for Windows 95 files, which are stored on the enclosed Data Disk.

Unlike a class, this book allows you to proceed at your own pace. And we'll be right there to guide you along every step of the way, providing landmarks to help you chart your progress and hold to a steady course.

When you're done working your way through this book, you'll have a solid foundation of skills in:

- Creating, editing, printing, storing, and retrieving text documents

- Modifying a document's appearance (typestyles and sizes, page layout, and so on)

- Checking documents for spelling, grammar, style, and wording errors

- Creating, modifying, printing, storing, and retrieving AutoText entries (files that hold frequently used text you can insert in your documents without retyping)

- Creating, modifying, and enhancing tables

- Creating and modifying multicolumn text

- Inserting, sizing, moving, and modifying graphics (on-screen pictures)

- Creating and generating form letters

- Using templates and styles to simplify the creation of documents

This foundation will enable you to quickly and easily create sophisticated, professional-quality documents.

WHO THIS BOOK IS FOR

This book was written with the beginner in mind. Although experience with word processing and personal computers is certainly helpful, little or none is required. You should know how to turn on your computer and use your keyboard. We explain everything beyond that.

HOW TO USE THIS BOOK

You can use this book as a learning guide, a review tool, and a quick reference.

 AS A LEARNING GUIDE

Each chapter covers one broad topic or set of related topics. Chapters are arranged in order of increasing proficiency; skills you acquire in one chapter are used and elaborated on in later chapters. For this reason, you should work through the chapters in strict sequence.

Each chapter is organized into explanatory topics and step-by-step activities. Topics provide the theory you need to master Word for Windows 95; activities allow you to apply this theory to practical, hands-on examples.

You get to try out each new skill on a specially prepared sample Word for Windows 95 file stored on the enclosed Data Disk. This saves you typing time and allows you to concentrate on the technique at hand. Through the use of sample files, hands-on activities, illustrations that give you feedback at crucial steps, and supporting background information, this book provides you with the foundation and structure to learn Word 7.0 for Windows 95 quickly and easily.

 AS A REVIEW TOOL

Any method of instruction is only as effective as the time and effort you are willing to invest in it. For this reason, we strongly encourage you to spend some time reviewing the book's more challenging topics and activities.

 AS A QUICK REFERENCE

General procedures such as opening a document or italicizing selected text are presented as a series of bulleted steps; you can find these bullets (•) easily by skimming through the book. These procedures can serve as a handy reference.

At the end of every chapter, you'll find a quick reference that lists the mouse/keyboard actions needed to perform the techniques introduced in that chapter.

SPECIAL LEARNING FEATURES

The following features of this book will facilitate your learning:

- Carefully sequenced topics that build on the knowledge you've acquired from previous topics

- Frequent hands-on activities that sharpen your Word for Windows 95 skills

- Numerous illustrations that show how your screen should look at key points during these activities

- The Data Disk, which contains all the files you will need to complete the activities (as explained in the next section)

- Easy-to-spot, bulleted procedures that provide the general, step-by-step instructions you'll need to perform Word for Windows 95 tasks

- A quick reference at the end of each chapter, listing the mouse/keyboard actions needed to perform the techniques introduced in the chapter

 THE DATA DISK

 One of the most important learning features of this book is the *Data Disk*, the 3½-inch floppy disk that accompanies the book. This disk contains the sample Word for Windows 95 files you'll retrieve and work on throughout the book. To perform the activities in this book, you will first need to create a work directory on your hard disk (see Chapter 1). You'll then copy the sample files from the Data Disk to your work directory. This directory will also hold all the Word for Windows files that you will be creating, editing, and saving during the course of this book.

WHAT YOU NEED TO USE THIS BOOK

To run Word 7.0 for Windows 95 and complete this book, you need a computer with a hard disk and at least one floppy-disk drive, a monitor, a keyboard, and a mouse (or compatible tracking device). Although you don't absolutely need a printer, we strongly recommend that you have one.

Windows 95 must be installed on your computer; if it is not, see your Windows 95 reference manuals for instructions. Word for Windows 95 must also be installed; for help see Appendix A.

 ### COMPUTER AND MONITOR

You need an IBM or IBM-compatible personal computer and monitor that are capable of running Microsoft Windows (version 3.1 or higher). We recommend that you use a 386 or higher (486, and so on) computer.

You need a hard disk with at least 26 megabytes (26 million bytes) of free storage space (if Word 7.0 for Windows 95 is not yet installed) or 1 megabyte of free space (if Word 7.0 for Windows 95 is installed).

Finally, you need an EGA or higher (VGA, SVGA, and so on) graphics card and monitor to display Windows 95 and Word for Windows 95 at their intended screen resolution. (**Note:** The Word for Windows 95 screens shown in this book are taken from a VGA monitor. Depending on your monitor type, your screens may look slightly different.)

 ### KEYBOARD

IBM-compatible computers come with various styles of keyboards; these keyboards function identically, but have different layouts. Figures I.1, I.2, and I.3 show the three main keyboard styles and their key arrangements.

Figure I.1 **IBM PC–style keyboard**

Figure I.2 **XT/AT–style keyboard**

Figure I.3 **The 101-key Enhanced Keyboard**

Word for Windows 95 uses all main areas of the keyboard:

- The *function keys*, which enable you to access Word for Windows 95's special features. On the PC-, XT-, and AT-style keyboards, there are 10 function keys at the left end of the keyboard; on the 101-key Enhanced Keyboard there are 12 at the top of the keyboard.

- The *typing keys*, which enable you to enter letters, numbers, and punctuation marks. These keys include the Shift, Ctrl, and Alt keys, which you need to access several of Word for Windows 95's special features. The typing keys are located in the main body of all the keyboards.

- The *numeric keypad*, which enables you either to enter numeric data or to navigate through a document. When Num Lock is turned on, you use the numeric keypad to enter numeric data, just as you would on a standard calculator keypad. When Num Lock is turned off, you use the numeric keypad to navigate through a document by using the cursor-movement keys: Up, Down, Left, and Right Arrows; Home, End, PgUp (Page Up), and PgDn (Page Down). To turn Num Lock on/off, simply press the Num Lock key. To enter numeric data when Num Lock is off, use the number keys in the top row of the typing area.

- The *cursor-movement keypad*, which is available only on Enhanced Keyboards, enables you to navigate through a document by using the Home, End, Page Up, and Page Down keys. The cursor-movement keypad works the same when Num Lock is turned on or off. This enables you to use the numeric keypad for numeric data entry (that is, to keep Num Lock on) and still have access to cursor-movement keys.

MOUSE OR OTHER TYPE OF TRACKING DEVICE

You need a mouse or other type of tracking or pointing device to work through the activities in this book. Any standard PC mouse or tracking device (a trackball, for example) will do.

Note: Throughout this book, we direct you to use a mouse. If you have a different tracking device, simply use your device to perform all the mousing tasks: pointing, clicking, dragging, and so on.

 ## PRINTER

Although you don't absolutely need a printer to work through the activities in this book, we strongly recommend that you have one. A laser printer is ideal, but an ink-jet or dot-matrix will do just fine. Your printer must be selected for use with Word for Windows 95; for help, see Appendix A.

CONVENTIONS USED IN THIS BOOK

The following conventions used in this book will help you learn Word 7.0 for Windows 95 easily and efficiently.

- Each chapter begins with a short introduction and ends with a summary that includes a quick-reference guide to the techniques introduced in the chapter.

- Main chapter topics (large, capitalized headings) and subtopics (headings preceded by a cube) explain Word for Windows 95 features.

- Hands-on activities allow you to practice using these features. In these activities, keystrokes, menu choices, and anything you are asked to type are printed in boldface. Here's an example from Chapter 2:

> **4.** Choose **File, Open** to display the Open dialog box.

- Activities adhere to a *cause-and-effect* approach. Each step tells you what to do (cause) and then what will happen (effect). From the preceding example,

    Cause: Choose the menu command **File, Open**.

    Effect: The Open dialog box is displayed.

- A plus sign (+) is used with the Shift, Ctrl, and Alt keys to indicate a multikey keystroke. For example, "press **Ctrl+F10**" means "Press and hold down the Ctrl key, then press the F10 key, and then release them both."

- To help you distinguish between steps presented for reference purposes (*general procedures*) and steps you should carry out at your computer as you read (*specific procedures*), we use the following system:

    - A bulleted step, like this, is provided for your information and reference only.

    1. A numbered step, like this, indicates one in a series of steps that you should carry out in sequence at your computer.

BEFORE YOU START

Each chapter's activities proceed sequentially. In many cases, you cannot perform an activity until you have performed one or more of the activities preceding it. For this reason, we recommend that you allot enough time to work through an entire chapter in one continuous session.

Feel free to take as many breaks as you need. Stand up, stretch, take a walk, drink some decaf. Don't try to absorb too much information at one time. Studies show that people assimilate and retain information most effectively when it is presented in digestible chunks and followed by a liberal amount of hands-on practice.

You are now ready to begin. Good learning and...*bon voyage!*

CHAPTER 1: GETTING STARTED

A Quick Review of Mouse Skills

Introduction to Word

Please Read This—It's Important!

The Word Application and Document Windows

Exiting Word

Welcome to Word for Windows 95—from here on referred to simply as Word—and the exciting world of word processing! In this chapter, we'll get you up and running in Word and introduce you to the Word working environment. Then you'll learn how to exit the program.

When you're done working through this chapter, you will know

- How to use the mouse

- How to start Word

- How to exit Word

A QUICK REVIEW OF MOUSE SKILLS

The *mouse* is a hand-operated device that enables you to communicate with Word by manipulating (selecting, deselecting, moving, deleting, and so on) graphical and text objects that are displayed on your computer screen. When you move the mouse across the surface of your mouse pad (or roll a trackball in its base), a symbol called the *mouse pointer* moves across the screen. You use this mouse pointer to point to the on-screen object that you want to manipulate. The mouse has two or more buttons. You use these buttons to communicate with Word in various ways, as detailed in Table 1.1.

Table 1.1   **Mousing Techniques**

Technique	How to Do It
Point	Move the mouse until the tip of the mouse pointer is over the desired object. "Point to the word *File*" means "move the mouse until the tip of the mouse pointer is over the word *File*."
Click	Press and release the left or right mouse button. When we want you to click the left mouse button, we'll simply say "click." For example, "click on the word *File*" means "point to the word *File* and then press and release the left mouse button." When we want you to click the right mouse button, we'll say so. For example, "point to the Standard toolbar and click the right mouse button."

Table 1.1   **Mousing Techniques (Continued)**

Technique	How to Do It
Double-click	Press and release the left mouse button twice in rapid succession. "Double-click on the Preview 1 file" means "point to the file name *Preview 1* and then press and release the left mouse button twice in rapid succession."
Choose	Click on a menu command or a dialog-box button. "Choose File, Open" means "click on the word *File* (in the menu bar), and then click on the word *Open* (in the File menu)."
Drag	Press and hold the left mouse button while moving the mouse. "Drag the scroll box upward" means "point to the scroll box, press and hold the left mouse button, move the mouse upward, and then release the mouse button."
Scroll	Click on a scroll arrow or within a scroll bar, or drag a scroll box.
Select	Click on an object (to select the entire object), or drag over part of a text object (to select part of the text). "Select the Chapter 2 file" means "click on the file name *Chapter 2*." "Select the first four letters of the title *Global Travel*" means "drag over the letters *Glob*."
Check	Click on a check box to check (turn on) that option. "Check the Match Case option" means "click on the Match Case check box to check it."
Uncheck	Click on a check box to uncheck (turn off) that option. "Uncheck the Match Case option" means "click on the Match Case check box to uncheck it."

Note: Read through the table to familiarize yourself with standard Word mousing techniques. Do not, however, try to memorize these techniques. Instead, use this table as a quick reference, referring to it whenever you need to refresh your memory.

INTRODUCTION TO WORD

A *word processor* (such as Word) is a computer program that enables you to create, edit, print, and save documents for future retrieval and revision. You enter text into the computer by using a keyboard. As you type, your words are displayed on a monitor, or screen, and are stored temporarily in computer memory as you are creating the document (and permanently on disk once you save it) rather than on paper.

One of the chief advantages of a word processor over a conventional typewriter is that a word processor enables you to make changes to a document without retyping the entire document. For example, you can create a letter in a word processor and then, after you are finished, go back and change margins, add sentences, delete words, move paragraphs, correct spelling errors, and so on. You can do all of this without retyping the original text.

 ## CREATING YOUR WORK FOLDER

Throughout this book, you'll be creating, editing, and saving a number of files. To keep these files in one place, you'll need to create a work folder for them on your hard disk. Your work folder will also hold the sample files contained on the enclosed Data Disk.

Note: Before you start Word, both Microsoft Windows 95 and Word for Windows 7.0 must be installed on your hard disk. If either of these programs is not installed, please install it now. For help installing Windows 95, see your Windows documentation. For help installing Word for Windows 7.0, see Appendix A of this book.

Let's create our work folder:

1. Turn on your computer. After a brief internal self-check, Windows 95 will load and prompt you for a password.

2. Type your password and press **Enter**. Momentarily, the Windows 95 desktop will be displayed (see Figure 1.1).

3. From the Windows 95 desktop, click on the **Start** button to open the Start menu. Point to Programs to open the Programs menu, and select **Windows Explorer**. The Windows

Figure 1.1 **The Windows 95 desktop**

Explorer can be used to manage the folders and files on your computer.

4. In the Tree pane, click on the plus sign (+) to the left of the My Computer branch to expand it so that you can view both the floppy-disk drive and the hard drive. (The branch might already be expanded.) This branch may also contain folders, such as the Control Panel and Printers folders.

5. Click on the hard-disk icon **(C:)**. From the menu bar, choose **File, New, Folder** to create a new folder. You will copy the contents of the Data Disk into this folder. The new folder is displayed in the Contents pane and is highlighted so that you can rename it now.

6. Type **Word Work** and press **Enter** to assign the name to the new folder.

7. Select (click on) the hard-disk icon **(C:)** and choose **File, Properties** to view the amount of available hard-disk space. On the General tab, the number of free bytes is displayed. If you have fewer than **1,000,000** free bytes (1MB), you will not be

able to create your work folder and perform the hands-on activities in this book (while still maintaining an adequate amount of free hard-disk space for your other computer activities). In this case, you will have to delete enough files from your hard disk to increase the bytes-free total to at least 1,000,000. To do this, refer to your Windows 95 reference manual, or better yet, enlist the aid of an experienced Windows 95 user. (**Note:** Make sure you back up all your important files before deleting them!)

8. Click on **Cancel** to close the Properties dialog box. (Do *not* proceed to step 9 until you have made room for the Data Disk files on your computer.)

9. Remove the Data Disk from its envelope at the back of this book. Insert the Data Disk (label up) into the appropriately sized disk drive. Determine whether this is drive A or drive B. (On a single floppy-disk system, the drive is generally designated as A. On a double floppy-disk system, the upper or left drive is generally designated as A and the lower or right as B.)

10. The easiest way to copy the files from the floppy disk to your Word Work folder is by dragging them. Display the contents of the **3 1/2 Floppy (A:)** branch. (Use the same technique that you used in step 4.) Then, choose **Edit, Select All** from the menu to select all the files in the Contents pane.

11. Drag the selected files to the Word Work folder in the Tree pane. (The folder name should be highlighted before you release the mouse button.) As the files are copied, a message box graphically displays the files flying from one folder to another.

All the files that you need for this book are now stored in your Word Work folder. You can create a shortcut to this folder and display it on your desktop. A shortcut will give you easy access to the files in the folder. This procedure is strictly optional; you don't need the shortcut to work through the chapters in the book. However, if you would like to create such a shortcut, you can use the following drag-and-drop technique.

• If the Windows Explorer window is maximized, click on the *Restore* button (in the upper-right corner of the window) so that you can see part of the desktop.

- Select the *Word Work* folder icon. Press and hold the right mouse button and drag the icon to the desktop. Release the mouse button and choose *Create Shortcut(s) Here* from the shortcut's object menu.

Important Note: The hands-on activities in this book assume that your work folder is on the hard drive and is named Word Work. If you specified a different location or name for this folder, remember to substitute this location and/or name whenever we mention the Word Work folder.

 ## STARTING WORD

Before you start Word, both Microsoft Windows 95 and Word for Windows 7.0 must be installed on your hard disk. If either of these programs is not installed, please install it now. For help installing Windows 95, see your Windows documentation. For help installing Word for Windows 7.0, see Appendix A of this book.

You also need to have created a work folder on your hard disk and copied the files from the enclosed Data Disk to this folder. If you have not done this, please do so now; for instructions, see "Creating Your Work Folder" earlier in this chapter.

Note: In this book, we present two types of procedures: bulleted and numbered. A *bulleted* procedure—one whose steps are preceded by a bullet (•)—serves as a general reference; you should read its steps without actually performing them. A *numbered* procedure—one whose steps are preceded by numbers (1., 2., and so on)—is a specific hands-on activity; you should perform its steps as instructed.

To start Word,

- Turn on your computer.

- Enter your Windows 95 password.

- From the Start menu, open the Programs menu, and select *Microsoft Word*. If you have installed Microsoft Office, you might need to move through additional layers of the Start menu to locate Word; for example, you might have to choose *Start, Programs, Microsoft Office, Microsoft Word*.

Note: To start Word, we must first locate the program in the Start menu. Because Windows 95 is a customizable program, we cannot know the details of your Windows 95 setup. So please bear with us as we search for your Microsoft Word program.

With Windows 95 already running, let's start Word:

1. Click on the **Start** button in the taskbar.

2. Highlight (point to) **Programs** to display the available programs (see Figure 1.2; your menu choices will vary). Depending on your Windows 95 setup, you might need to search through a few layers of menus to find Microsoft Word (or you might have created a shortcut to it).

Figure 1.2   **The Start and Programs menus**

3. Click on the **Microsoft Word** choice to start the program. Your screen should match—or closely resemble—Figure 1.3. If your Word window does not fill the entire screen, click on the **Maximize** button, in the upper-right corner of the screen.

PLEASE READ THIS—IT'S IMPORTANT!

Like Windows 95, Word can be customized. Depending on how you (or perhaps a colleague) have set up your Word program, it

Figure 1.3   **Word 7.0, after start-up**

may look very different from another user's Word setup, or from the Word setup used in this book.

To write this book for an "invisible" audience—with hundreds, if not thousands, of different Word setups—we had to assume that you are running Word with the same *default* (standard) settings that were automatically chosen when you first installed the application. Of course, this assumption may be false. You or a colleague may have customized your Word program to show additional toolbars, run in full-screen view, display on-screen text as 20-point Gargantuan Urdu, hide the formula and status bars, and so on.

Here's our recommendation: First of all, relax. Chances are your program settings are fine. But if you should run into a snag while working through this book—for example, if your screen displays differ markedly from ours, or if tools we ask you to use are missing from your screen—simply use your ever-increasing Word expertise to make the changes necessary to match your Word setup as closely as possible to ours.

THE WORD APPLICATION AND DOCUMENT WINDOWS

Word is built around a set of interactive *windows*—rectangular, on-screen boxes through which you communicate with the Word program and create your documents. When you start Word, two windows appear on the screen, one nestled snugly within the other. The larger of these, called the *application window*, frames the entire screen; you use it to communicate with the Word program. (The terms *program* and *application* are synonymous.) The smaller window, called the *document window*, fits seamlessly within the application window; you use it to create and edit your Word documents.

Table 1.2 and Figure 1.4 show the screen elements with which you need to be familiar when using Word.

Table 1.2   **Screen Elements of Word**

Term	Definition
Application window	Larger of two start-up windows; provides interface between user and Word
Document window	Smaller of two start-up windows; holds currently active Word document
Control-menu icons	Located in upper-left corner of screen; control size and position of application window (upper icon) and document window (lower icon)
Title bar	Located at top of screen; displays name of application (Microsoft Word) and active document (Document1, in this case)
Maximize/Restore buttons	Located in upper-right corner of screen; control size of application window (upper box) and document window (lower box)
Minimize buttons	Located to left of Maximize/Restore buttons; reduces application and document windows

Table 1.2   **Screen Elements of Word (Continued)**

Term	Definition
Menu bar	Located below title bar; lists Word menu options
Standard toolbar	Located below menu bar; provides quick access to Word's most frequently used commands and utilities
Formatting toolbar	Located below Standard toolbar; provides quick access to Word's most frequently used formatting commands
Ruler	Located below Formatting toolbar; provides ongoing page measurement as well as quick access to margins, tabs, and indents
Scroll bars	Located along right side and bottom of document window; used to display different areas of active document (each scroll bar contains a pair of directional scroll arrows)
View buttons	Located left of horizontal scroll bar; used to change document display to Normal view (leftmost button), Page Layout view (middle button), and Outline view (rightmost button)
Status bar	Located below horizontal scroll bar; displays variety of information relating to active document

Let's take a closer look at some of these screen elements. (We'll discuss the remaining elements over the next few chapters.)

1. Click on the application-window **Control-menu** icon to open its drop-down menu. (Do *not* double-click on the Control-menu icon, as this would cause you to exit Word.) Note the

Figure 1.4   The Word application window

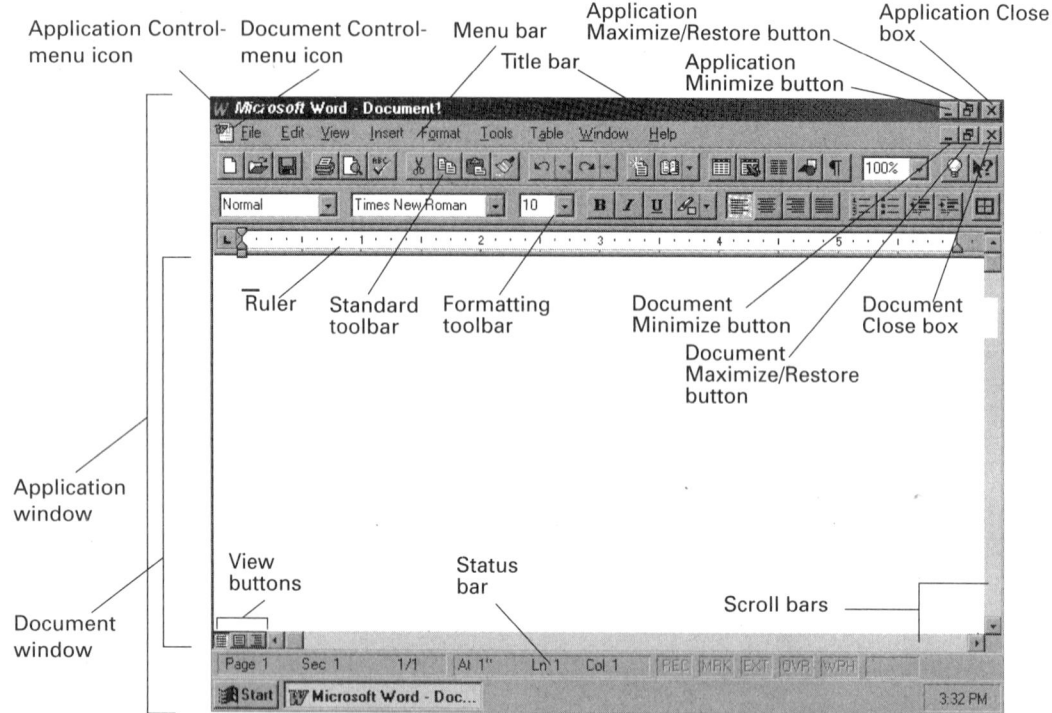

Control menu options: Restore, Move, Size, Minimize, and so on.

2. Click on the application-window **Control-menu** icon again to close its drop-down menu.

3. Now click on the document-window **Control-menu** icon to open its drop-down menu. Note that the document-window Control-menu options are very similar to the application window Control-menu options you saw in the previous step.

4. Click on the document-window **Control-menu** icon again to close its drop-down menu.

5. Click on the application-window **Maximize/Restore** button to restore (shrink) the application window. Note that the Maximize/Restore button now contains the graphic of a single large window, indicating that its function is to maximize (rather than to restore) the window.

6. Click on the application-window **Maximize/Restore** button again to maximize the application window to fill the entire screen.

7. Now click on the document-window **Maximize/Restore** button (at the right edge of the menu bar) to restore the document window. Note that the Maximize/Restore button moves to the upper-right corner of the restored (shrunken) document window. Note also that when the document window is restored, it gets its own title bar (in this case, it reads *Document1*).

8. Click on the document-window **Maximize/Restore** button again to maximize the document window to fit snugly within the application window. Note that when the document window is maximized, it loses its title bar, and the document title (Document1) appears in the application-window title bar.

USING THE MENU BAR TO ISSUE COMMANDS

To perform a word processing task (such as retrieving a document from disk, formatting text, printing a document, and so on), you must issue the appropriate Word command. You can do this by:

• Using the mouse to choose the command from the menu bar

• Using the mouse to choose the command from one of the toolbars or the ruler

• Using the mouse to choose the command from a shortcut menu

• Using the keyboard to enter a keyboard shortcut

For example, to italicize text, you could

- Use the mouse to choose the *Font* command from the Format option in the menu bar, and then select the *Italic* option.

- Use the mouse to click on the *Italic* button on the Formatting toolbar.

- Use the mouse to choose the *Font* command from the short-cut menu, and then select the *Italic* option.

- Use the keyboard to press *Ctrl+I* (press and hold the Ctrl key, press and hold the I key, and then release both keys), the keyboard shortcut for italicizing text.

Please do not perform any of these actions now.

Using the menu bar is the only method that allows you to issue every available Word command. The toolbars and ruler provide a subset of Word's most frequently used commands, as do the shortcut menus and the keyboard. For this reason, we'll begin our exploration of commands by using the menu-bar approach.

Let's issue some commands by using the menu bar:

1. Point to the **File** option (move the mouse pointer until its tip is over the word *File* in the menu bar). Press and hold down the left mouse button. (Do not release this button until we tell you to do so in step 4.) The drop-down File menu opens, displaying a set of file-related commands: *New, Open, Close, Save, Save As,* and so on.

2. Observe the message in the status bar at the bottom of your screen. Word displays a brief description of the currently selected item—the drop-down File menu, in this case.

3. Without releasing the button, drag the mouse pointer down to highlight the **Save As** command. Note that the status bar now displays a brief description of the File, Save As command.

4. Release the mouse button (finally!) to open the Save As dialog box (see Figure 1.5). *Dialog boxes* prompt you to enter information relating to the selected command (File, Save As, in this case). You will work extensively with dialog boxes during the course of this book.

5. Click on the **Cancel** button in the upper-right corner of the Save As dialog box to close it without making any changes.

Figure 1.5   **The Save As dialog box**

6. Click on the **Edit** option in the menu bar. The drop-down Edit menu opens, displaying Word's editing commands. Note that you can either press and hold the mouse button as you did in step 1, or click (press and release) the button as you did here to open a drop-down menu.

7. Observe that several Edit commands are dimmed (displayed in light letters): *Cut, Copy, AutoText, Links,* and so on. Word dims menu commands to show that they are unavailable in the current context. For example, the Copy command is dimmed because you have not selected any text to copy.

8. Observe also that several commands are followed by ellipses (*Find..., Replace..., Go To...,* and so on). When you choose a command with an ellipsis, Word displays a dialog box prompting you for further information; for example, when you choose Find..., Word displays a dialog box prompting you for the word(s) you want to find. When you choose a command without an ellipsis, Word simply carries out the command; for example, when you choose Select All, Word immediately (with no intervening dialog box) selects all the text in the current document. To keep this book easy to read, we chose not to print command ellipses. In step 3 of this activity, for example, we asked you to drag the mouse pointer to the Save As command, though *Save As...* is how the command actually appears on your screen.

9. Click on **Edit** again to close the Edit menu.

EXITING WORD

Earlier you learned that there are multiple ways to issue many of the commands available in Word. Exiting Word is no exception; for example, you could exit the program by using any one of the following techniques:

- Choose *File, Exit* from the menu.

- Click on the application-window *Control-menu* icon, and choose *Close*.

- Double-click on the application-window *Control-menu* icon.

- Click on the application-window *Close* box.

The method that you choose to issue any command is to some extent a matter of preference. For example, if you're one who computes by mouse alone, you might not want to learn any keyboard shortcuts; if, on the other hand, you're a dyed-in-the-wool keywhacker, you might be violently allergic to mouse pointers.

For the remainder of this book, rather than confuse you with a plethora of techniques to accomplish the same thing, we will, in each case, try to provide you with what we believe is the simplest method of accomplishing a task. For the long haul, it's up to you to determine which techniques will be the most comfortable for you.

Let's exit Word:

1. Observe the button to the right of the application-window Maximize/Restore button: This is the Close button. (Notice also that the document window contains a Close box of its own, which allows you to close the document without exiting Word.)

2. Click on the application-window **Close** button to exit Word.

SUMMARY

In this chapter, you learned how to start and exit Word, and you've been introduced to the Word environment.

Here's a quick reference guide to the Word features introduced in this chapter:

Desired Result	How to Do It
Start Word	Start Windows; choose **Start, Programs**; locate and click on **Microsoft Word** choice
Exit Word	Click on application-window **Close** box

In the next chapter, we'll show you the basics of using Word: how to enter and edit text, how to save the text in a file, how to create a new document, how to print a document, and how to navigate in Word. You'll also learn how to obtain helpful Word tips, open a file, display different portions of a document, search for text in a document, control document magnification, and obtain online help.

A NOTE ON HOW TO PROCEED

If you wish to stop here, please feel free to do so now. If you feel energetic and wish to press onward, please proceed directly to the next chapter. Remember to allot enough time to work through an entire chapter in one sitting.

CHAPTER 2: WORD BASICS

In this chapter, we'll lead you through one complete Word work session: You'll start the Word program, create and edit a document, save and print the document, create and save a new document, and learn some important navigation techniques. This, in a nutshell, is the procedure you'll use in your day-to-day word processing work with Word.

You'll also learn how to use the mouse *and* the keyboard to navigate through a multipage document. It's essential for you to master these navigational techniques as early as possible in your Word career. The more comfortable you feel moving around within a document, the more you'll be able to concentrate on the contents of the document itself.

When you're done working through this chapter, you will know

- How to enter text

- How to insert, delete, and replace text

- How to save and name a document

- How to print and close a document

- How to create a new document

- How to open a file

- How to use the mouse to scroll through a document

- How to use the keyboard and menus to move through a document

- How to use the Find command to search for text

- How to use the Zoom Control box to change the document magnification

- How to use Word Help to obtain on-line help

ENTERING TEXT

Word is a WYSIWYG (What You See Is What You Get) program; that is, the screen shows you (more or less) exactly how your document will look when you print it. WYSIWYG programs are not subject to the arcane codes and inaccurate page layouts that plague non-WYSIWYG programs. Word's "WYSIWYGness" encourages you to work in a "visual-intuitive" style in which you treat the word processor as a computerized extension of a typewriter.

Over the next several sections, we'll discuss the basics of entering text in a Word document.

 ### THE TEXT AREA

When you start Word, a new document window automatically opens, providing you with a blank text area in which you can type your desired text. Word automatically selects a whole slew of critical document settings, including margins, font and font size, line spacing, tab stops, page dimensions, and many other document attributes. Because Word preselects these settings—which are called defaults—you can start to type immediately, without first having to specify any of the settings yourself.

The characters you type are inserted in front of a blinking vertical bar called the insertion point. To move the insertion point—and thus change where your typing appears in the document—you simply move the mouse pointer and click at the desired new place in the text.

Let's examine Word's text area (see Figure 2.1):

1. Observe the *insertion point* (the blinking vertical bar). Its location determines where the next character you type will be entered into your document. Note that the insertion point of a new document always appears in the upper-left corner (that is, at the beginning) of the document window.

2. Observe the *end mark*. This is the broad horizontal line that indicates the end of the document. The end mark cannot be formatted or deleted (erased), and you cannot place the insertion point beyond it.

3. Observe the mouse pointer. The pointer becomes an *I-beam* (as shown in Figure 2.1) when it is within the text area.

Figure 2.1   **The text area**

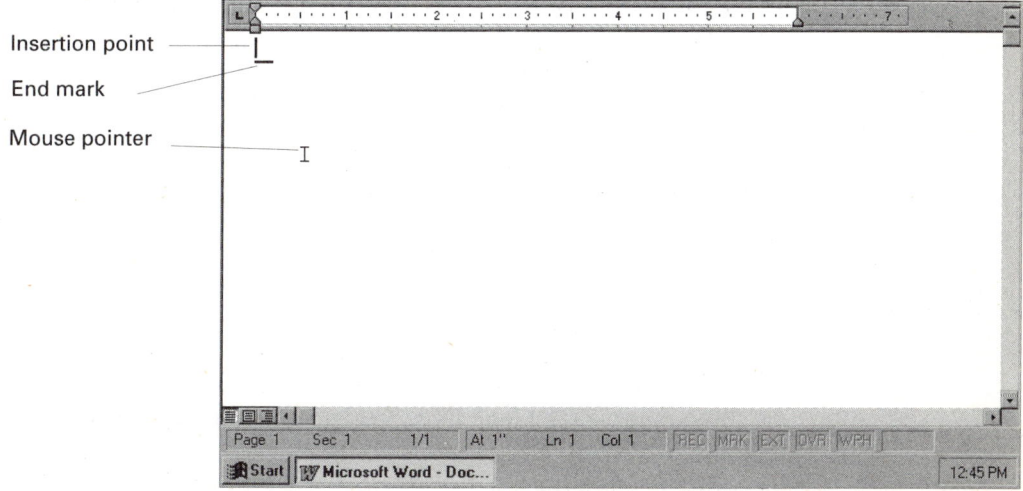

Insertion point

End mark

Mouse pointer

When you move it outside the text area, it becomes an arrow. Take a moment to verify this.

WORD-WRAP AND THE ENTER KEY

The Enter key on your keyboard is similar to—but not exactly the same as—the Return key on a typewriter. On a typewriter, you need to hit the Return key whenever you want to end a line. In Word, when a word does not fit on a line, it automatically flows to the beginning of the next line. This feature is called *word-wrap*. However, you do need to press Enter to

- End a short line (one that doesn't reach the right margin)

- End a paragraph

- Create a blank line

Let's type some text in our new document window and practice using the Enter key. (We'll demonstrate word-wrap in "Using the Backspace Key to Delete Text" later in this chapter.)

1. Observe the status bar. The vertical page position measurement (*At*) and the line number (*Ln*) reflect the current position of the insertion point.

2. Type **Julie Nichols** to enter the characters at the insertion point, and press **Enter** to end the line. Note that the status bar At and Ln numbers show the new insertion point position. Also, notice that Word has placed a wavy, red line beneath *Nichols*, suggesting that this "word" might be misspelled. This is because the *Automatic Spell Checking* option (on the Spelling tab of the Options dialog box) is turned on by default. We'll take a closer look at this feature in Chapter 7. For now, let's continue creating our letter.

3. Type **3325 Fillmore Avenue** and press **Enter**.

4. Type **North Hills, NY 14052** and press **Enter**.

5. Press **Enter** to create a blank line.

6. Type **Dear Janet:** and then press **Enter** twice to end the line and create one blank line. Your screen should now match Figure 2.2.

Figure 2.2   **Entering text in a document**

> Julie Nichols
> 3325 Fillmore Avenue
> North Hills, NY 14025
>
> Dear Janet:

NONPRINTING CHARACTERS

You can choose to have Word display a number of special characters on the screen that show the places in the text where you pressed the spacebar, or the Enter and Tab keys. These *nonprinting* characters (so called because they do not appear on paper when you print the document) are often useful to see. This is particularly true when you are working with heavily formatted documents and need to keep track of your tabs, spaces, blank lines, and so on.

To display Word's nonprinting characters, you click on the Show/Hide button in the Standard toolbar

Let's display the nonprinting characters of our active document:

1. Examine the screen. Each line of text is short, not reaching the right margin. Note that there are no characters marking the ends of these lines.

2. Click on the **Show/Hide** button to display Word's special formatting characters.

3. Examine the screen. Each time you pressed Enter in the previous activity, Word placed a paragraph mark (¶) in the document. Each time you pressed the spacebar, Word placed a space mark (·) in the document. These nonprinting characters only appear on the screen when the Show/Hide button is depressed; they will not appear in your printed document.

4. Click on the **Show/Hide** button again to hide the nonprinting characters. Clicking on this button *toggles* the display between its Show and Hide modes.

5. Click on the **Show/Hide** button again to display the nonprinting characters.

USING THE TAB KEY TO ALIGN TEXT HORIZONTALLY

Tabs enable you to align text horizontally. These lines are properly aligned:

```
Line 1 ....
Line 2 ....
```

These are not:

```
Line 1 ....
        Line 2 ....
```

Pressing the Tab key moves the insertion point to the next tab stop to the right. *Tab stops* are fixed horizontal positions within a line. By default, Word's tab stops are set at 0.5" increments. Pressing Tab once moves the insertion point 0.5" to the right; pressing Tab again moves it another 0.5", for a total of 1" (0.5" + 0.5") from the left margin; and so on. (We created the properly aligned example just shown by pressing Tab once at the beginning of each line. We created the improperly aligned example by using the spacebar to insert blank spaces at the beginning of each line.)

USING THE BACKSPACE KEY TO DELETE TEXT

You can use the Backspace key to delete text one character at a time. Simply press Backspace to delete the single character immediately to the left of the insertion point.

Let's experiment with Word's Tab, Backspace, and word-wrap features:

1. Press **Tab** to insert a tab at the beginning of the line. This moves the insertion point to the first tab stop, 0.5" to the right. Note that Word displays the tab mark (→), since the Show/Hide button is still depressed from our last exercise. As with the paragraph and space marks, this tab mark will not appear on the printed page.

2. Press **Tab** again to insert another tab. This moves the insertion point to the second tab stop, 1" from the left margin.

3. Press **Backspace** to remove the second tab character.

4. Type **I have been happy with the service provided by Global Travel.** (Include the period.) Then press the **spacebar** to insert a space before the next sentence.

5. Type **I would like additional information** and then examine the screen. Note that the word *information* automatically wraps to the next line, even though you did not press Enter. This is an example of word-wrap. (**Note:** Depending on the printer you are using, your sentence may wrap at a different place.)

6. Complete the sentence by typing **about your program.** and press **Enter** twice to end the paragraph and add one blank line above the next paragraph.

PRACTICE YOUR SKILLS

Complete the entire letter as shown in Figure 2.3.

Figure 2.3   **The completed letter in show mode**

```
Julie·Nichols¶
3325·Fillmore·Avenue¶
North·Hills,·NY··14052¶
¶
Dear·Janet:¶
¶
    →    I·have·been·happy·with·the·service·provided·by·Global·Travel.··I·would·like·additional·
information·about·your·program.¶
    →    Since·the·company·is·opening·a·new·office·in·Paris·sometime·this·year,·your·worldwide·services·
would·be·most·beneficial·to·us.··I·look·ahead·to·hearing·from·you.¶
¶
Yours·truly,¶
¶
Edward·Brooks¶
Amalgamated·Widgets,·Inc.¶
```

EDITING A DOCUMENT

As mentioned in the introduction to this chapter, one of the strongest arguments for switching from a typewriter to a word processor is the greatly increased ease of editing your documents. In the time it would take you just to pencil in your desired changes to a typewritten document (without actually retyping it), you could incorporate these changes into a word-processed document, print it, and save it on a hard or floppy disk for future revision.

In the next several sections, we'll discuss the basics of text editing in Word.

INSERTING TEXT

By default, Word runs in *insert* mode; as you type, text to the right of the insertion point is pushed further to the right to make room for your new text. To insert text in a document, perform these two steps:

- Place the insertion point (use the mouse to position the I-beam and click) where you want to insert your new text.

- Type the new text.

Let's practice inserting text in a document:

1. Point to the left of the *p* in *program*, which is located in the second sentence of the paragraph beginning with *I have.* Click the mouse button to place the insertion point directly before the *p* in *program.* (Do not place the insertion point before the space preceding the *p*.) This is where you will insert your new text.

2. Type **corporate travel** and press the **spacebar**. Note that the existing text is pushed to the right of the inserted text.

SELECTING TEXT

At times, you'll find it more convenient to work with a block of text than with a single character. For example, if you needed to underline a sentence in a paragraph, you would not want to underline each character separately (a multistep, tedious task); rather, you would want to underline the entire sentence at once (a single-step, straightforward task).

To work with a block of text, you must first select it. In the next activity (in the section "Deleting Text") you'll select text by using the following method:

- Point to the first (or final) character of the text to be selected.

- Press and hold the left mouse button.

- Drag across the text to the final (or first) character to be selected.

- Release the mouse button.

Note: As just indicated, you can select text downward (from the first to the last character) or upward (from the last to the first character). Both methods are effective; use whichever you feel more comfortable with.

DELETING TEXT

As you know, pressing Backspace deletes the character to the left of the insertion point. To delete the character immediately to the right of the insertion point, press the Delete key (on the cursor-movement keypad of an enhanced keyboard) or the Del key (on the numeric keypad).

Note: If you use the Del key on the numeric keypad, make sure that Num Lock is off. (To turn Num Lock on/off, press the Num Lock key.) If Num Lock is on, Del functions as a decimal point key; when you press it, Word displays a period (.) on the screen instead of performing the deletion.

To delete a block of selected text:

- Select the text.

- Press *Del* (or *Delete*).

Let's begin by deleting text one character at a time:

1. Place the insertion point directly to the left of the *A* in *Avenue*, which is located in the heading at the top of the page.

2. Press **Del** (or **Delete**) six times to delete the word *Avenue*. (To keep things simple, we'll only mention the Del key from here on. Feel free, however, to use the Delete key instead, if you wish.)

3. Type **Circle**.

4. Place the insertion point to the right of the *y* in *happy*, located in the paragraph beginning with *I have*.

5. Press **Backspace** five times to delete the word *happy*.

6. Type **very pleased**.

Now let's delete a block (in this case, a single word) of selected text:

1. Point to the left of the *m* in *most* in the first sentence of the paragraph beginning *Since the company*.

2. Press and hold the (left) mouse button. Then drag over *most* and its trailing space (the space that follows the word) to select the text. Do not select the space before *most*. Release the mouse button.

3. Press **Del** to delete the selected text.

 ## REPLACING TEXT

You already learned how to insert new text within a document. At times, however, you may want to replace existing text with new text. For example, you may want to replace the standard letter salutation "Dear Sir or Madam" with "To Whom It May Concern." One way you can do this is by inserting the new text and then deleting the old text. This, however, doubles your work and can grow very tiresome, particularly when you are replacing many blocks of text. Fortunately, Word provides a more convenient solution.

To replace existing text with new text:

• Select the text to be replaced.

• Type the new text.

Let's use this technique to replace some text in our letter:

1. Select the name **Janet** in the salutation *Dear Janet:* (be careful not to include the *:* in the selection).

2. Type **Julie** to replace *Janet* with *Julie*.

PRACTICE YOUR SKILLS

Make the following additional corrections to your letter:

1. Delete *the* (in the paragraph that begins *Since the company*) and replace it with **our**.

2. Delete *ahead* (in the same paragraph) and replace it with **forward**.

3. Delete *Yours truly* in the closing and replace it with **Sincerely**.

4. Check your work against Figure 2.4.

Figure 2.4   **The edited letter**

Julie·Nichols¶
3325·Fillmore·Circle¶
North·Hills,·NY··14052¶
¶
Dear·Julie:¶
¶
→   I·have·been·very·pleased··with·the·service·provided·by·Global·Travel.··I·would·like·additional·
information·about·your·program.¶
¶
→   Since·our·company·is·opening·a·new·office·in·Paris·sometime·this·year,·your·worldwide·services·
would·be·beneficial·to·us.··I·look·forward·to·hearing·from·you.¶
¶
Sincerely,¶
¶
Edward·Brooks¶
Amalgamated·Widgets,·Inc.¶

SAVING A DOCUMENT

Before you save it, a document exists only in computer memory, a temporary storage area. For permanent storage, you must save the document as a file on a hard or floppy disk. Word provides two commands you can use to save your documents: File, Save As and File, Save. Let's explore the differences between these commands.

THE FILE, SAVE AS COMMAND

You use the *File, Save As* command to save a document for the first time, to save a document with a new name, or to save a document in a different location (on another disk or in another folder).

To save a document using File, Save As:

- Choose *File, Save As* (that is, choose the Save As command from the File menu) to open the Save As dialog box.

- Select the location (drive and folder) in which you wish to save the document, if this location is not already selected.

- In the File Name box, type the name of the file.

- Click on *Save*.

THE SAVE COMMAND

You use the *Save* command (rather than Save As) to save a document with its current name and in its current location. Save updates a saved document; it replaces the last-saved version of the document with the new version of the document on your screen. For example, let's say you'd used Save As to save a business report to your reports folder as *Report 1,* and then you'd gone back and revised the report by adding an extra closing paragraph. If you then issued the Save command, the new (extra paragraph) report version would replace the last-saved (no extra paragraph) version on the disk. Once you've used Save As to name and save a document, you should generally use Save for all subsequent updates of that document. However, if you later want to rename it or save it in a different location (while retaining a copy of the original file in the current location), you should use Save As.

SAVING GUIDELINES

You should save your active documents frequently; every 10 to 15 minutes is a good rule of thumb. That way, if something happens to your computer memory (for example, a power failure, which erases the contents of memory), you will have a recent copy of the document safely stored on disk. This precaution will keep your eventual retyping to a minimum.

Word provides an automatic save option. When this option is turned on, Word automatically saves all your active documents at a specified time interval (for example, every 10 minutes), making it unnecessary for you to save your documents manually (by issuing Save commands). This feature is a godsend for those who just can't seem to remember to save as often as they should.

Let's take a moment to make sure that your automatic save option is turned on:

1. Choose **Tools, Options** (click on **Tools**, and click on **Options**) to open the Options dialog box.

2. Click on the **Save** tab to display the available Save options.

3. Observe the Automatic Save Every ____ Minutes option. If this option is unchecked (turned off)—that is, if the square box preceding *Automatic* is empty—check it (turn it on) by clicking on the square box to fill it with an X.

4. If the rectangular box between *Every* and *Minutes* does not contain the value *10*, select its current value (by dragging over it), and then type **10**.

5. Your option should now read *Automatic Save Every 10 Minutes*. This means that Word will automatically save all your active documents every ten minutes.

6. Click on **OK** to close the Options dialog box.

NAMING A DOCUMENT

When you save a document for the first time, you must name it. Follow these guidelines when naming documents:

- A file name can contain from 1 to 255 letters (uppercase and/or lowercase), numbers, spaces, or the following special characters: ! @ # $ % ( ) - _ { } ' ~

- A file name should be descriptive so that you can remember the file's contents (for example, My Essay on Life rather than X117-A).

Let's save our new document:

1. Choose **File, Save As** to open the Save As dialog box. Since our document is new (unsaved, as of yet) we're using Save As—rather than Save—to save it. In the Save In box, the My Documents folder is currently displayed.

2. Click on the **Up One Level** button to display the contents of the folder up one level.

Repeat this procedure, as necessary, until drive C (or whatever drive your hard disk is) is displayed. The drive's contents are displayed in the large box below the Save In box.

3. If necessary, use the horizontal scroll bar to display the Word Work folder. This is the work folder we created in Chapter 1; here you will store and retrieve all of the documents you work with in this book.

4. Double-click on the **Word Work** folder to display its contents (see Figure 2.5).

Figure 2.5   **Saving the new file in the Word Work folder**

5. Select (drag over) the contents of the File Name box. Notice that Word has quite sensibly used information in our document to suggest a descriptive file name; however, we'll make up our own name.

6. Type **My Letter to Global Travel** to name the document, and click on **Save** to save the document as a disk file in your Word Work folder.

7. Observe the title bar. Note that it has changed to display the document's name, *My Letter to Global Travel*.

DOCUMENT PROPERTIES

Word provides an option called Prompt For Document Properties. By default, this option is disabled. When this option is turned on, the first time you save a new document, Word displays the Document Properties dialog box. This box prompts you for supplementary information about the document, including the subject, author, keywords, comments, and a descriptive title. This option allows for quite a bit of detail in describing a document. You can also choose to skip any, or all, of these categories. The Document Properties option is especially useful for keeping track of author names and for storing comments and notes relating to a document.

To enable/disable the Document Properties feature:

• Choose *Tools, Options*.

- Click on the *Save* tab.
- Check/Uncheck (click on) the *Prompt For Document Properties option.*
- Click on *OK*.

PRINTING A DOCUMENT

By default, Word prints one copy of the entire active document. You can, however, choose to print the current page only, multiple pages, multiple copies, or selected text. You can also print to a document rather than to a printer. (We'll discuss these print options in Chapter 6.)

To print the active document:

- Choose *File, Print.*
- Select the desired options from the Print dialog box.
- Click on *OK*.

Now let's print our document:

1. Choose **File, Print** to open the Print dialog box (see Figure 2.6). Notice that this dialog box contains a number of options for printing your documents.

Figure 2.6   **The Print dialog box**

2. Click on **OK** to print the document. (Or, if you do not have a printer, click on **Cancel** to cancel the Print command and return to your document.)

3. If your document failed to print, make sure your printer is on-line, then try again. If it still won't print, refer to Appendix A for help in selecting your printer.

CLOSING A DOCUMENT

When you're finished working with a document—that is, after you've completed, saved, and (if desired) printed it—you should close the document window. To do this:

• Click on the document-window *Close* box.

Let's close our document, since we've saved and printed it:

1. Click on the document-window **Close** box (the one below its application-window counterpart) to close the document and remove it from memory.

2. Observe the screen. Word remains loaded, but there is no active document. The title bar displays only *Microsoft Word*, the menu bar contains only the File and Help choices, and the ruler and scroll bars have disappeared.

CREATING A NEW DOCUMENT

After you've closed the active document, you're ready—if you choose—to create a new document. To do this:

• Click on the *New* button in the Standard toolbar.

Word will open a new, blank document window.

Let's create a new document and then save it:

1. Click on the **New** button to open a new, blank document window. Notice that the title bar reads *Document2*.

2. Type **This is my second document.**

3. Choose **File, Save As** to open the Save As dialog box.

4. If necessary, select (drag over) the text in the File Name box, and type **My Second Document** to name the document. Note that the Word Work folder is still selected; Word remembered it from the last time we selected it, earlier in this chapter.

5. Observe that the Save button (in the dialog box) is enclosed in a border that is somewhat darker than the other buttons in the dialog box. This means that Save is the default button. To choose a default button, you simply press **Enter**.

6. Press **Enter** to choose **Save** instead of clicking on the button with the mouse.

7. Click on the document-window **Close** box to close the new document.

OPENING A FILE

Opening (retrieving) a *file* (a document that is stored on a disk) enables you to revise previously saved documents and then reprint and resave them.

Note: The terms *file* and *document* are two different ways of looking at the same thing. When referring to a text object on your screen, we call it a *document*; when referring to this same text object stored on a disk, we call it a *file*.

To open a file:

• Click on the *Open* button in the toolbar to display the Open dialog box.

• Select the desired drive and folder, if necessary.

• In the list of files, double-click on the desired file (or click on the file, and then click on *Open*).

When you open a file, Word places a copy of the file in a document window on your screen. Because this is a *copy* of the file, and not the original, you can revise it to your heart's content without changing the original document stored on your disk. You will, however, change the original document if you save your revised document as a file with the same name, and in the same location, as the original. For this reason, if you want to preserve the original document, make sure to give your revised file a new name.

Word also provides a convenient file-opening shortcut; it keeps track of the last four files that you worked on and displays their names at the bottom of the drop-down File menu. To open one of these documents, simply choose File and click on the desired document name.

Let's begin by opening a file that's stored in our Word Work folder:

1. Click on the **Open** button in the toolbar.

The Open dialog box appears (see Figure 2.7). The contents of your Word Work folder should be displayed; notice the folder name in the Look In box.

Figure 2.7   **The Open dialog box**

2. In the list of files, double-click on the **Navigation** file. A copy of the file appears in an active document window. Notice that the title bar reads *Microsoft Word - Navigation*.

Now let's try the shortcut method for opening this same file. First we'll close it:

1. Click on the document-window (*not* the application-window) **Close** box to close the Navigation file.

2. Open the File menu (click once on **File** in the menu bar). Notice that *Navigation* appears in the recently accessed files section at the bottom of the menu.

3. Choose (click on) **Navigation** to open the file.

SCROLLING THROUGH A DOCUMENT

At normal (100%) magnification, a Word document window can only display about half of a standard business-size (8.5 by 11-inch) page on the screen. To view the remainder of the page (or other pages within the document), you can use the mouse in conjunction with the vertical and horizontal scroll bars to *scroll* through the document. The vertical scroll bar controls up-down scrolling; the horizontal scroll bar controls side-to-side scrolling.

Scrolling through a document changes the document display, but does *not* change the position of the insertion point. For example, if the insertion point is at the top of page 2 and you use the vertical scroll bar to scroll down to page 8, the contents of page 8 will be displayed on the screen, but the insertion point will still be at the top of page 2. If you then begin to type, your text is entered at the insertion point on page 2, not on page 8. (You'll learn how to change both the document display *and* the insertion point position in the next section.)

Table 2.1 lists Word's vertical and horizontal scrolling options and how to perform them. Figure 2.8 identifies screen elements used for scrolling.

Table 2.1   **Vertical and Horizontal Scrolling Options**

To Scroll	Do This
Up or down one line at a time	Click on up or down scroll arrow
To top, bottom, or middle of document	Drag vertical scroll box to top, bottom, or middle of scroll bar
Up or down one screen at a time	Click in shaded area above or below vertical scroll box

Table 2.1   **Vertical and Horizontal Scrolling Options (Continued)**

To Scroll	Do This
Left or right one character at a time	Click on left or right scroll arrow
To left edge, right edge, or middle of document	Drag horizontal scroll box to left, right, or middle of scroll bar
Left or right one screen at a time	Click in shaded area to left or right of horizontal scroll box

Figure 2.8   **Scrolling terminology**

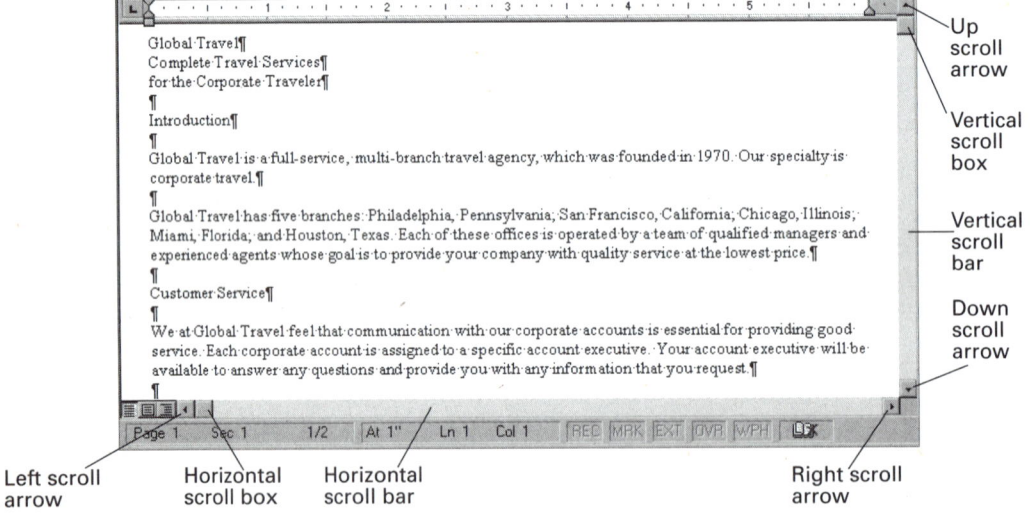

Let's practice scrolling through the active document, Navigation:

1. Click on the **down scroll** arrow several times to scroll down through the document one line at a time. Note that the insertion point does not move.

2. Click on the **up scroll** arrow several times to scroll up through the document.

3. Drag the **vertical scroll** box to the bottom of the scroll bar to scroll to the bottom of the document.

4. Drag the **vertical scroll** box to the middle of the scroll bar to scroll to the middle of the document. Observe the *page break*—the dotted line marked *Page Break* that indicates where one page ends and the next begins. (You may need to scroll to see this.) Because Navigation is a two-page document, the page break is located about halfway through the document.

5. Drag the **vertical scroll** box to the top of the scroll bar to scroll to the top of the document. Notice that, throughout all of your scrolling, the insertion point has remained at the top of the document.

6. Click in the **vertical scroll** bar below the vertical scroll box to scroll one screen length down through the document. Do this as many times as necessary to scroll to the bottom of the document.

7. Click in the **vertical scroll** bar above the vertical scroll box to scroll one screen length up through the document. Do this as many times as necessary to scroll to the top of the document.

Let's take a moment to observe a common scrolling mistake. Assume you wanted to enter your initials at the end of the active document:

1. Drag the **vertical scroll** box to the bottom of the scroll bar to display the end of the document.

2. Type your initials. The text is inserted at the top of the document (where your insertion point is located), not at the end (where you scrolled to). Note that Word automatically repositions the document to display the inserted text. To avoid making such a mistake, remember these two facts:

   • Text that you type is always inserted at the insertion point.

   • The insertion point does not move when you use the mouse to scroll through your document.

3. Use **Backspace** to erase your initials.

MOVING THROUGH A DOCUMENT

When you *scroll* through a document, you change the document display but not the insertion point. When you *move* through a document, you change both the document display *and* the insertion point. For this reason, you should scroll when you just want to view different parts of a document, and you should move when you want to view and modify a document.

 USING THE KEYBOARD

Table 2.2 lists several ways to move through a document by using the keyboard.

Table 2.2   **Keyboard Movement Techniques**

To Move	Press
Up one screen	PgUp (or Page Up on enhanced keyboards)
Down one screen	PgDn (or Page Down)
To top of document	Ctrl+Home
To end of document	Ctrl+End
To beginning of line	Home
To end of line	End

Now let's practice using the keyboard to move—rather than to scroll—through a document.

Note: If you intend to use the PgDn and PgUp keys on the numeric keypad, make sure that Num Lock is off.

1. Press **PgDn** (or **Page Down**) twice to move two screen lengths down through the document. Notice that the insertion point has moved along with the document display.

2. Press **PgUp** (or **Page Up**) twice to move two screen lengths up through the document. Notice that the insertion point has moved.

3. Press **Ctrl+End** (press and hold down the **Ctrl** key, press the **End** key, and then release both keys) to move to the end of the document.

4. Press **Ctrl+Home** (press **Ctrl**, press **Home**, and then release both) to move to the beginning of the document.

Let's redo our initial-writing task, this time using the correct method:

1. Press **Ctrl+End** to move to the end of the document.

2. Type your initials. They now appear in the desired location, because you used Ctrl+End (not the scroll bar) to move the insertion point along with the document display.

USING *GO TO* TO MOVE TO A PAGE

You can use the Go To command to move to the top of a specified page in the active document. This technique is particularly useful when you are moving through a long (multipage) document.

To move to the top of a page:

• Press *F5* (or choose *Edit, Go To*).

• Type the page number and then click on *Go To* (or press *Enter*).

• To move to a different page, repeat the previous step.

• When you're finished using Go To, click on the *Close* box (or click on the *Close* button).

Let's use the Go To command to move through a document:

1. Press **F5** to open the Go To dialog box (see Figure 2.9).

Figure 2.9   **The Go To dialog box**

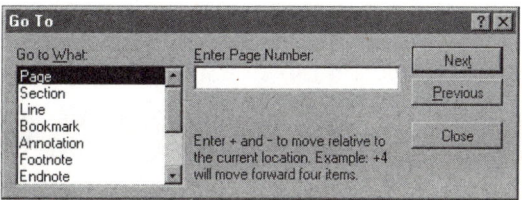

2. In the Enter Page Number text box, type **2** to specify the destination page. Then click on **Go To** to move (the document display and the insertion point) to the top of page 2. Notice that your current page number is displayed in the status bar. The Go To dialog box remains on the screen, allowing you to move to another page.

3. *Enter* **1**—that is, type **1** and then press **Enter**—to move to the top of page 1. (From here on, we'll use "enter text" to mean "type *text* and then press *Enter*.")

4. Click on the **Close** box to close the Go To dialog box.

PRACTICE YOUR SKILLS

1. Use Go To to move to the top of page 2.

2. Use Go To to move to the top of page 1, and then attempt to move to the top of page 3. Since this document does not have a page 3, Word moves you to the top of the final page (2).

3. Close the Go To dialog box.

 ### USING FIND TO SEARCH FOR TEXT

One of Word's most powerful features is its ability to locate a specific word or phrase in a document. You can use this feature to move rapidly to any desired document location. For example, you can move to the sentence containing the phrase "We would like to establish…," even if you have no idea on which page this sentence appears.

To use Edit, Find to search for text within a document:

• Choose *Edit, Find* or press *Ctrl+F* to open the Find dialog box.

• In the Find What text box, type the *search text* (the text that you want to find).

• Select any desired search options (as explained in the paragraph following this bulleted procedure).

• Click on *Find Next* (or press *Enter*); Word finds and highlights the first occurrence of your search text.

Repeat the previous step as many times as necessary until you have searched through the entire document (or cancel your search at any time by clicking on *Cancel*).

- When Word has finished searching the document, it displays a message informing you so. Click on *OK* (or press *Enter*) to close this message box.

- If desired, perform another search by repeating the previous five steps.

- When you are finished searching, click on *Cancel* to close the Find dialog box.

Edit, Find provides several options that allow you to refine your text searches. By checking (turning on) the *Match Case* option, you can locate only words that exactly match the case (capitalization) of your search text. By checking the *Find Whole Words Only* option, you can tell Find to locate only whole words that match your search text. By checking the *Search Up* option, you can search from the insertion point upward, instead of in the default downward direction.

Let's experiment with the Edit, Find command:

1. Your insertion point should be at the top of page 2. If it is not, use Go To to move it there.

2. Choose **Edit, Find** to open the Find dialog box (see Figure 2.10).

3. In the Find What box, type **vacation**. This is the word we're going to search for. Before we actually perform the search, we need to verify that the search options are correctly set.

Figure 2.10   **The Find dialog box**

4. If necessary, uncheck all of the following options: **Match Case, Find Whole Words Only, Use Pattern Matching, Sounds Like,** and **Find All Word Forms**. Verify that the Search list box is set to *All* (if not, select this option by clicking on the **down arrow** next to the Search list box and then clicking on **All**); this option tells Word to search the entire document. If the **No Formatting** button is active—that is, if it is not dimmed—click on it; this tells Word to ignore the formatting (font, style, and so on) of your search word (*vacation*).

5. Click on **Find Next** (or press **Enter**) four times, pausing each time to examine the found word; when a word is found, it is highlighted in the document. Word finds the following occurrences of *vacation*:

   Vacations

   vacation

   Vacation

   Vacation

   Word found the second occurrence (*vacation*) because it exactly matches your search text (*vacation*). It found the last two occurrences (*Vacation*), because by unchecking the Match Case option, you told it to ignore capitalization. It found the first occurrence (*Vacations*), because by unchecking the Find Whole Words Only option, you told it to find not just *vacation*, but to find all words that contain *vacation* (*Vacations* contains *vacation*).

6. Click on **Find Next** (or press **Enter**) again. A *message box* appears, informing you that Word has finished searching the document. Click on **OK** (or the **Close** box) to close this box.

7. Click on **Cancel** (or the **Close** box) to close the Find dialog box.

Now let's refine our search by using the Match Case and Find Whole Words Only options:

1. With the insertion point at the top of page 2, press **Ctrl+F** (you do not need to capitalize shortcut-key letters) to open the Find dialog box.

2. Check the **Find Whole Words Only** option.

3. Click on **Find Next** (or press **Enter**) three times, pausing to examine each found word. This time, only three occurrences are found: *vacation*, *Vacation*, and *Vacation*. *Vacations* is not

found, because you told Word to find only whole-word matches of *vacation*.

4. Click on **Find Next** (or press **Enter**) again; the end-of-document message box appears. Click on **OK** to close this box, but do not close the Find dialog box.

5. Check the **Match Case** option; both Match Case and Find Whole Words Only should now be checked. Click on **Find Next** (or press **Enter**) two times. Only one occurrence of your search text is found: *vacation*. *Vacation* is not found, because you told Word to find only case-matching occurrences of *vacation*.

6. Click on **OK** to close the search-finished message box.

PRACTICE YOUR SKILLS

1. Uncheck the **Match Case** and **Find Whole Words Only** options, and search your entire active document for *news*. There are three matches.

2. Check the **Find Whole Words Only** option and repeat this search. There is one match.

3. Uncheck **Find Whole Words Only,** check **Match Case**, and repeat the search. There are two matches.

4. Close the Find dialog box.

 ## USING THE ZOOM BOX TO CHANGE DOCUMENT MAGNIFICATION

Word allows you to change the level of magnification at which your documents are displayed on the screen. By default, documents are displayed at 100 percent magnification (where the screen display matches the actual document size), but you can adjust this magnification to anywhere from 10 percent to 200 percent.

Lower magnifications (from 99 percent to 10 percent) shrink the on-screen document, allowing you to view more of a page at once. Higher magnifications (from 101 percent to 200 percent) enlarge the on-screen document, allowing you to view text and graphics close up to perform detail work.

To change the magnification of the active document:

- Click on the *down arrow* to the right of the percentage displayed in the *Zoom Control* box to open a drop-down list of magnification options.

- Click on your desired magnification. Clicking on the *Page Width* option shrinks a page so that its extra-wide text lines fit on-screen.

Let's change the magnification of our document:

1. Move the insertion point to the top of the document.

2. Observe the Zoom Control box. Notice that it reads *100%*, meaning that the active document is displayed at 100 percent (actual-size) magnification.

3. Click on the **down arrow** to the right of the percentage in the Zoom Control box to open its drop-down list of magnification options.

4. Click on the **50%** option to shrink the document to half its actual size.

5. Using the technique outlined in the previous two steps, change the magnification to **150%** (see Figure 2.11). Note how much less of the text fits on-screen.

6. Change the magnification back to **100%**.

OBTAINING ONLINE HELP

Word Help is an extensive online help system that provides you with "how-to" information on every aspect of the Word program. The beauty of Word Help is its accessibility. No matter what you are doing in Word (choosing a command from the menu, editing a document, filling in a dialog box, and so on), Help is only a keystroke—or mouse click—away.

Figure 2.11 **The document at 150% magnification**

THE HELP TOPICS WINDOW

The Word Help Topics window provides an overview of the topics for which Help information is available. To use the Help Topics window:

- Press *F1* (or choose *Help, Microsoft Word Help Topics*) to open the Help Topics window, which contains the following tabs designed to give you access to information in different ways:

  - *Contents*, which displays a list of common procedures, which contain further subtopics that expand in outline style.

  - *Index*, which contains a comprehensive list of word terms and procedures.

  - *Find*, which allows you to search for specific information. (The first time you use this feature, Word guides you through the creation of a database of information that is customized to your particular setup.)

- *Answer Wizard*, which you can use for step-by-step guidance.

- To exit Word Help, click on its *Close* box.

Note: All the tabs available in the Help Contents window contain built-in instructions for their use.

Let's briefly explore the use of the Help Topics window:

1. Press **F1** to open the Help Topics window, and select (click on) the Contents tab (see Figure 2.12).

Figure 2.12   **The Contents tab in the Help Topics window**

2. In the list of topics, double-click on **Typing, Selecting, and Editing**. A group of subtopics is displayed below our selection (the subtopics are indented).

3. Double-click on **Going to a Specific Page or Other Location**. Eureka! More subtopics.

4. Double-click on **Go to a page, bookmark, footnote, table, annotation, graphic**. Another help box opens; it describes the procedure for using Go To (see Figure 2.13).

5. Exit Word Help by clicking on its **Close** box.

Figure 2.13   **Getting help on using Go To**

USING F1 TO OBTAIN CONTEXT-SENSITIVE HELP

Word Help also offers you *context-sensitive* help—help related to your current working context. For example, if a dialog box is open and you ask for context-sensitive help, Help displays information about that dialog box. Used in this manner, Help can quickly provide information about specific dialog boxes, menu commands, or areas of the screen. You can use either of the following methods to obtain context-sensitive help:

- Press *F1*; Word displays the Help window related to your current working context.

- Press *Shift+F1*; the mouse pointer changes to an arrow with a question mark attached. Make any menu choice, or click on any button or any part of the application window, and Word will open the related Help window.

Let's use the F1 key to obtain context-sensitive help:

1. Open the Go To dialog box (press **F5**).

2. Press **F1** to open the Help window for the Go To command. Voilà! We have used more direct means to get help about Go To. You can see that using context-sensitive help can be the more expedient way of getting help on a topic.

3. Click anywhere on the screen to close the Help window.

4. Close the Go To dialog box.

5. Click on the document-window **Close** box to close the document. When prompted to save the changes, click on **No**.

PRACTICE YOUR SKILLS

You've learned a great deal thus far. The following two activities allow you to apply this knowledge to practical word processing tasks. Please don't think of these activities as tests, but rather as opportunities to hone your Word skills. It is only through repetition that you'll internalize the techniques you've learned.

In this activity, you will create and edit the document shown in two different stages in Figures 2.14 and 2.15. Then you'll produce the final document shown in Figure 2.16.

1. Enter the text shown in Figure 2.14. Where the text *(today's date)* appears, enter the current date.

2. Edit the letter as shown in Figure 2.15.

Figure 2.14   **The first draft of My Practice 2A**

(today's date)

Katherine Carlisle
1822 W. 18th Avenue
New York, NY 10021

Dear Katherine:

Thank you for accepting the invitation to the announcement press conference in June. Because your generous orders, the entrance fee of $25.00 has been waived.

We look ahead to seeing you there!

Yours truly,

Dwight Minnley
Conference Director

Figure 2.15   **Editing My Practice 2A**

(today's date)

Katherine Carlisle
1822 W. 18th ~~Avenue~~ **Street**
New York, NY 10021

Dear Katherine:

Thank you for accepting ~~the~~ **our** invitation to the **product-**announcement press conference in June. Because **of** your generous orders, the entrance fee ~~of $25.00~~ has been waived.

We look ~~ahead~~ **forward** to seeing you there!

~~Yours truly,~~ **Sincerely,**

Dwight Minnley
Conference Director

Figure 2.16   **The corrected My Practice 2A**

(today's date)

Katherine Carlisle
1822 W. 18th Street
New York, NY 10021

Dear Katherine:

Thank you for accepting our invitation to the product-announcement press conference in June. Because of your generous orders, the entrance fee has been waived.

We look forward to seeing you there!

Sincerely,

Dwight Minnley
Conference Director

3. Save the document to your Word Work folder under the name My Practice 2A.

4. Print the document and compare the results with Figure 2.16.

5. Close the document window.

In the next activity, you will create and edit the document shown in two stages in Figures 2.17 and 2.18 to produce the final document shown in Figure 2.19.

1. Open a new document window.

2. Enter the text shown in Figure 2.17.

3. Edit the letter as shown in Figure 2.18.

4. Save the document to your Word Work folder under the name **My Practice 2B**.

5. Print the document and compare the results with Figure 2.19.

6. Close the document window.

7. Exit Word.

Figure 2.17   **The first draft of my Practice 2B**

(today's date)

Jayne L. Corkley
1029 Bodera Drive
Baltimore, MD 21227

Dear Jayne:

      Please accept this as a reminder to attend our product-announcement press conference in June. Because you are a valued customer, we want to make all effort to provide you with the support and services you need to make the conference a surreal one.

      Attached you will find a map to your hotel and the conference center. After you sign up at our registration desk, on the first day of the conference, your name will be entered into our mailing list. This will ensure that you receive product information and dates for future press conferences.

      Thank you for your interest and welcome to our growing list of customers.

Sincerely,

Dwight Minnley

Figure 2.18   **Editing My Practice 2B**

(today's date)

Jayne L. Corkley
1029 Bodera Drive
Baltimore, MD 21227

Dear Jayne:

~~Please accept this as~~ **This is** a reminder to attend our ~~product announcement~~ press conference in June. Because you are a valued customer, we want to make ~~all~~ **every** effort to provide you with the support and services you need to make the conference a ~~surreal~~ **successful** one.

~~Attached~~ **Enclosed** you will find a map to your hotel and the conference center. After you sign up at ~~our~~ **the** registration desk, ~~on the first day of the conference,~~ your name will be entered into our **national** mailing list. This will ensure that you receive product information and dates for future press conferences.

Thank you for your interest and welcome to our growing list of **satisfied** customers.

Sincerely,

Dwight Minnley

Figure 2.19   **The corrected My Practice 2B**

(today's date)

Jayne L. Corkley
1029 Bodera Drive
Baltimore, MD 21227

Dear Jayne:

This is a reminder to attend our press conference in June. Because you are a valued customer, we want to make every effort to provide you with the support and services you need to make the conference a successful one.

Enclosed you will find a map to your hotel and the conference center. After you sign up at the registration desk, your name will be entered into our national mailing list. This will ensure that you receive product information and dates for future press conferences.

Thank you for your interest and welcome to our growing list of satisfied customers.

Sincerely,

Dwight Minnley

SUMMARY

In this chapter, you learned the basics of the document creation-revision-saving-printing cycle, a procedure you'll use frequently in your daily word processing work. You now know how to enter, insert, delete, and replace text; how to save, name, print, and close a document; and how to create a new document. You also learned how to navigate in Word. You now know how to obtain Word tips, open a file, scroll and move through a document, search for text, control document magnification, and obtain on-line help. Congratulations! You're well on your way to mastering Word.

Here's a quick reference guide to the Word features introduced in this chapter:

Desired Result	How to Do It
End paragraph or short line	Press **Enter**
Create blank line	Press **Enter**
Display/hide nonprinting characters	Click on **Show/Hide** button
Align text horizontally	Use **Tab** key
Delete character to left of insertion point	Press **Backspace**
Select text	Point to first (or final) character of text, press and hold mouse button, drag across text to final (or first) character, release mouse button
Delete character to right of insertion point	Press **Del**
Delete selected text	Select text, press **Del**
Replace selected text	Select text, type replacement text
Save document for first time	Choose **File, Save As**

Desired Result	How to Do It
Rename document or save it to new location	Choose **File, Save As**
Save previously saved document under same name/location	Click on **Save** button
Turn on automatic save option	Choose **Tools, Options**; click on **Save** tab; check **Automatic Save Every _____ Minutes** option; if desired, change number of minutes between auto-saving; click on **OK**
Print active document	Choose **File, Print**
Close active document	Click on document-window **Close** box
Create new document	Click on **New** button
Open file	Click on **Open** button, select drive and folder, double-click on file name
Open recently used document	Choose **File**, click on document name at bottom of File menu
Scroll up or down one line	Click on **up** or **down scroll** arrow
Scroll to top, bottom, or middle of document	Drag **vertical scroll** box to top, bottom, or middle of scroll bar
Scroll up or down one screen	Click in **vertical scroll** bar above or below scroll box
Scroll left or right one column	Click on **left** or **right scroll** arrow
Scroll to left edge, right edge, or middle of document	Drag **horizontal scroll** box to left, right, or middle of scroll bar

Desired Result	How to Do It
Scroll left or right one screen	Click in **horizontal scroll** bar to left or right of scroll box
Move up one screen	Press **PgUp**
Move down one screen	Press **PgDn**
Move to beginning of document	Press **Ctrl+Home**
Move to end of document	Press **Ctrl+End**
Move to beginning of line	Press **Home**
Move to end of line	Press **End**
Move to top of page	Press **F5**; type page number and click on **OK**; repeat previous step, if desired; when finished, click on **Close**
Search for text	Choose **Edit, Find** (or press **Ctrl+F**); type search text; select desired search options; click on **Find Next** (or press **Enter**); if desired, perform another search; when finished, click on **Close**
Change document magnification	Open Zoom Control box; click on desired magnification option
Open Help Topics window	Press **F1**
Obtain context-sensitive help	Press **F1**; or press **Shift+F1**, make menu choice, or click on any button or part of application window
Exit Help	Double-click on Help window **Close** box

In the next chapter, you'll learn how to edit text. The editing process includes replacing found text, moving text, and copying text. You'll also be introduced to a handy way to undo an action when you change your mind about an editing decision.

IF YOU'RE STOPPING HERE

If you need to break off here, please exit Word (for help, see "Exiting Word" in Chapter 1). If you want to proceed directly to the next chapter, please do so now.

CHAPTER 3: EDITING TEXT

Techniques for
Selecting Text

Using Replace to
Replace Found Text

Moving and
Copying Text

Using Undo to
Reverse Your Last
Operation

In Chapter 2, you learned the basics of editing—how to insert, select, replace, and delete text. In this chapter we'll introduce you to some of Word's more advanced editing techniques. You'll learn sophisticated ways to select text and then move and copy this text to other locations in your document. You'll find out how to use the Replace command (Find's more powerful cousin) to find text and replace it with new text of your choice. Finally, we'll show you how to use the Undo command to rescue yourself from a potentially catastrophic word processing mistake.

When you're done working through this chapter, you will know

- How to use the mouse, the keyboard, and menus to select text
- How to use the Replace command to replace found text
- How to move and copy text
- How to use the Undo command to reverse your last operation

TECHNIQUES FOR SELECTING TEXT

Before you can move or copy text, you must select it. You can do this by using the mouse, the keyboard, or menus. Table 3.1 lists Word's text selection techniques.

Table 3.1   **Text Selection Techniques**

Selection Technique	How to Do It
Dragging	Point at one end of text you want to select; press and hold mouse button; move (drag) mouse pointer to other end of text; release mouse button; all text between ends is selected
Using Shift	Place insertion point at one end of text; press and hold Shift; then click at other end of text you want to select (do not drag); release Shift; all text between ends is selected
Selecting word	Point anywhere inside word and double-click mouse button; trailing space is automatically selected along with word
Selecting sentence	Point anywhere inside sentence; press and hold Ctrl key; then click mouse button; release Ctrl; end punctuation and trailing spaces are automatically selected along with sentence

Table 3.1   **Text Selection Techniques (Continued)**

Selection Technique	How to Do It
Selecting line	Point in *selection bar* area (blank vertical bar on left side of document window) next to line and click mouse button; all text on line is selected
Selecting multiple lines	Point in selection bar next to first or last line of text you want to select; press and hold mouse button; then drag down or up; release mouse button; all lines you "dragged" are selected
Selecting paragraph	Point in selection bar next to paragraph and double-click mouse button; ending paragraph mark is selected along with paragraph
Selecting entire document	Choose Edit, Select All; or, point anywhere in selection bar, press and hold Ctrl; click mouse button; then release Ctrl
Extending existing selection	While holding Shift, click beyond existing selection; selection extends to that point
Shortening existing selection	While holding Shift, click inside existing selection; selection shortens to that point
Deselecting existing selection	Make another selection; or, click mouse button in the text area anywhere outside existing selection

If you are not running Word, please start it now (for help, see "Starting Word" in Chapter 1). Let's begin this chapter's activities by opening a new document file and then using the mouse-dragging method to select text:

1. Click on the **Open** button to display the Open dialog box.

2. If your **Word Work** folder is not already selected, select it now.

3. In the list of files, double-click on **Editing** to open the document file.

4. Point to the left of the *C* in *Corporate* in the third line of the document.

5. Drag to the right to select **Corporate** and the trailing space.

6. Release the mouse button. Your screen should resemble Figure 3.1.

Figure 3.1   **Dragging the mouse to select text**

Global·Travel¶
Complete·Travel·Services¶
for·the·Corporate·Traveler¶
¶
Introduction¶
¶
Global·Travel·has·five·branches:·Philadelphia,·Pennsylvania;·San·Francisco,·California;·Chicago,·Illinois;·
Miami,·Florida;·and·Houston,·Texas.·Each·of·these·offices·is·operated·by·a·team·of·qualified·managers·and·
experienced·agents·whose·goal·is·to·provide·your·company·with·quality·service·at·the·lowest·price.¶
¶
Global·Travel·is·a·full-service,·multi-branch·travel·agency,·which·was·founded·in·1970.·Our·specialty·is·
corporate·travel.¶
¶
Customer·Service¶
¶
The·corporate·travel·division·of·Global·Travel·is·designed·to·offer·the·best·and·most·professional·service·
available·to·your·business·travelers.·We·encourage·you·to·tour·our·facility·and·meet·our·staff·at·your·
convenience.¶
¶

Now let's use the whole-word selection technique:

1. Point to the word *five* in the first paragraph of the document.

2. Double-click the mouse button to select the entire word **five**. Note that selecting *five* deselects *Corporate*.

3. Examine the selected text. The trailing space after *five* is also selected.

Now let's use the selection bar to select text:

1. Move the mouse pointer into the selection bar—the blank vertical bar between the left edge of the document window and the left edge of the document text (see Figure 3.2). Note that the pointer changes from an I-beam into an arrow.

2. Point in the selection bar next to the line beginning with *Global Travel is a full-service.* Click the mouse button to select the entire line.

Figure 3.2   ## The selection bar

Selection bar

Global·Travel¶
Complete·Travel·Services¶
for·the·Corporate·Traveler¶
¶
Introduction¶
¶
Global·Travel·has·five·branches:·Philadelphia,·Pennsylvania;·San·Francisco,·California;·Chicago,·Illinois;·
Miami,·Florida;·and·Houston,·Texas.·Each·of·these·offices·is·operated·by·a·team·of·qualified·managers·and·
experienced·agents·whose·goal·is·to·provide·your·company·with·quality·service·at·the·lowest·price.¶
¶
Global·Travel·is·a·full-service,·multi-branch·travel·agency,·which·was·founded·in·1970.·Our·specialty·is·
corporate·travel.¶
¶
Customer·Service¶
¶
The·corporate·travel·division·of·Global·Travel·is·designed·to·offer·the·best·and·most·professional·service·
available·to·your·business·travelers.·We·encourage·you·to·tour·our·facility·and·meet·our·staff·at·your·
convenience.¶

3. Point in the selection bar next to *Global Travel has five branches.* Double-click the mouse button to select the entire paragraph.

4. Point in the selection bar next to *Introduction*. Press and hold the mouse button, and then drag down to the paragraph mark before *Customer Service* to select multiple lines of text. Release the mouse button.

Let's use the Shift key to select a block of text and then extend and shorten this selection:

1. Place the insertion point before the *C* in *Corporate* in the third line of the document.

2. Press and hold **Shift**; then click the mouse pointer in the space after *five* to select all the text from *Corporate* to *five*. Release **Shift** (see Figure 3.3).

Figure 3.3   ## Selecting text with the mouse and the Shift key

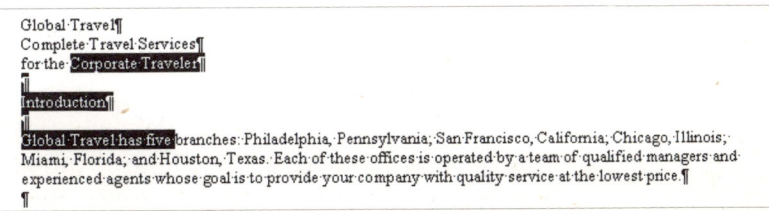

Global·Travel¶
Complete·Travel·Services¶
for·the·Corporate·Traveler¶
¶
Introduction¶
¶
Global·Travel·has·five·branches:·Philadelphia,·Pennsylvania;·San·Francisco,·California;·Chicago,·Illinois;·
Miami,·Florida;·and·Houston,·Texas.·Each·of·these·offices·is·operated·by·a·team·of·qualified·managers·and·
experienced·agents·whose·goal·is·to·provide·your·company·with·quality·service·at·the·lowest·price.¶
¶

3. Point to the right of the *s* in *Texas* in the next line down (but do *not* click). Press and hold **Shift**; then click the mouse button to extend the selection through to the end of *Texas*. Release **Shift**.

4. Point to the left of the *P* in *Philadelphia*. Note that the pointer appears as an arrow (instead of an insertion point) when you point to selected text. Press and hold **Shift**; then click the mouse button to shorten the selection. Release **Shift**.

Finally, let's use the menu to select the entire document:

1. Choose **Edit, Select All** to select the entire document.

2. Click anywhere within the text area to *deselect*.

PRACTICE YOUR SKILLS

1. Select the first sentence of the paragraph beginning with *Global Travel is a full-service*, using the mouse-dragging technique.

2. Deselect.

3. Select the same sentence as in step 1, this time using the mouse in conjunction with **Ctrl** to select the entire sentence without dragging. (For help, refer to Table 3.1, earlier in this chapter.)

4. Use the double-clicking technique to select each of the following words in the first paragraph: *Global, Philadelphia, Texas, qualified, price*. Note that double-clicking selects the trailing space after a word, but not the trailing comma (as in *Philadelphia,*) or period (as in *Texas.* and *price.*).

5. Use the selection-bar technique to select the first line of the document. Extend the selection to include the first four lines. Shorten the selection to include the first two lines.

6. Place the insertion point at the top of the document.

USING REPLACE TO REPLACE FOUND TEXT

In Chapter 2, you learned how to use Find to search for text in a document. Here you'll learn how to use the Replace command to search for text and replace it with new text of your choice.

Replace is one of Word's most powerful commands. Let's say you typed a 100-page document that made frequent reference to a man named *Pablo Sitauskus* and then you found out that the correct spelling was *Sitauskis*. Normally you'd have to find each occurrence of *Sitauskus* and retype it—an ugly task considering the length of the document. Using Edit, Replace, however, you could issue a single command that would automatically (and rapidly) replace every occurrence of *Sitauskus* with *Sitauskis*.

To use Replace to replace found text in a document:

- Choose *Edit, Replace* to open the Replace dialog box.

- In the Find What text box, type the *search text* (the text you wish to find).

- In the Replace With text box, type the *replace text* (the text you wish to replace the search text).

- If necessary, check your desired search option(s)—*Match Case, Find Whole Words Only, Use Pattern Matching, Sounds Like,* or *Find All Word Forms.*

- If necessary, click on the Search list box and select *Down* (to search from the insertion point to the end of the document), *Up* (to search from the insertion point to the beginning of the document), or *All* (to search the entire document).

- Click on *Find Next* (or press *Enter*); Word highlights the first occurrence of your search text.

- Click on either *Replace* (to replace the found text and search for the next occurrence), *Find Next* (to leave the found text unchanged and search for the next occurrence), or *Replace All* (to replace all occurrences of the search text throughout the rest of the document).

- Repeat the previous step as many times as necessary until you have searched through the entire document, or cancel your search at any time by clicking on *Cancel*.

- Close the Replace dialog box.

Let's use the procedures just described to find and replace some text in the active document:

1. Choose **Edit, Replace** to open the Replace dialog box (see Figure 3.4).

Figure 3.4 **The Replace dialog box**

2. In the Find What text box, type **20**. This is the text we will search for and replace.

3. Press **Tab** to select the Replace With text box and then type **50**. This is the text that will replace the search text (*20*).

4. Uncheck (deselect) the **Find Whole Words Only** and **Match Case** options, if necessary.

5. If necessary, click on **All** in the Search list box to search the entire document.

6. Click on **Find Next** to find the first occurrence of *20*. (You may need to move the dialog box to see the text.)

7. Click on **Replace** to replace *20* with *50* and to search for the next occurrence of *20*.

8. Click on **Find Next** to leave *20-30%* unchanged and search for the next occurrence of *20*.

9. Click on **Replace** to replace *20* with *50* and search for the next occurrence of *20*. The message

        Word has finished searching the document.

    is displayed.

10. Click on **OK** to remove the message. Because there are no more occurrences of *20*, the insertion point moves back to where it was in the document when you began the search.

11. Click on **Close** to close the Replace dialog box.

You'll have a chance to use the Replace All command in the "Practice Your Skills" section at the end of this chapter.

MOVING AND COPYING TEXT

Another of Word's powerful editing features is its ability to move and copy text within a document. You can, for example, quickly and easily move a table of numbers from the top of the fifth page of a business report to the bottom of the 11th page, or copy a four-line address to several locations within the body of a letter.

THE CLIPBOARD

Windows provides a temporary storage area called the *Clipboard* for those times when you move or copy text. When selected text is *cut* (removed) or copied, it is placed on the Clipboard. *Pasting* inserts a copy of the Clipboard contents before the insertion point. You'll notice that the Paste button on the toolbar resembles a clipboard. An entry remains on the Clipboard, either until you cut or copy another entry to it, or until you exit Windows.

MOVING TEXT

To move text within a document:

* Select the text to be moved.

* Click on the *Cut* button in the toolbar to cut the selected text from the document and place it on the Clipboard.

* Place the insertion point where you want to move this text.

* Click on the *Paste* button to paste the cut text before the insertion point.

Let's practice moving text from one location to another within a document:

1. If you aren't at the beginning of the document, press **Ctrl+Home** to move there, and then drag in the selection bar to select the paragraph beginning with *Global Travel is a full-service* and the blank line below it.

2. Click on the **Cut** button to remove the selected text from the document and place it on the Windows Clipboard.

3. Place the insertion point before the *G* in *Global Travel has five*.

4. Click on the **Paste** button to paste a copy of the Clipboard contents before the insertion point (see Figure 3.5).

Figure 3.5   **Page 1 of Editing, after pasting**

Global·Travel¶
Complete·Travel·Services¶
for·the·Corporate·Traveler¶
¶
Introduction¶
¶
Global·Travel·is·a·full-service,·multi-branch·travel·agency,·which·was·founded·in·1970.·Our·specialty·is·
corporate·travel.¶
¶
Global·Travel·has·five·branches:·Philadelphia,·Pennsylvania;·San·Francisco,·California;·Chicago,·Illinois;·
Miami,·Florida;·and·Houston,·Texas.·Each·of·these·offices·is·operated·by·a·team·of·qualified·managers·and·
experienced·agents·whose·goal·is·to·provide·your·company·with·quality·service·at·the·lowest·price.¶
¶
Customer·Service¶
¶
The·corporate·travel·division·of·Global·Travel·is·designed·to·offer·the·best·and·most·professional·service·
available·to·your·business·travelers.·We·encourage·you·to·tour·our·facility·and·meet·our·staff·at·your·
convenience.¶
¶

COPYING TEXT

To copy text within a document:

• Select the text to be copied.

• Click on the *Copy* button in the toolbar to copy the selected text to the Clipboard.

• Place the insertion point where you want to copy this text.

• Click on the *Paste* button to paste the Clipboard text before the insertion point.

Now let's practice copying text within a document:

1. Select the first four lines of the document (the three-line page heading and the blank line below it).

2. Click on the **Copy** button to place a copy of the selected text on the Clipboard. Note that the selected text is not removed from the document, as it was when you used Cut.

3. Use **F5** (Go To) to place the insertion point at the top of page 2.

4. Click on the **Paste** button to paste a copy of the Clipboard contents before the insertion point (see Figure 3.6).

Figure 3.6   **Page 2 of Editing, after pasting**

```
Global·Travel¶
Complete·Travel·Services¶
for·the·Corporate·Traveler¶
¶
Discounts¶
¶
Global·Travel·guarantees·the·lowest·air·fares·available.·Due·to·the·volume·of·tickets·that·we·issue,·several·
of·the·large·air·carriers·offer·us·special·discounts·that·we·can·pass·on·to·our·clients.¶
¶
Our·quality-control·specialists·check·each·of·your·tickets·to·guarantee·that·you·have·received·the·lowest·
rate·available.·In·addition,·each·ticket·is·checked·to·ensure·that·it·includes·seating·assignments·and·
boarding·passes·before·it·is·delivered·to·you.¶
¶
Deliveries¶
¶
Our·courier·makes·daily·deliveries,·both·in·the·morning·and·afternoon,·to·offices·within·50·miles·of·our·
local·branch.·All·of·our·offices,·each·located·across·from·the·local·airport,·have·drive-up·windows.·If·you·
make·last-minute·travel·plans·with·us·you·can·pick·up·your·ticket·right·at·the·drive-up·window.¶
¶
```

PRACTICE YOUR SKILLS

1. Place the insertion point at the top of page 3.

2. Paste the contents of the Clipboard at the insertion point. Because a copy of the text is still on the Clipboard, you do not need to copy the text again before pasting.

3. Save the document as **My Editing**.

USING UNDO TO REVERSE YOUR LAST OPERATION

Word provides an Undo command that allows you to reverse (undo) one or more of the most recent operations that you have performed.

Use either of the following Undo methods to reverse your last operation:

- Click on the *Undo* button in the toolbar.

- Choose *Edit, Undo.*

You can also repeat an action that you've canceled (with Undo) by using the Redo command. (This is the equivalent of choosing the Repeat option from the Edit menu.) To repeat an action that you've undone, click on the Redo button in the toolbar.

Note: It is possible to Undo or Redo any of several actions, not just the most recent one. To list several of the most recent procedures that you've performed or undone, click on the down arrow button immediately to the right of the Undo or Redo button, respectively. Then drag to select the operation that you wish to undo or redo.

Let's delete a block of text from My Editing and then use the Undo feature to undelete this text:

1. Select the heading *Flight Insurance* near the top of page 3.

2. Press **Del** to delete the text. (Because you used Del rather than Cut or Copy, the text has not been placed on the Clipboard.)

3. Click on **Edit** to display the Edit drop-down menu. Observe the Undo option at the top; it reads *Undo Clear.* The Edit, Undo option changes to reflect the operation to be undone. Close the Edit menu.

4. Click on the **Undo** button to restore your deleted text.

Now let's use the Undo button to reverse a potentially catastrophic text-replacement mistake:

1. Select the entire document. (Choose **Edit, Select All**.)

2. Type your first initial. Word prompts:

   > Are you sure you want to replace the current selection?

   This prompt is intended as a safeguard to prevent you from accidentally replacing (thus deleting) the entire contents of your document. For now, we'll ignore its warning.

3. Press **Enter** (or click on **Yes**) to replace the entire document with your first initial. Surprise! All that's left in the document window is a single letter. We should have taken Word's warning more seriously.

4. Click on the **Undo** button to restore the original text. All is well.

5. Deselect to avoid deleting the entire document again.

6. Click on the **Save** button to update the document—that is, to save it with the same name and in the same location.

7. Close the document window.

PRACTICE YOUR SKILLS

In Chapters 2 and 3, you've learned how to navigate within a document, and how to select, replace, move, and copy text. The following two Practice Your Skills activities give you the opportunity to apply these techniques to realistic word processing situations.

Follow these steps to produce the final document shown in Figures 3.7 and 3.8 from the original document Practice 3A.

1. Open **Practice 3A** (Chapter 2).

2. Replace all occurrences of *Mayco* with **Macco**. (**Hint:** Click on **Replace All** in the Replace dialog box.)

3. Move the second paragraph on page 1 (beginning with *Congratulations to all*), and the blank line below it, to before the first paragraph on page 1 (beginning with *As we expected*).

Figure 3.7   **Page 1 of My Practice 3A**

Macco Plastics Inc.
Quarterly Sales Report
First Quarter

1. Introduction

Congratulations to all of you! An initial review of the sales figures for the nation reveals a surge in sales in all of Macco's sales areas. Major new clients have been added and many new products are on the way.

As we expected when we entered the field, computer-related products, such as keyboard housings and protective carrying cases, are accounting for a major portion of this upswing.

2. Regional Updates

Midwestern Territory

After several years of falling sales due to the slump in the auto industry, Blair Williams and his folks have something to celebrate. The recent boom in auto manufacturing has led to renewed demand of Macco Products in Detroit.

Northeastern Territory

John Martinson and his group are doing a great job in Nashua. They have secured major contracts for a wide range of new and existing products. Much of this business is coming from Computer Equipment Corporation, a major client of Macco's.

Southern Territory

Mark Daley and his group have done a fine job of maintaining relations with Becker's Product Development Division in Boca Raton. They have been working closely with Becker to decrease manufacturing costs.

3. Computer Study

A companywide study will begin in March, under the direction of Cathy Donaldson and Bill Schuster in data processing, to determine how to most effectively implement automation in our firm. We will be making a large commitment to productivity gains via computerization sometime late this year.

Figure 3.8   **Page 2 of My Practice 3A**

Macco Plastics Inc.
Quarterly Sales Report
First Quarter

4. Quarterly Meeting

The quarterly meeting will take place in Memphis this time. You will find the agenda attached to this report.

5. Conclusion

If the recovery continues at the current pace, this year should be a banner year for all of us at Macco. We want to thank all of you for the outstanding jobs you have done and, most important, for standing by Macco in hard times. Keep up the good work!

John Smith
Regional Coordinator
Macco Plastics Inc.

4. Copy the three-line heading and the blank line below it on the top of page 1 to the top of page 2.

5. Save the document as **My Practice 3A** (Chapter 2).

6. Print the document and compare it to Figures 3.7 and 3.8 (Chapter 2).

7. Close the document (Chapter 2).

Follow these steps to produce the final document shown in Figures 3.9 and 3.10 from the original document Practice 3B:

1. Open **Practice 3B** (Chapter 2).

2. Replace all case-matching occurrences of *Territory* with **Region**.

3. Move the heading *3. Computer Study* and the subsequent paragraph and paragraph marks on page 1 to before the heading *2. Regional Updates*.

4. Change *3. Computer Study* to **2. Computer Study** (Chapter 2).

5. Change *2. Regional Updates* to **3. Regional Updates** (Chapter 2).

6. Add the current date as a fourth line to the three-line heading on the top of page 1 (Chapter 2).

7. Copy the entire date line into the heading on the top of page 2.

8. Save the document as **My Practice 3B** (Chapter 2).

9. Print the document and compare it to Figures 3.9 and 3.10 (Chapter 2).

10. Close the document (Chapter 2).

SUMMARY

In this chapter, you learned how to use the mouse, keyboard, and menus to select text; how to use the Edit, Replace command to replace found text; how to move and copy text; and how to use the Undo command to reverse one or more of your most recent operations.

Figure 3.9   **Page 1 of My Practice 3B**

Macco Plastics Inc.
Quarterly Sales Report
First Quarter
(today's date)

1. Introduction

Congratulations to all of you! An initial review of the sales figures for the nation reveals a surge in sales in all of Macco's sales regions. Major new clients have been added and many new products are on the way.

As we expected when we entered the field, computer-related products, such as keyboard housings and protective carrying cases, are accounting for a major portion of this upswing.

2. Computer Study

A companywide study will begin in March, under the direction of Cathy Donaldson and Bill Schuster in data processing, to determine how to most effectively implement automation in our firm. We will be making a large commitment to productivity gains via computerization sometime late this year.

3. Regional Updates

Midwestern Region

After several years of falling sales due to the slump in the auto industry, Blair Williams and his folks have something to celebrate. The recent boom in auto manufacturing has led to renewed demand of Macco Products in Detroit.

Northeastern Region

John Martinson and his group are doing a great job in Nashua. They have secured major contracts for a wide range of new and existing products. Much of this business is coming from Computer Equipment Corporation, a major client of Macco's.

Southern Region

Mark Daley and his group have done a fine job of maintaining relations with Becker's Product Development Division in Boca Raton. They have been working closely with Becker to decrease manufacturing costs.

Figure 3.10   **Page 2 of My Practice 3B**

Macco Plastics Inc.
Quarterly Sales Report
First Quarter
(today's date)

4. Quarterly Meeting

The quarterly meeting will take place in Memphis this time. You will find the agenda attached to this report.

5. Conclusion

If the recovery continues at the current pace, this year should be a banner year for all of us at Macco. We want to thank all of you for the outstanding jobs you have done and, most important, for standing by Macco in hard times. Keep up the good work!

John Smith
Regional Coordinator
Macco Plastics Inc.

Here's a quick reference guide to the Word features introduced in this chapter:

Desired Result	How to Do It
Select text by dragging	Point at one end of text to be selected; press and hold mouse button; drag mouse pointer to other end of text; release mouse button
Select text by using Shift	Place insertion point at one end of text; press and hold **Shift**; click at other end of text; release **Shift**
Select word	Point anywhere inside word and double-click
Select sentence	Point anywhere inside sentence; press and hold **Ctrl**; click mouse button; release **Ctrl**
Select line	Point in selection bar next to line and click
Select multiple lines	Point in selection bar next to first or last line of text to be selected; press and hold mouse button; drag down or up; release mouse button
Select paragraph	Point in selection bar next to paragraph and double-click
Select entire document	Choose **Edit, Select All**; or, point anywhere in selection bar; press and hold **Ctrl**, click mouse button; release **Ctrl**
Extend existing selection	While holding **Shift**, click beyond existing selection
Shorten existing selection	While holding **Shift**, click inside existing selection
Deselect existing selection	Make another selection; or, click in text area anywhere outside existing selection

Desired Result	How to Do It
Replace found text in document	Choose **Edit, Replace**; type search text in Find What text box; type replace text in Replace With text box; select desired search options; click on **Find Next** (or press **Enter**) to find first occurrence; click on either **Replace, Find Next**, or **Replace All**; repeat previous step as many times as necessary until you have searched through entire document (or cancel search at any time by clicking on **Cancel**); close **Replace** dialog box
Move text within document	Select text to be moved; click on the **Cut** button; place insertion point where you want to move text; click on **Paste** button
Copy text within document	Select text to be copied; click on **Copy** button; place insertion point where you want to copy text; click on **Paste** button
Undo last operation	Click on **Undo** button

In the next chapter, you'll learn the basics of character formatting—how to apply and remove character styles (such as bold and italic) and how to change fonts (typestyles) and point sizes of your text.

CHAPTER 4: CHARACTER FORMATTING

Applying Font
Styles

Applying Fonts
and Point Sizes

T he overall effectiveness of a document is directly related to the way it looks. A brilliantly written business report, for example, can be severely undermined by an inappropriate typestyle, print too small to read comfortably, a dizzying barrage of italics or underlining, tables whose columns don't line up, an overbusy page layout, and so on. These next three chapters are devoted to *formatting*—controlling the way your documents look. We'll proceed logically: This chapter covers Word's smallest formatting units, *characters*; Chapter 5 covers its intermediate units, *paragraphs*; and Chapter 6 covers its largest units, *pages*.

When you're done working through this chapter, you will know

- How to apply and remove font styles
- How to change fonts and point sizes

APPLYING FONT STYLES

You can enhance the appearance of your documents and empha-size selected text through the application of font styles (bold, italic, underline, and so on). In this book, for example, we chose to bold certain headings (such as **Desired Result** and **How to Do It**, which appear in each chapter's Summary) and italicize new terms (such as *font styles*). Word provides two methods for apply-ing font styles: the Font dialog box (accessed by issuing the For-mat, Font command) and the font style buttons in the Formatting toolbar.

USING THE FONT DIALOG BOX TO APPLY FONT STYLES

To use the Font dialog box to apply font styles:

- Select the desired text.
- Choose *Format, Font* to open the Font dialog box.
- Click the *Font* tab, if necessary.
- Select your desired font style options.
- Click on *OK* (or press *Enter*) to apply your chosen styles.

To use the Font dialog box to remove font styles, follow the proce-dure just described, selecting *Regular* in the Font Style list.

If you are not running Word, please start it now. Let's begin by opening a new document and modifying its font styles:

1. Click on the **Open** button to display the Open dialog box.

2. If your Word Work folder is not already selected, select it now.

3. In the list of file names, double-click on **Character Formatting** to open the document.

4. Select **Introduction**, near the top of the document.

5. Choose **Format, Font** to open the Font dialog box. Notice that the Font dialog box contains two tabs: the Font tab and the Character Spacing tab (see Figure 4.1). (If you cannot see the contents of the Font tab, click on it to display them.) Under Font Style, the current selection is *Regular*. The Preview box, in the lower-right portion of the dialog box, displays the currently selected text.

Figure 4.1   **The Font dialog box**

6. In the Font Style list box, select (click on) the **Bold** option. Note that the Preview box shows you how your style choice (Bold) will look when applied to the selected text.

7. Click on **OK** (or press **Enter**) to bold your selected text and return to the document.

8. Deselect **Introduction** to verify that it is bolded. You can see font styles better when the text is deselected.

9. Select **Customer Service**, the next heading on page 1.

10. Choose **Format, Font** to open the Font dialog box. Under Font Style, select the **Bold** option, and then click on **OK** (or press **Enter**) to bold *Customer Service*.

Now let's see how to remove the font style that you just applied and then restore it:

1. If *Customer Service* is not selected, select it now.

2. Choose **Format, Font**.

3. Under Font Style, select **Regular**, and then click on **OK** (or press **Enter**) to unbold *Customer Service*.

4. Choose **Edit, Undo Font Formatting** to reverse step 3—that is, to rebold *Customer Service*.

Let's use the Font dialog box to apply multiple styles (italic and underline) to your document's first line:

1. Select **Global Travel**, the first line.

2. Choose **Format, Font**.

3. Under Font Style, select **Italic**. Observe the Preview box text; the text is italicized.

4. Click on the **down arrow** next to the Underline list box to display Word's underline options. Click on **Single** to apply a single underline. Observe the Preview box; the text is now italicized *and* underlined.

5. Click on **OK** (or press **Enter**) to italicize and underline your selected text, *Global Travel*. Deselect the text to see the multiple styles more clearly.

6. Select **Global Travel** again.

7. Choose **Format, Font**.

8. Select the **Regular** font style, and then click on **OK** to remove the italic character style. Deselect *Global Travel* to verify that the italics (but not the underline) have been removed, as shown in Figure 4.2.

USING THE FORMATTING TOOLBAR TO APPLY FONT STYLES

Located just below the Standard toolbar, the Formatting toolbar provides quick access to font style options, including bold, italic, and underline.

To use the Formatting toolbar to apply font styles:

• Select the desired text.

Figure 4.2   **Global Travel, after removing italics**

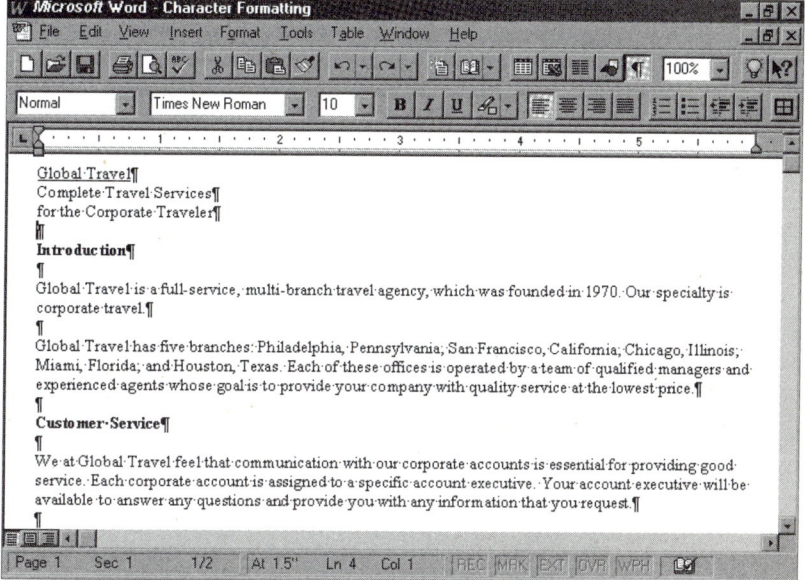

- Click on the desired font style button.

To use the Formatting toolbar to remove font styles:

- Select the desired text.

- Click on the button of the font style you wish to remove.

When you wish to remove all font styles from your selected text, use this shortcut: Press *Ctrl+Spacebar*.

Let's practice using the Formatting toolbar to apply font styles:

1. Move to the top of the document.

2. Select the paragraph beginning with *Global Travel has five branches* (double-click in the selection bar). Do not include the blank line below it.

3. Click on the **Bold** button in the Formatting toolbar to bold the entire paragraph. Note that the button now appears to be pushed in.

B

4. Choose **Format, Font**. Note that the Bold font style is selected. Regardless of how you apply font styles—by using the Formatting toolbar or the Font dialog box—these styles are reflected in both places.

5. Select the **Regular** font style, and then click on **OK**. Observe the Bold button; it no longer appears pushed in.

6. Click on the **Bold** button to rebold the selected text.

7. Click on the **Italic** button to italicize the text.

8. Click on the **Underline** button to single-underline the text (see Figure 4.3).

Figure 4.3   **Selected text with bold, italic, and underline font styles**

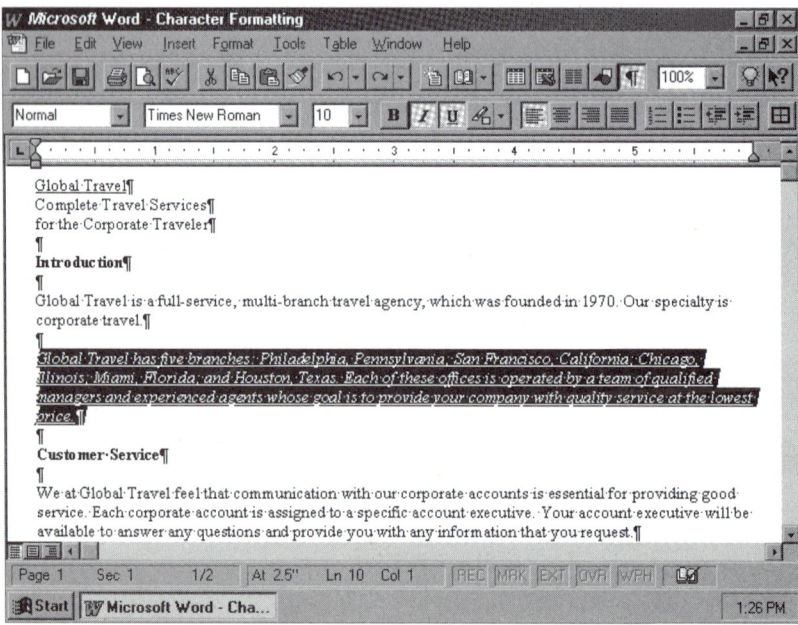

Now let's use the Ctrl+Spacebar technique to remove all font styles from your selected text:

1. If the paragraph *Global Travel has five branches* is not selected, select it now.

2. Press **Ctrl+Spacebar** to remove all font styles from the selected text. Note that this removal is reflected in the font style buttons on the Formatting toolbar.

PRACTICE YOUR SKILLS

1. Verify that your font style removal is also reflected in the Font dialog box.

2. Select the entire document and then italicize it.

3. Use the **Undo** button to reverse step 2.

4. Remove the underline from the first line of the heading (Global Travel); then bold and italicize it.

COPYING FONT STYLES

Once you have applied one or more font styles to your selected text, you can easily reapply (repeat) these styles to newly selected text. To do this:

• Select the new text.

• Choose *Edit, Repeat Font Formatting*, or press the *F4* (Repeat) shortcut key.

Note: If you wish to use the technique just described to repeat multiple font styles (for example, bold *and* italic), you must have applied these font styles through the Font dialog box. If you attempt to repeat multiple font styles that you applied by using the Formatting toolbar, only the last font style you applied will be repeated.

Let's use the F4 key to repeat font styles:

1. Scroll to the bottom of the document. (Drag the vertical scroll box to the bottom of the scroll bar.)

2. Select **Flight Insurance**.

3. Choose **Format, Font**.

4. Select the **Italic** font style. In the Underline list box, click on **Single**. Then click on **OK** to italicize and underline the selected text.

5. Select **Telex**.

6. Open the Edit menu (click on **Edit**). Observe the shortcut key for the Repeat Font Formatting command—it is Ctrl+Y. Close the Edit menu (click on **Edit** again).

7. Press **F4** (Repeat) to repeat your last font style. Note that the selected text (*Telex*) is now italicized and underlined.

8. Use **Go To** to move to the top of page 2.

9. Select **Complete Travel Services**. Click on the **Bold** button, then click on the **Italic** button to bold and italicize the selected text.

10. Move to the top of the document and select **Complete Travel Services**.

11. Press **F4** (Repeat) to attempt to repeat your bold/italic styles. Deselect and observe the text. Because you used the Formatting toolbar instead of the Font dialog box, pressing F4 repeated only the *last* font style: italic.

12. Reselect **Complete Travel Services** and click on the **Bold** button to correct the style.

13. Save the disk file as **My Character Formatting** (use **File, Save As**).

PRACTICE YOUR SKILLS

1. Bold the heading International Travel.

2. Use **F4** (Repeat) to bold the remaining headings: *Corporate Profiles, Worldwide Services, Discounts, Deliveries, Auto Rentals, Hotel Accommodations, Additional Services, Personal Vacations, Flight Insurance,* and *Telex*.

3. Remove the italics and underlining from *Flight Insurance* and *Telex*.

4. Use the **Font** dialog box to bold and italicize (choose the **Bold Italic** option) *for the Corporate Traveler* at the top of page 1.

5. Use **F4** to repeat these multiple styles to *Global Travel* and *for the Corporate Traveler* at the top of page 2.

6. Compare your document to the printouts depicted in Figures 4.4 and 4.5.

7. Update the disk file (click on the **Save** button).

APPLYING FONTS AND POINT SIZES

You can change the shape and size of your selected text by changing the text's *font* and *point size*. The font determines the shape (typestyle) of the text; the point size determines the size of the font (one point equals $\frac{1}{72}$ of an inch). The sentence you are reading, for example, is printed in 10-point Univers font. You can use the Font dialog box or the Formatting toolbar to apply fonts and point sizes.

Note: The specific fonts and point sizes that Word makes available for your use are dependent upon your currently selected printer. PostScript-type laser printers, for example, offer a large variety of fonts and point sizes, whereas low-end dot-matrix printers offer a much more limited selection.

 ### USING THE FONT DIALOG BOX TO APPLY FONTS AND POINT SIZES

To use the Font dialog box to apply fonts and point sizes:

• Select the desired text.

• Choose *Format, Font* to open the Font dialog box.

• Select your desired font and/or point size.

• Click on *OK* (or press *Enter*).

Let's select some text and use the Font dialog box to change its font and point size:

1. Move to the top of the document.

2. Select the lines **Complete Travel Services** and **for the Corporate Traveler** in the heading at the top of page 1.

3. Choose **Format, Font**.

4. Scroll through the Font list box to view your available fonts. Note that the font names are listed in alphabetical

Figure 4.4   **Page 1 of My Character Formatting**

Global Travel
Complete Travel Services
for the Corporate Traveler

Introduction

Global Travel is a full-service, multi-branch travel agency, which was founded in 1970. Our specialty is corporate travel.

Global Travel has five branches: Philadelphia, Pennsylvania; San Francisco, California; Chicago, Illinois; Miami, Florida; and Houston, Texas. Each of these offices is operated by a team of qualified managers and experienced agents whose goal is to provide your company with quality service at the lowest price.

Customer Service

We at Global Travel feel that communication with our corporate accounts is essential for providing good service. Each corporate account is assigned to a specific account executive. Your account executive will be available to answer any questions and provide you with any information that you request.

The corporate travel division of Global Travel is designed to offer the best and most professional service available to your business travelers. We encourage you to tour our facility and meet our staff at your convenience.

International Travel

We offer complete international itinerary assistance. We maintain a supply of passport and visa applications so that we can provide the necessary papers to our clients with minimum delay. Our International Rate Program guarantees you fast and accurate pricing, no matter how complicated the itinerary.

Corporate Profiles

Your company profile will be stored in our computer, and individual profiles will be maintained on each frequent traveler. Each profile will contain information regarding passport information, seating preference, car rental preference, frequent-flyer membership number, and corporate discount numbers. This information ensures that we can provide frequent travelers fast, cost-effective itineraries.

Worldwide Services

Global Travel's Reservation Center will handle all of your weekend and after-hour reservations and changes. The reservation center can be dialed toll-free 24 hours a day. The worldwide service emergency numbers will be clearly marked on your travel itineraries.

Figure 4.5 **Page 2 of My Character Formatting**

Global Travel
Complete Travel Services
for the Corporate Traveler

Discounts

Global Travel guarantees the lowest air fares available. Due to the volume of tickets that we issue, several of the large air carriers offer us special discounts that we can pass on to our clients.

Our quality-control specialists check each of your tickets to guarantee that you have received the lowest rate available. In addition, each ticket is checked to ensure that it includes seating assignments and boarding passes before it is delivered to you.

Deliveries

Our courier makes daily deliveries, both in the morning and afternoon, to offices within 20 miles of our local branch. All of our offices, each located across from the local airport, have drive-up windows. If you make last-minute travel plans with us you can pick up your ticket right at the drive-up window.

Auto Rentals

We guarantee the lowest prices on all car rentals. We will match the type of car with the information provided in the profile for each of your frequent travelers. Each car that is rented through Global Travel carries an extra $50,000 worth of liability insurance.

Hotel Accommodations

Our Corporate Hotel Program is the most competitive and comprehensive program in the world, offering corporate travelers cost savings and extra amenities in most business locations. Global Travel has access to more than 10,000 hotels worldwide, with a range of rooms from economy to luxury. This selection offers your corporate travelers the accommodations they want with a cost savings of 10-30% off the regular rates.

Additional Services

Global Travel also provides the following services for our corporate customers:

Personal Vacations

Our corporate clients are invited to discuss their vacation and personal travel plans with an agent from Global Travel's Vacation Division. Our Vacation Division is skilled in both domestic and international travel.

Flight Insurance

We will supply all clients with $250,000 worth of flight insurance for every trip arranged through Global Travel.

Telex

Service is available for international hotel confirmations.

order. Observe the current font (*Times New Roman*) and the representative text in the Preview box.

5. Select **Arial**. You will need to scroll up through the list to find it. Observe the change in the Preview box text.

6. Scroll through the Size list box to view the available point sizes for the Arial font.

7. Select **12**. Observe the change in the Preview box text.

8. Click on **OK** to apply your chosen font and point size to the selected text. Deselect and compare your screen to Figure 4.6.

Figure 4.6   **Lines 2 and 3 of the heading, after changing the font and point size**

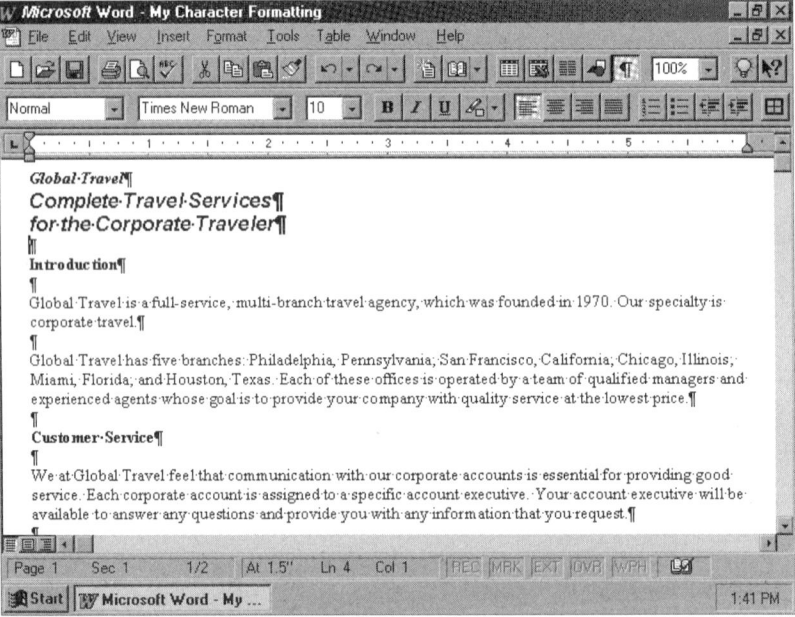

In a previous activity, you used F4 (Repeat) to repeat font styles. Now let's use F4 to repeat the font and point size:

1. Move to the top of page 2.

2. Select **Complete Travel Services** and **for the Corporate Traveler**, lines 2 and 3 in the page heading.

3. Press **F4** to repeat your last font style. Because you used the Font dialog box instead of the Formatting toolbar when you applied the font and point size on page 1, the selected text changes to Arial *and* 12 point.

4. Update the document.

USING THE FORMATTING TOOLBAR TO APPLY FONTS AND POINT SIZES

To use the Formatting toolbar to apply fonts and point sizes:

- Select the desired text.

- Click on the down arrow of the *Font* or *Size* list boxes (respectively, the second and third boxes from the left in the Formatting toolbar).

- Select your desired font or point size.

Let's use the Formatting toolbar to change the font and point size:

1. Select **Global Travel**, the first line on page 2.

2. Open the Font list box in the Formatting toolbar (click on the **down arrow** to the right of the box). It currently displays *Times New Roman*. Select **Arial**.

3. Open the Size list box in the Formatting toolbar. Note that the box currently displays *10*. Select **24** (you'll need to scroll).

PRACTICE YOUR SKILLS

1. Move to the top of page 1.

2. Change the font and point size of the first line, *Global Travel*, to **Arial** and **24**. (Hint: Use the **Formatting** toolbar.)

3. Deselect and compare your screen to Figure 4.7.

4. Save the disk file and close the document.

SUMMARY

In this chapter, you learned the basics of character formatting. You now know how to apply and remove font styles, and how to change fonts and point sizes.

Figure 4.7   **Global Travel, after changing the font and point size**

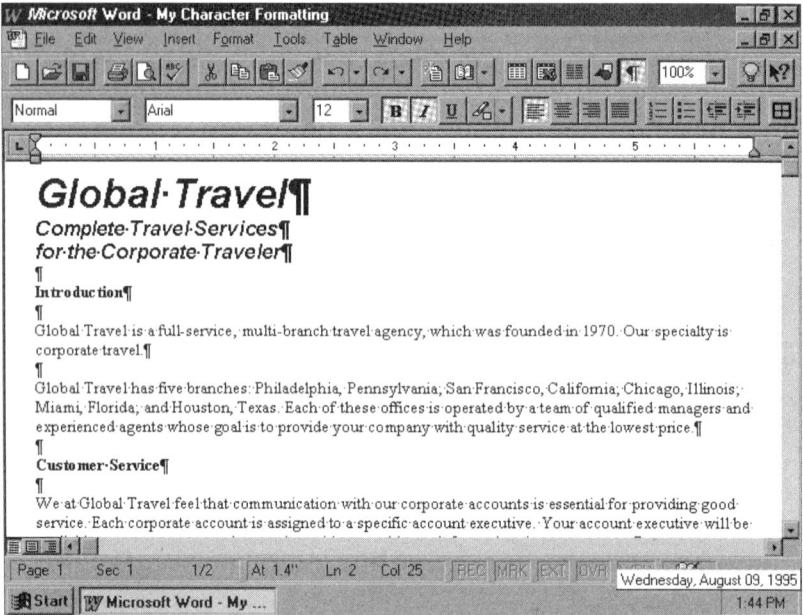

Here's a quick reference guide to the Word features introduced in this chapter:

Desired Result	How to Do It
Use Font dialog box to apply font styles	Select desired text; choose **Format, Font**; select desired font style options; click on **OK**
Use Font dialog box to remove font styles	Follow procedure just described; choose **Regular** font style option
Use Formatting toolbar to apply font styles	Select desired text; click on desired font style button
Use Formatting toolbar to remove font styles	Select desired text; click on button of font style you wish to remove
Remove all font styles from selected text	Press **Ctrl+Spacebar**

Desired Result	How to Do It
Repeat font formatting	Select new text; choose **Edit, Repeat Font Formatting** (or press **F4**)
Use Font dialog box to apply fonts and point sizes	Select desired text; choose **Format, Font**; select desired font and/or point size; click on **OK**
Use Formatting toolbar to apply fonts and point sizes	Select desired text; click on **down arrow** of Font or Size boxes; select desired font or point size

In the next chapter, you will learn the basics of paragraph formatting. You'll find out how to work with tab stops and paragraph indents, create new lines within a paragraph, align paragraphs, and set line spacing.

CHAPTER 5: PARAGRAPH FORMATTING

Working with Tabs

Setting Indents and Line Breaks

Using Shift+Enter to Create a New Line

Setting Paragraph Alignment

Setting Line Spacing

In Chapter 4, you learned the basics of character formatting. In this chapter, we'll move on to Word's intermediate unit of formatting: the paragraph. Many important document layout features are controlled at the paragraph level, including tab stops, indents, text alignment, and line spacing. Mastering paragraph formatting will greatly assist you in presenting professionally laid out, attractive documents.

When you're done working through this chapter, you will know

- How to set, change, and clear tab stops
- How to set and repeat paragraph indents
- How to create new lines within a paragraph
- How to align paragraphs
- How to set line spacing

WORKING WITH TABS

As you learned in Chapter 1, you use tabs to align text at preset tab stops across the page. This type of alignment is particularly important in tables, where several categories of information must line up in precise columns. In the first part of this chapter, you'll learn how to set, change, and clear custom tab stops.

SELECTING PARAGRAPHS FOR PARAGRAPH FORMATTING

Before you set custom tab stops, you must first select the desired paragraph or paragraphs. As you learned in the last chapter, when you select a paragraph for character formatting (character styles, font, point size, and so on), you must select the entire paragraph. However, when you select a paragraph for *paragraph formatting* (tab stops, indents, line spacing, and so on), you *do not* have to select the entire paragraph. To select a *single* paragraph for paragraph formatting, place the insertion point anywhere in the paragraph. You do not have to select (highlight) any characters. To select *multiple* paragraphs for paragraph formatting, select (highlight) a portion of each paragraph.

The techniques just described are paragraph selection shortcuts. If you feel more comfortable selecting entire paragraphs for paragraph formatting, please do so.

TAB TYPES

There are four types of tab stops available in Word. Figure 5.1 illustrates how tab stops align on your computer screen, and Table 5.1 defines each tab type.

Figure 5.1   **Tab types**

Table 5.1   **The Four Tab Types**

Type	How Tab Affects Text
Left-aligned	Text flows to the right of the tab stop.
Centered	Text is centered on the tab stop.
Right-aligned	Text flows to the left of the tab stop.
Decimal-aligned	Text aligns on the decimal point (used for numbers).

Note: By default, left-aligned tab stops are set at 0.5" increments between the margins (0.5", 1", 1.5", and so on). These default tab stops are displayed as small vertical lines at the bottom of the ruler (examples shown shortly).

SETTING CUSTOM TAB STOPS

Word allows you to create your own custom tab stops, and in doing so, to clear its default tab stops. To set custom tab stops:

- Select the desired paragraph(s).

- Click on the *Tab Alignment* button at the left of the tab ruler until the desired tab type is displayed.

- Point at the desired tab-stop position in the ruler, and click the mouse button.

Your custom tab stop is set and all default tab stops to the left of your custom stop are automatically cleared.

As you click on the Tab Alignment button, it changes to indicate the type of tab: *left-aligned, centered, right-aligned,* or *decimal-aligned.* This is illustrated in Figure 5.2.

Figure 5.2   **The four tab indicators**

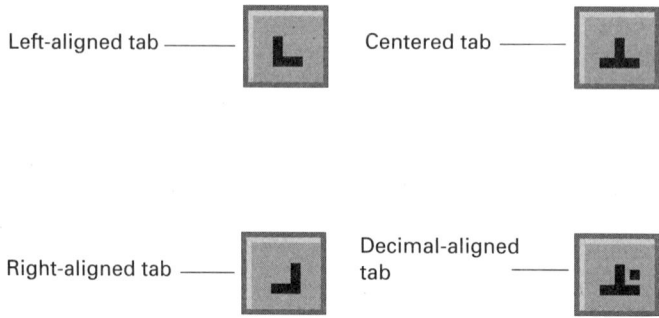

If you are not running Word, please start it now.

Note: The further you progress in this book, the more succinct our activity instructions tend to be. For example, instead of saying "Click on the Open button, select the Word Work folder, and then double-click on Paragraph Formatting to open it," we now simply say "Open Paragraph Formatting from your Word Work folder." If you are unsure of how to perform a certain Word task, use the Index, the end-of-chapter quick reference guides, or Word Help to jog your memory.

Let's open a new document and begin our exploration of tabs by adding text to a tabbed table:

1. Open **Paragraph Formatting** from your Word Work folder.

2. Move to the top of page 2.

3. Examine the tabbed table following the heading *Discounts*. Note that the Paris and Sydney savings percentages (*20%* and *10%*) are misaligned. We will fix this in the next activity.

4. Place the insertion point in the first blank line after the tabbed table.

5. Press **Tab** to move the insertion point to the first tab stop (0.5" to the right) and then type **Hong Kong**.

6. Press **Tab** to move to the second tab stop (1" to the right) and then type **25%**.

7. Press **Enter** to create a new blank line. Compare your screen to Figure 5.3.

Figure 5.3   **Adding text to the Discounts tabbed table**

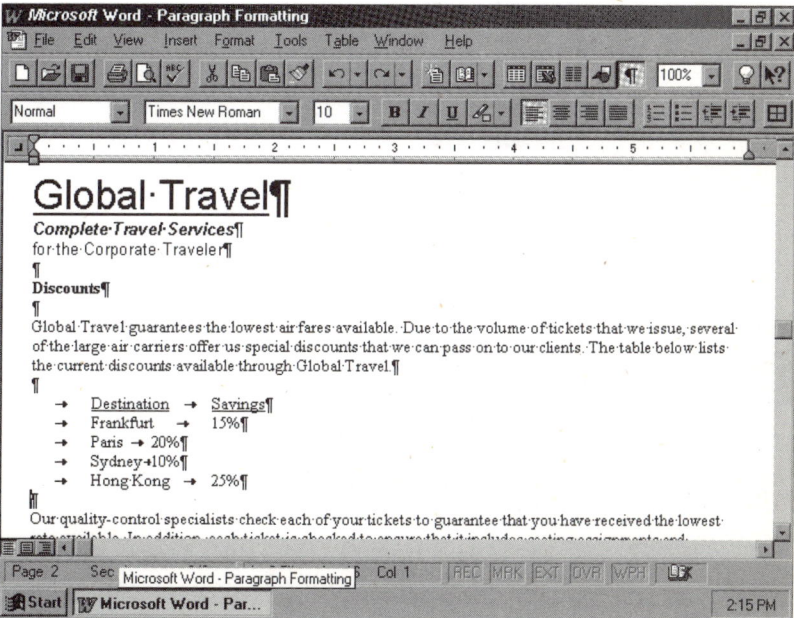

Now let's set some new left-aligned tab stops to fix the Paris and Sydney savings-percentage misalignments. First we need to select the entire table (all five lines). Let's use our multiple paragraph selection shortcut to do this:

1. Select all the text from *Savings* (in the first line) up to and including *Hong* (in the last line). Even though the first and last lines of the table are only partially highlighted, they are fully selected. Any paragraph formatting changes you now make will apply equally to all five lines.

2. Observe the ruler. The tick marks below the ruler measurements indicate that Word's default tab stops are set every half inch (0.5").

3. Observe that the Tab Alignment button is currently set to create a left-aligned tab (see Figure 5.2). Text flows to the right of a left-aligned tab stop. The Tab Alignment button determines the alignment of the *next* tab stop that you set; a left-aligned tab stop is the default.

4. Point directly at the **1"** tick mark in the ruler. Click the mouse button to set a left-aligned tab stop at 1". Note that the default tab stop to the left of 1" has automatically been cleared.

5. Observe the text. The first column in the tabbed table is now 1" from the left margin.

PRACTICE YOUR SKILLS

1. Set a second left-aligned tab stop at **2.5"**. The second column in the table is now properly aligned.

2. Deselect the table, and compare your screen to Figure 5.4.

SETTING DIFFERENT TYPES OF TABS

As mentioned in the previous section, Word provides four types of tab stops: left-aligned, centered, right-aligned, and decimal-aligned. Let's use the ruler and the tab buttons to experiment with these:

1. Scroll down to the tabbed table following the heading *Hotel Accommodations*, near the middle of page 2.

Figure 5.4   **Setting tab stops for the Discounts table**

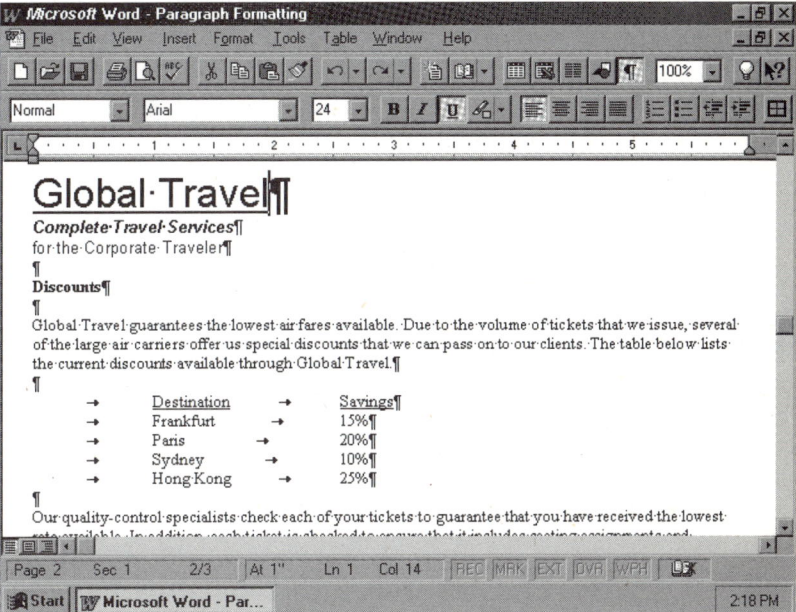

2. Use the multiple paragraph selection shortcut to select the body (lower four lines) of the tabbed table.

3. Click once on the **Tab Alignment** button. It is now set to insert a centered tab (see Figure 5.2). Click a second time; it is set to insert a right-aligned tab. Click a third time; it is set to insert a decimal-aligned tab. Click once again; the Tab Alignment button cycles back to the left-alignment setting.

4. Click twice on the **Tab Alignment** button to right-align the next tab stop you set.

5. Set a right-aligned tab stop at **3.5"**.

6. Click on the **Tab Alignment** button to decimal-align the next tab stop you set. Notice the decimal point in the button's icon. Decimal tabs are used to align numbers containing decimals.

7. Set a decimal tab stop at **5"**. Notice that the tab markers on the ruler reflect the type of tab set at each location.

PRACTICE YOUR SKILLS

1. Prepare to set tab stops for the heading (top line) of the tabbed table. (**Hint:** Use the single paragraph selection short-cut—place the insertion point anywhere within the heading.)

2. Set a centered tab stop at **2.5"**.

3. Set a right-aligned tab stop at **5"**. Note that the heading and body columns are misaligned. We will fix this in the next activity.

 CHANGING THE POSITIONS OF CUSTOM TAB STOPS

Word allows you to quickly and easily change the positions of your custom tab stops. To do this:

• Select the desired paragraph(s).

• In the ruler, drag the custom tab stop to a new position.

 CLEARING CUSTOM TAB STOPS

Word also allows you to quickly clear (delete) your custom tab stops. To do this:

• Select the desired paragraph(s).

• Drag the custom tab stop down into the text area.

Now let's fix the Hotel Accommodations table's misalignment by changing and clearing tabs:

1. Select the body (four lines) of the tabbed table.

2. Drag the decimal tab stop at 5" to **4.75"** to adjust the position of the table's numbers.

3. Place a centered tab stop at **2.5"**. Note that this causes a se-vere misalignment. Why? Because there is now an undesired tab stop in the ruler (the right-aligned tab stop at 3.5"), which prevents the final column of text (*Daily Rate*) from moving to its intended decimal tab-stop location at 4.75".

4. Drag the undesired right-aligned tab stop at 3.5" down off the ruler into the text area, and then release the mouse but-ton to clear this tab stop. Note that the misalignment prob-lem has been fixed.

5. Deselect and compare your screen to Figure 5.5.

6. Save the disk file as **My Paragraph Formatting** (use **File, Save As**).

Figure 5.5   **The Hotel Accommodations table, properly aligned**

USING THE TABS DIALOG BOX TO MANAGE CUSTOM TAB STOPS

We've shown you how to use the ruler to manage your custom tab stops. This is generally the preferred method of tab management because it is quick, easy, and provides immediate visual feedback. You can, however, perform all of the tab-management tasks already presented in this chapter (setting, changing, and clearing tab stops) by using the Tabs dialog box (see Figure 5.6).

The advantage of using the Tabs dialog box is that you can specify exact tab-stop positions that you couldn't choose by using the mouse and ruler (for example, 3.12" or 6.78"). The disadvantages are that you must type in your tab-stop positions and that you only see how your tab-stop settings affect the selected paragraph(s) when you exit the Tabs dialog box.

Figure 5.6   **The Tabs dialog box**

To use the Tabs dialog box for managing your custom tab stops:

• Select the desired paragraph(s).

• Choose *Format, Tabs* to open the Tabs dialog box.

Note: The Tabs dialog box in Figure 5.6 reflects the settings for the tabbed table line beginning with *Madrid*.

• Enter your desired settings to change or clear tab stops.

• Click on *OK* (or press *Enter*).

Note: We recommend that you use the ruler for managing your custom tab stops, except in those rare instances when you need to set an exact tab-stop position that you cannot choose with the mouse and the ruler.

SETTING INDENTS AND LINE BREAKS

Margins define the upper, lower, left, and right page boundaries of an entire document (see "Setting Margins" in Chapter 6 for details on this Word feature). *Indents* define the left and right boundaries of selected paragraphs within a document.

By default, a paragraph's left and right indents are set equal to the document's left and right margins. However, you can modify a paragraph's left and/or right indents without changing the document's margins. Figure 5.7 illustrates the relationship between margins and indents.

Figure 5.7   Margins and indents

First-line-indent marker

Decrease Indent button

Increase Indent button

Left-indent marker

Right-indent marker

Margin

Margin

Indents

INDENT MARKERS

The ruler provides *indent markers* (displayed as triangles—see Figure 5.7) that you can use to control the positions of a selected paragraph's indents. There are three types of indent markers as shown in Figure 5.7.

Indent Marker Type	Location and Function
First-line indent	Upper-left triangle in the ruler; controls the left boundary for the first line of a paragraph

Indent Marker Type	Location and Function
Left indent	Lower-left triangle in the ruler; controls the left boundary of every line in a paragraph but the first
Right indent	Triangle on the right end of the ruler; controls the right boundary for every line in a paragraph

SETTING INDENTS

Word allows you to quickly and easily set indents. To do this:

- Select the paragraph(s) you wish to indent.

- Drag the appropriate indent marker to your desired new position in the ruler.

By default, if you drag the left-indent marker, the first-line-indent marker does not move along with it. To left-indent every line of a paragraph, move both these markers by dragging the small box below the left-indent marker.

THE INCREASE INDENT AND DECREASE INDENT BUTTONS

If you wish to increase or decrease the left indentation of a paragraph, using existing tabs, you can also use the Increase Indent and Decrease Indent buttons in the Formatting toolbar (see Figure 5.7). The left border of the paragraph automatically moves to the next tab stop in the chosen direction. To do so:

- Select the paragraph(s) you wish to affect.

- To increase the left indent to the next tab stop, click on the *Increase Indent* button. To decrease the left-indent to the previous tab stop, click on the *Decrease Indent* button.

REPEATING PARAGRAPH FORMATTING

In the last chapter, you learned how to repeat character formatting. Word also allows you to repeat paragraph formatting. To do this:

- Format a paragraph.

- Select a new paragraph.
- Choose *Edit, Repeat Formatting* (or press *F4*).

Let's set some indents and then repeat them:

1. Move to the top of page 3.

2. Place the insertion point in the *Personal Vacations* heading. This heading is indented 0.5" from the left margin.

3. Observe the ruler. The left-indent marker and the first-line-indent marker (the lower and upper triangles near the left end of the ruler, respectively) are both at 0.5".

4. Place the insertion point in the paragraph beginning with *Our corporate clients*. This paragraph is not indented. Observe the ruler. The indent markers are set even with the margins.

5. Drag the **right-indent** marker—the triangle at the right end of the ruler—to **5.5"**. (Use the measurement in the center of the ruler as a guide.) A right indent creates a different right boundary for the selected paragraph.

6. Point the tip of the mouse pointer at the **left-indent** marker (the lower-left triangle), and drag the **left-indent** marker to 0.5" to change the left boundary of all lines of the paragraph but the first one.

7. Now, drag the **first-line-indent** marker to 0.5" to also change the left boundary of the first line of the paragraph. The entire paragraph now has a left indent of 0.5".

Now let's repeat our indent formatting:

1. Place the insertion point in the paragraph beginning with *We will supply all clients* (the next multiple-line paragraph on page 3).

2. Choose **Edit, Repeat Formatting** (or press **F4**) to repeat your indent formatting. Observe the new indents.

PRACTICE YOUR SKILLS

1. Format the paragraph beginning with *Telex service is available* with left and first-line indents at **0.5"** and a right indent at **5.5"**. (**Hint:** Use **F4**.)

2. Compare your screen to Figure 5.8.

Figure 5.8   **MYCHAP5.DOC, after indent formatting**

SETTING HANGING INDENTS

The term *hanging indent* is used to describe a format in which a paragraph's first line is left-indented less than all of its subsequent lines. In effect, the first line *hangs* over the rest. Hanging indents are commonly used for the paragraphs in bulleted or numbered lists, such as the list of bulleted instructions that appears next or the lists of numbered instructions in the activities throughout this book.

To create a hanging indent:

• Select the desired paragraph(s).

• If necessary, drag the *first-line indent* marker (the upper-left triangle) to the desired position.

• Drag only the *left-indent* marker (the lower-left triangle—not the small box below it) to the desired position (to the right of the first-line-indent marker).

Now let's set some hanging indents and then repeat them:

1. Scroll up to the heading *Newsletter* (near the bottom of page 2).

2. Place the insertion point in the paragraph beginning with *1. Travel Costs*.

3. Drag the **left-indent** marker (the lower-left triangle in the ruler) to **0.5"**. Observe your hanging indent: The second line is indented to 0.5", while the first line remains at the left margin—that is, unindented.

PRACTICE YOUR SKILLS

1. Repeat a 0.5" hanging indent for the paragraphs beginning with *2. Special Fares* and *3. Travel Basics*. (**Hint:** Use **F4**.)

2. Deselect, if necessary, and compare your screen to Figure 5.9.

Figure 5.9   **Setting hanging indents**

USING THE PARAGRAPH DIALOG BOX TO MANAGE YOUR INDENTS

As you've learned in previous sections of this chapter, you can manage custom tab stops by using the Formatting toolbar and the ruler or the Tabs dialog box. Similarly, you can manage indents by using the ruler or the Paragraph dialog box. The same advantages and disadvantages apply to both situations (you may want to review the section on the Tabs dialog box, earlier in this chapter). Again, we recommend that you use the ruler for managing your indents, except in those instances when you need to set an exact indent position that you cannot choose with the mouse and the ruler.

To use the Paragraph dialog box to manage your indents:

• Select the desired paragraph(s).

• Choose *Format, Paragraph* to open the Paragraph dialog box.

• Enter your desired indent settings.

• Click on *OK* (or press *Enter*).

USING SHIFT+ENTER TO CREATE A NEW LINE

When you press Enter to create a new line in a document, you also create a new paragraph. At times, this may be undesirable. For example, let's say that you wanted to insert a new line in the middle of a list within a hanging-indent paragraph. If you pressed Enter to create the new line, you would lose your indent. (Remember, pressing Enter creates a new first-line paragraph, and the first line of a hanging-indent paragraph is not indented.) To remedy this problem, Word allows you to use Shift+Enter to create a new line without creating a new paragraph. To do so:

• Place the insertion point where you want to end the current line and create a new line.

• Press *Shift+Enter;* Word inserts a *newline character* (↵) and creates a new line (without creating a new paragraph).

Let's create some new lines without creating new paragraphs:

1. In the paragraph beginning with *3. Travel Basics*, place the insertion point to the left of the hyphen (-) in *- safer and*.

2. Press **Shift+Enter** to create a new line without creating a new paragraph. Your hanging indent is maintained. Note

that pressing Shift+Enter ends the line with a newline character (↵) instead of with the usual paragraph mark.

3. Press **Shift+Enter** to insert a blank line while maintaining the
   hanging indent. Notice that the newline character is also displayed on the blank line (see Figure 5.10).

Figure 5.10   **Inserted newline characters**

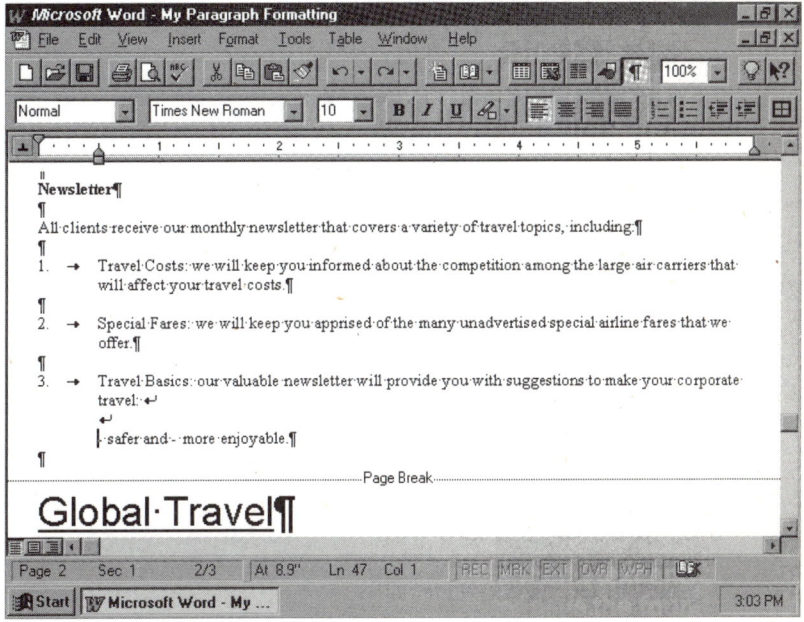

4. Place the insertion point to the left of the second hyphen (-)
   in the same paragraph, - *more enjoyable*.

5. Press **Shift+Enter** twice to create two new lines.

SETTING PARAGRAPH ALIGNMENT

Paragraph alignment determines how text is positioned between
the left and right indents. Word provides four types of paragraph
alignment. Figure 5.11 illustrates how paragraph alignment appears on your computer screen, and Table 5.2 defines each type
of paragraph alignment.

Figure 5.11   **Paragraph alignment types**

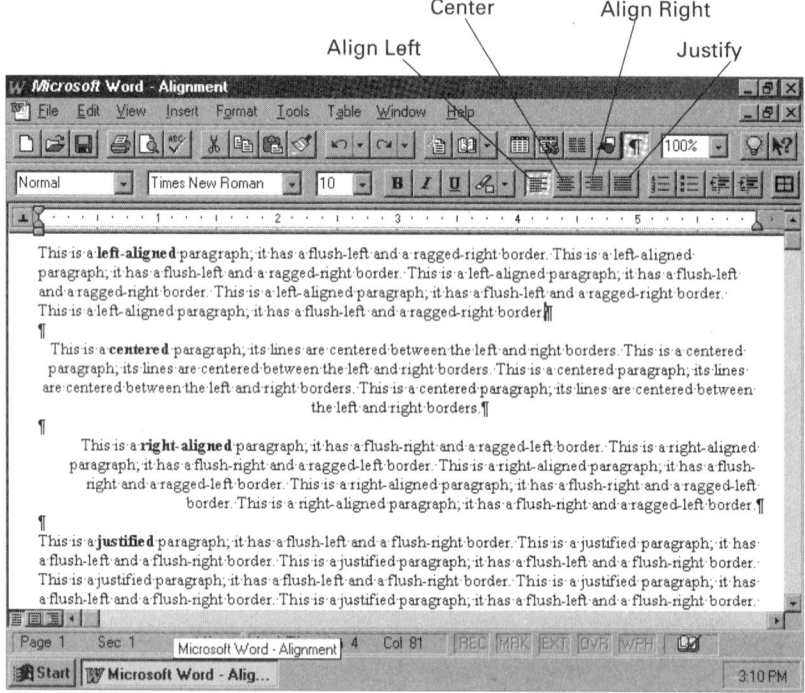

Table 5.2   **The Four Paragraph Alignment Types**

Type	Alignment
Left-aligned	Lines of text are *flush-left* (aligned evenly along the left indent) and *ragged-right* (aligned unevenly along the right indent). Left-aligned is the default paragraph-alignment setting.
Centered	Lines of text are centered between the indents. Both the left and right sides of a centered paragraph are ragged.

Table 5.2 **The Four Paragraph Alignment Types (Continued)**

Type	Alignment
Right-aligned	Lines of text are flush-right and ragged-left, the opposite of left-aligned.
Justified	Lines of text are both flush-left and flush-right. In a justified paragraph, Word adjusts the spacing between words so that they stretch from the left indent to the right indent.

To set paragraph alignment:

- Select the desired paragraph(s).

- Click on the appropriate alignment button in the Formatting toolbar (see Figure 5.11).

Note: You can also use the Alignment option in the Paragraph dialog box to align paragraphs; but, once again, we recommend using the Formatting toolbar.

Let's begin our paragraph-alignment activities by centering some paragraphs:

1. Place the insertion point anywhere within the first line of the document, *Global Travel*. Observe the text-alignment buttons (see Figure 5.11). The Align Left button is currently selected.

2. Click on the **Center** button in the Formatting toolbar (see Figure 5.11) to center each line of the selected paragraph between the left and right indents. In this example, the paragraph contains only one line.

3. Select lines 2 and 3 of the heading.

4. Click on the **Center** button to center both paragraphs.

5. Deselect and compare your screen with Figure 5.12.

Figure 5.12   **Centered paragraphs**

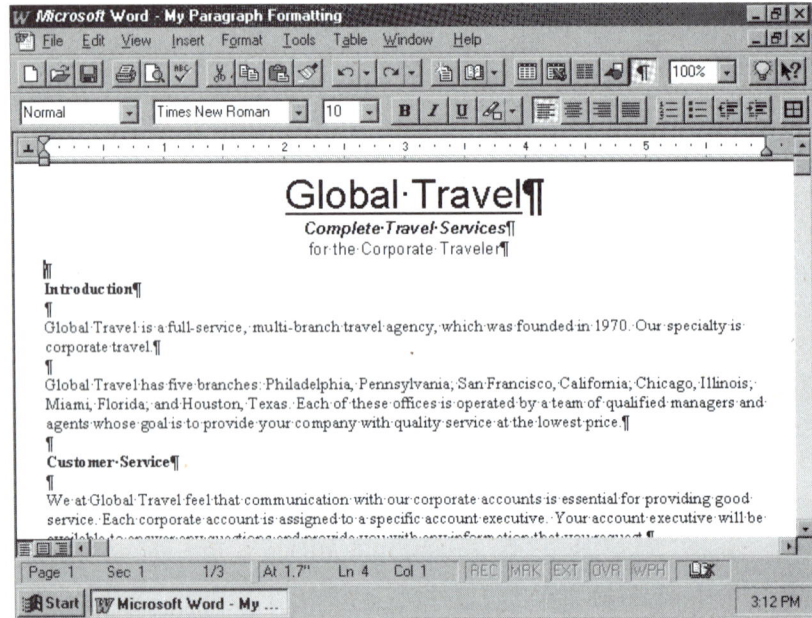

Now let's try the other paragraph alignments:

1. Place the insertion point in the paragraph beginning with *Global Travel has five branches* (the second multiple-line paragraph on page 1). Observe the last word in each line of the selected paragraph: Because the paragraph is left-aligned, text does not always reach the right indent before wrapping to the next line.

2. Click on the **Justify** button (see Figure 5.11). Observe the last word in each line: Word increases the spacing between words in the selected paragraph to fill each line (except the last line, which is too short) so that the text is even with both the left and right indents.

3. Click on the **Align Right** button (see Figure 5.11). Observe the text: Text in the current paragraph now aligns only with the right-indent marker.

4. Click on the **Align Left** button to return the paragraph to its original alignment.

PRACTICE YOUR SKILLS

1. Center all three lines of the heading on the top of page 2.

2. Repeat step 1 for the three-line heading on the top of page 3. (**Hint**: Use **F4**.)

3. Update the disk file.

SETTING LINE SPACING

Line spacing is the vertical distance between lines of text. Word provides six line-spacing options:

- *Single* (the default setting) sets the line spacing to one single line; Single always maintains a minimum of 12-point ($1/6"$) spacing.

- *1.5 lines* sets the line spacing to a line-and-a-half.

- *Double* sets the line spacing to two lines.

- *At Least* allows you to specify a custom minimum line spacing.

- *Exactly* allows you to specify exact line spacing that will not adjust according to font size.

- *Multiple* sets the line spacing to accommodate more than one line; the default is three lines.

To set line spacing:

- Select the desired paragraph(s).

- Choose *Format, Paragraph* to open the Paragraph dialog box; you cannot set line spacing by using the Standard toolbar, Formatting toolbar, or ruler.

- Display the Indents and Spacing folder (click on its tab), if necessary.

- Select your desired line-spacing setting from the *Line Spacing* list box.

- Click on *OK* (or press *Enter*).

Let's use the above procedure to change the line spacing of our document:

1. Move to the top of the document.

2. Select the entire document (choose **Edit, Select All**).

3. Choose **Format, Paragraph**. Examine the Indents and Spacing tab (see Figure 5.13). Unlike the Formatting toolbar and ruler, the Paragraph dialog box provides access to *all* paragraph-formatting options and allows you to type in exact measurements.

Figure 5.13   **The contents of the Indents and Spacing tab**

4. Click on the **down arrow** of the **Line Spacing** list box to open the box and display the line-spacing choices.

5. Select **1.5 Lines** and then click on **OK** (or press **Enter**). Observe the text. The line spacing has changed from 1 to 1.5 lines (see Figure 5.14).

6. Choose **Format, Paragraph** and then open the **Line Spacing** list box (click on its **down arrow**).

7. Select **Double** and then click on **OK**. Observe the text. The line spacing has changed to 2 lines from its previous value of 1.5 lines.

8. Choose **Format, Paragraph** and then open the **Line Spacing** list box.

9. Select **Single** and then click on **OK**. Observe the text. The line spacing has returned to its original value of 1 line.

10. Deselect the text to avoid inadvertently deleting the entire document.

Figure 5.14 **Changing the line spacing to 1.5 lines**

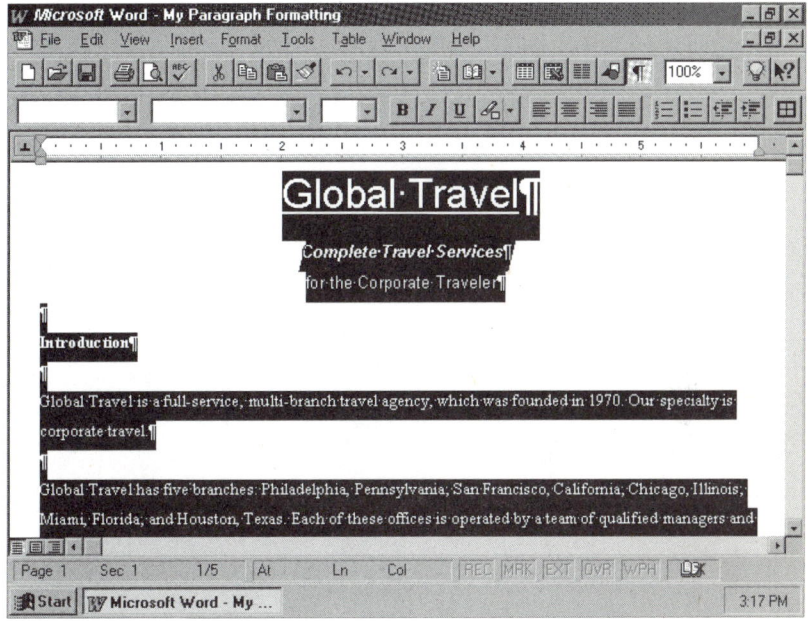

Up to now, you've always saved the changes you made to your active document before closing it. However, you can close a document without saving the changes. Let's see how:

1. Click on the **Close** button. Word prompts:

```
Do you want to save changes to My Paragrah
Formatting?
```

2. Click on **No** to save the document without saving the changes.

PRACTICE YOUR SKILLS

In Chapters 4 and 5, you learned the basics of character and paragraph formatting. The following two Practice Your Skills activities give you the opportunity to apply these formatting techniques to realistic word-processing situations.

Follow these steps to produce the final document shown in Figure 5.15 from the original document Practice 5A:

1. Open **Practice 5A** (Chapter 2).

Figure 5.15   **The completed document My Practice 5A**

Macco Plastics Inc.
Quarterly Sales Report
First Quarter

1. Introduction

Congratulations to all of you! An initial review of the sales figures for the nation reveals a surge in sales in all of Macco's sales regions. Major new clients have been added and many new products are on the way.

As we expected when we entered the field, computer-related products, such as keyboard housings and protective carrying cases, are accounting for a major portion of this upswing.

2. Computer Study

A companywide study will begin in March, under the direction of Cathy Donaldson and Bill Schuster in data processing, to determine how to most effectively implement automation in our firm. We will be making a large commitment to productivity gains via computerization sometime late this year.

3. Regional Updates

Midwestern Region

After several years of falling sales due to the slump in the auto industry, Blair Williams and his folks have something to celebrate. The recent boom in auto manufacturing has led to renewed demand of Macco Products in Detroit.

Northeastern Region

John Martinson and his group are doing a great job in Nashua. They have secured major contracts for a wide range of new and existing products. Much of this business is coming from Computer Equipment Corporation, a major client of Macco's.

Southern Region

Mark Daley and his group have done a fine job of maintaining relations with Becker's Product Development Division in Boca Raton. They have been working closely with Becker to decrease manufacturing costs.

Figure 5.15 **The completed document My Practice 5A (Continued)**

Macco Plastics Inc.
Quarterly Sales Report
First Quarter

4. Quarterly Meeting

The quarterly meeting will take place in Memphis this time. You will find the agenda attached to this report.

5. Conclusion

The following items will be discussed at the next managers' meeting:

A.   Marketing and sales strategies for the introduction of the new System 400 and System 500 product lines.

B.   Current available positions resulting from the early retirement program and normal attrition of personnel.

C.   Development of the new expense form to facilitate the prompt payment of - travel reimbursements - other out-of-pocket expenses and - commissions.

If the recovery continues at the current pace, this year should be a banner year for all of us at Macco. We want to thank all of you for the outstanding jobs you have done and, most important, for standing by Macco in hard times. Keep up the good work!

John Smith
Regional Coordinator
Macco Plastics Inc.

2. Select the entire document and remove all of its character formats (Chapters 3 and 4). (**Hint:** Use the **Ctrl+Spacebar** shortcut.)

3. Bold the following headings (Chapter 4):

   1. **Introduction**

   2. **Computer Study**

   3. **Regional Updates**

   4. **Quarterly Meeting**

   5. **Conclusion**

4. Using the Font dialog box, change the font and point size of the three-line heading on the top of page 2 to **12-point Arial** (Chapter 4).

5. Repeat the formatting in step 4 for the three-line heading on the top of page 1 (Chapter 4).

6. Scroll to the bottom of page 1 (Chapter 2).

7. In the paragraph beginning with *After several years* set left and first-line indents at **0.5"** and a right indent at **5.5"**.

8. Repeat the indents in step 7 for the paragraphs beginning with *John Martinson* and *Mark Daley.*

9. Center the three-line heading on the top of pages 1 and 2.

10. Save the disk file as **My Practice 5A** (Chapter 2).

11. Print the document and compare it to Figure 5.15 (Chapter 2).

12. Close the document (Chapter 2).

Follow these steps to produce the final document shown in Figure 5.16 from the original document Practice 5B.

1. Open **Practice 5B** (Chapter 2).

2. Using the Font dialog box, italicize the first line on page 1, *Macco Plastics Inc.*, and change the point size to 24-point (Chapter 4).

3. Repeat the formatting in step 2 for the first line on page 2 (Chapter 4).

Figure 5.16   **The completed document My Practice 5B**

Macco Plastics Inc.
Quarterly Sales Report
First Quarter

1. Introduction

Congratulations to all of you! An initial review of the sales figures for the nation reveals a surge in sales in all of Macco's sales regions. Major new clients have been added and many new products are on the way.

As we expected when we entered the field, computer-related products, such as keyboard housings and protective carrying cases, are accounting for a major portion of this upswing.

2. Computer Study

A companywide study will begin in March, under the direction of Cathy Donaldson and Bill Schuster in data processing, to determine how to most effectively implement automation in our firm. We will be making a large commitment to productivity gains via computerization sometime late this year.

3. Regional Updates

Midwestern Region

After several years of falling sales due to the slump in the auto industry, Blair Williams and his folks have something to celebrate. The recent boom in auto manufacturing has led to renewed demand of Macco Products in Detroit.

Northeastern Region

John Martinson and his group are doing a great job in Nashua. They have secured major contracts for a wide range of new and existing products. Much of this business is coming from Computer Equipment Corporation, a major client of Macco's.

Southern Region

Mark Daley and his group have done a fine job of maintaining relations with Becker's Product Development Division in Boca Raton. They have been working closely with Becker to decrease manufacturing costs.

Figure 5.16   **The completed document My Practice 5B (Continued)**

Macco Plastics Inc.

Quarterly Sales Report

First Quarter

4. Quarterly Meeting

The quarterly meeting will take place in Memphis this time. You will find the agenda attached to this report.

5. Conclusion

The following items will be discussed at the next managers' meeting:

A.   Marketing and sales strategies for the introduction of the new System 400 and System 500 product lines.

B.   Current available positions resulting from the early retirement program and normal attrition of personnel.

C.   Development of the new expense form to facilitate the prompt payment of

- travel reimbursements

- other out-of-pocket expenses and

- commissions.

If the recovery continues at the current pace, this year should be a banner year for all of us at Macco. We want to thank all of you for the outstanding jobs you have done and, most important, for standing by Macco in hard times. Keep up the good work!

John Smith
Regional Coordinator
Macco Plastics Inc.

4. Single-underline the following subheadings (near the bottom of page 1) (Chapter 4):

Midwestern Region

Northeastern Region

Southern Region

5. Clear (delete) the 2" left-aligned tab stop from the paragraph that begins with *B. Current available positions* (near the top of page 2).

6. Set a 0.5" hanging indent for the paragraph beginning with *A. Marketing and sales*.

7. Repeat the 0.5" hanging indent for the paragraphs beginning with *B. Current available positions* and *C. Development of the*.

8. In the paragraph beginning with *C. Development of the*, create new lines for:

- travel reimbursements

- other out-of-pocket expenses and

- commissions.

9. Save the disk file as **My Practice 5B** (Chapter 2).

10. Print the document and compare it to Figure 5.16 (Chapter 2).

11. Close the document (Chapter 2).

SUMMARY

In this chapter, you learned the basics of paragraph formatting. You now know how to set, change, and clear tab stops; how to set and repeat paragraph indents; how to create new lines within a paragraph; how to align paragraphs; and how to set line spacing.

Here's a quick reference guide to the Word features introduced in this chapter:

Desired Result	How to Do It
Select single paragraph for paragraph formatting	Place insertion point anywhere in paragraph

Desired Result	How to Do It
Select multiple paragraphs for paragraph formatting	Select (highlight) at least portion of each paragraph
Create custom tab stop	Select desired paragraph(s); select desired type of tab stop by clicking on **Tab Alignment** button until desired tab type appears; point at desired tab-stop position in ruler; click mouse button
Change position of custom tab stop	Select desired paragraph(s); drag custom tab stop (in ruler) to new position
Clear (delete) custom tab stop	Select desired paragraph(s); drag custom tab stop into text area
Use Tabs dialog box to manage custom tab stops	Select desired paragraph(s); choose **Format, Tabs** to open Tabs dialog box; enter desired settings to set, change, or clear tab stops; click on **OK**
Set indents	Select paragraph(s) you wish to indent; drag appropriate indent marker to desired position in ruler
Repeat paragraph formatting	Format paragraph(s); select new paragraph(s); choose **Edit, Repeat Formatting** or press **F4**
Create hanging indent	Select desired paragraph(s); if necessary drag **first-line-indent** marker to desired position; drag only **left-indent** marker to desired position
Use Paragraph dialog box to manage indents	Select desired paragraph(s); choose **Format, Paragraph** to open Paragraph dialog box; display Indents and Spacing tab, if necessary; enter desired indent settings; click on **OK**

Desired Result	How to Do It
Create new line without creating new paragraph	Place insertion point where you want to end current line and create new line; press **Shift+Enter**
Set paragraph alignment	Select desired paragraph(s); click on appropriate alignment button in Formatting toolbar
Set line spacing	Select desired paragraph(s); choose **Format, Paragraph** to open Paragraph dialog box; in Indents and Spacing tab, select desired line-spacing setting; click on **OK**

In the next chapter, you will learn the basics of page formatting. You'll find out how to work with headers and footers, how to use Print Preview to preview a printed document, how to set margins, how to use page breaks to paginate a document, how to work in Page Layout view, how to hyphenate text, and how to control the printing of your documents.

CHAPTER 6:
PAGE FORMATTING

Creating Headers
and Footers

Using Print
Preview to Preview
a Printed
Document

Setting Margins

Using Page Breaks
to Paginate a
Document

Working in Page
Layout View

Hyphenating Text

Controlling the
Printing of Your
Documents

In Chapters 4 and 5, you learned how to format your documents at the character and paragraph levels. In this chapter, we'll introduce Word's final level of formatting—*page formatting*. Many powerful formatting features are controlled at the page level, including headers and footers, margins, page breaks, hyphenation, and advanced printing options.

We'll also present two new methods for displaying your documents—*Print Preview* and *Page Layout* view—both of which are well-suited for page-level formatting tasks.

When you're done working through this chapter, you will know

- How to create, edit, and view headers and footers

- How to use Print Preview to preview a printed document

- How to set margins

- How to use page breaks to paginate a document

- How to work in Page Layout view

- How to hyphenate text

- How to control the printing of your documents

CREATING HEADERS AND FOOTERS

A *header* is text that is automatically printed at the top of every page in a document, and a *footer* is text that is automatically printed at the bottom of every page. Headers and footers are used extensively in word processing to do such things as number each page in a document, place the current date on each page, print the document title and/or author name on each page, and so on.

To create a header or footer, choose *Header and Footer* from the View menu. Word automatically switches to Page Layout view, opens the Header area, and displays the Header and Footer toolbar (see Figure 6.1). (You'll learn about Page Layout view later in this chapter.)

To open the Footer area from the Header area and vice versa, click on the *Switch Between Header and Footer* button (see Figure 6.1).

To enter header/footer information:

- In the Header or Footer area, type your desired header or footer text, using the Header and Footer toolbar buttons as desired (these buttons are discussed in the next section).

- Click on *Close* to accept the header or footer and close the Header or Footer area.

Figure 6.1 **The Header area and Header and Footer toolbar**

Show Previous   Show Next   Page Numbers   Time   Show/Hide Document Text

Switch Between Header and Footer

Same as Previous   Date   Page Setup

To delete a header or footer:

- Follow the previous procedure to open the Header or Footer area.

- Choose *Edit, Select All* to select the entire contents of the Header or Footer area.

- Press *Del* to delete these contents.

- Click on *Close* to close the Header or Footer area.

THE HEADER AND FOOTER TOOLBAR

You can use the Header and Footer toolbar buttons to insert the page number, the current date, or the current time into your header or footer (see Figure 6.1). When using the Date and Time buttons, keep in mind that your printout will reflect the date and time when you *print* the document, rather than the date and time when you first *created* the document.

The Show Previous, Show Next, and Same as Previous buttons are sometimes used in long documents that consist of more than one section, and in which each section has more than one header and/or footer. (You'll learn about sections in Chapter 11.) The Page Setup button opens the Page Setup dialog box, in which you can control, for example, your document's margins and the size of its pages. The Show/Hide Document Text button allows you to display the document text dimmed in the background or to remove it from the screen display (as in Figure 6.1).

 ## VIEWING HEADERS AND FOOTERS

Word provides five *views* (screen representations) for your documents: *Normal, Outline, Page Layout,* and *Master Document,* which are available through the View menu; and *Print Preview,* which is located in the File menu. The three most important views, and the ones we'll use in this book, are Normal, Page Layout, and Print Preview.

When you are working in Normal view (the view we've always used up to now), your headers and footers are not shown on-screen, though they will still appear if you print the document. To see your headers and footers on-screen, you must be in Print Preview or Page Layout view. These views will be discussed later in this chapter.

If you are not running Word, please start it now. Let's begin this chapter's activities by opening a new document and creating a header for it:

1. Open **Page Formatting** from your Word Work folder.

2. Choose **View, Header and Footer** to open the Header area and display the Header and Footer toolbar (see Figure 6.1).

3. Observe the Header area. Text entered here will automatically appear at the top of every page of your document.

4. Without clicking on any of the buttons, move the mouse pointer to each button. As in the main (Standard) and Formatting toolbars, the name of each button is displayed when you point to it.

5. Type **Global Travel**. Press **Tab** twice and then type **Travel Services**.

6. Observe the header text. Note that *Travel Services* is right-aligned. Observe the ruler. As long as the Header area is open, the ruler refers to the header, *not* to the document. Word has automatically set a centered tab stop at 3" (half-way between the left and right margins) and a right-aligned tab stop at 6" (at the right margin). These preset tab stops enable you to quickly and easily use tabs to center your header text or to align it with the right margin.

7. Click on **Close** in the Header and Footer toolbar to accept your header and close the Header area. Note that the ruler now refers to the document, not to the header. Note also that the header you just created is not displayed on the screen. Remember, headers and footers are only visible in Print Preview and Page Layout views.

Now let's create a footer:

1. Choose **View, Header and Footer**. The header you just created is again visible in the Header area.

2. Click on the **Switch Between Header and Footer** button (see Figure 6.1) to open the footer area.

3. Examine the Footer area. It is identical to the Header area. However, the text you type here will be displayed at the *bottom* of every page, instead of at the top.

4. Click on the **Date** button (see Figure 6.1) to insert the current date.

5. Press **Tab** twice to move to the right margin.

6. Type **Page** and then press the **Spacebar**.

7. Click on the **Page Numbers** button (see Figure 6.1) to insert the page number.

8. Close the Footer area (click on **Close**) to accept your footer and return to the document.

USING PRINT PREVIEW TO PREVIEW A PRINTED DOCUMENT

Print Preview provides a miniature view of how a document will look when it is printed. You can use Print Preview to examine and adjust the layout of a document before you actually print it.

You can edit text in Print Preview, but doing so is not very efficient and, depending on the system you are using, the response of the program can be slow. You can, however, control the placement of text on the page by changing the margins. You also can print the active document and view two or more pages at one time.

To use the Print Preview option:

• Click on the *Print Preview* button to open the Preview window.

• To print the document, click on the *Print* button in the Print Preview toolbar (see Figure 6.2).

Figure 6.2   **The Preview window**

- To view more than one page at a time, click on the *Multiple Pages* button in the Print Preview toolbar, and then drag over the grid to select the desired number of pages and their configuration (see the next exercise); to return to single-page view, click on the *One Page* button.

- To close the window, click on the *Close* button.

Let's use Print Preview to examine our header and footer:

1. Click on the **Print Preview** button in the toolbar to open the Preview window (see Figure 6.2). Click on the View Ruler button to display the horizontal and vertical rulers. Print Preview provides a miniature display of your document as it will print, including headers and footers. Remember, you cannot edit text in this view. Notice that, in addition to the horizontal ruler displayed above the document page, a vertical ruler is displayed at the left of the Preview window.

2. Click on the **Multiple Pages** button (see Figure 6.2) to display the Multiple Pages grid.

3. Drag down one row and three "pages" to the right, so that a **1 × 3** grid is selected (see Figure 6.3). Then release the mouse button to display a single row of (all) three pages of the document at one time. Compare your screen to Figure 6.4. Notice that the horizontal ruler, which functions in the same manner as the one in Normal document view, appears above the page that currently contains the insertion point (page 1).

4. Click on the **One Page** button to return to single-page view.

5. Click on the **bottom scroll** arrow (see Figure 6.2) to display page 2 of the document; then click again to display page 3. In Print Preview, each click scrolls one full page. Notice that the headers and footers appear on every page. Page Formatting is a three-page document. Click once again on the **bottom scroll** arrow to verify this; your computer may beep, and the screen display does not change, since there are no more pages to scroll to.

6. Click on the **top scroll** arrow (see Figure 6.2) twice to return to page 1.

Figure 6.3   **Specifying the number of pages to be previewed**

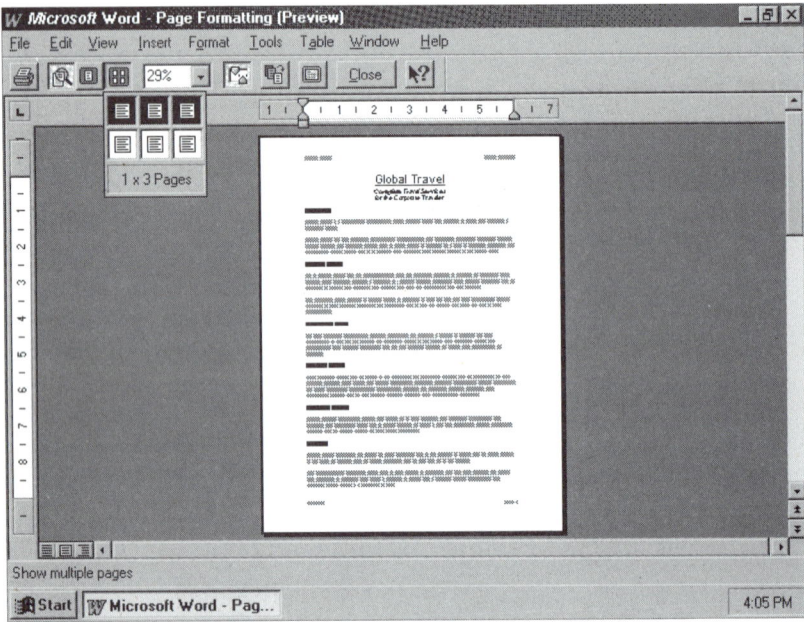

Figure 6.4   **Print Preview in Multiple Pages view**

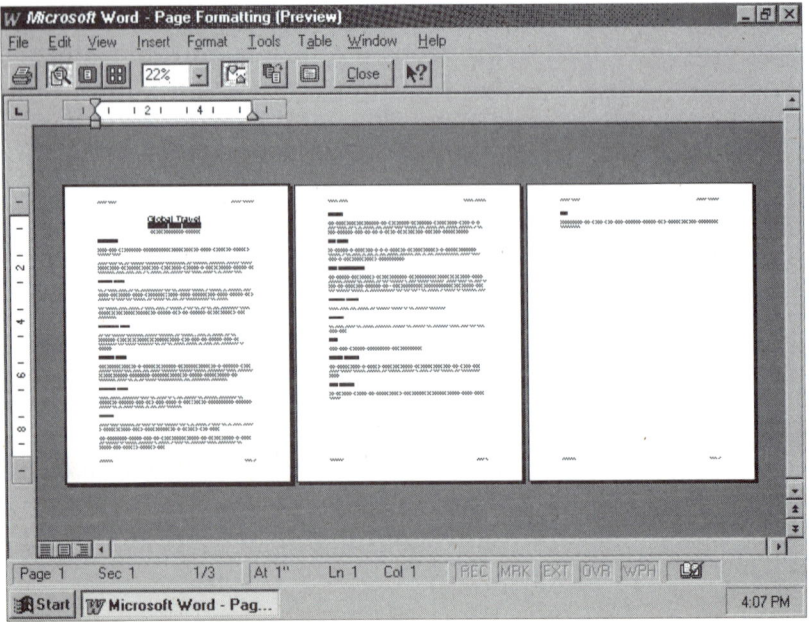

SETTING MARGINS

Margins determine the space between the four edges of the page and the text of the document. Figure 6.5 shows a Print Preview of a sample document with Word's default margin settings—the top and bottom margins are set to 1"; the left and right margins are set to 1.25". Figure 6.6 shows the same document with custom margins set to twice the default values—the top and bottom are set to 2"; the left and right are set to 2.5".

You can set a document's margins either from the Preview window (by dragging the margin boundaries) or in Normal or Page Layout view (by using the Page Setup dialog box).

Figure 6.5   **A sample document with default margins**

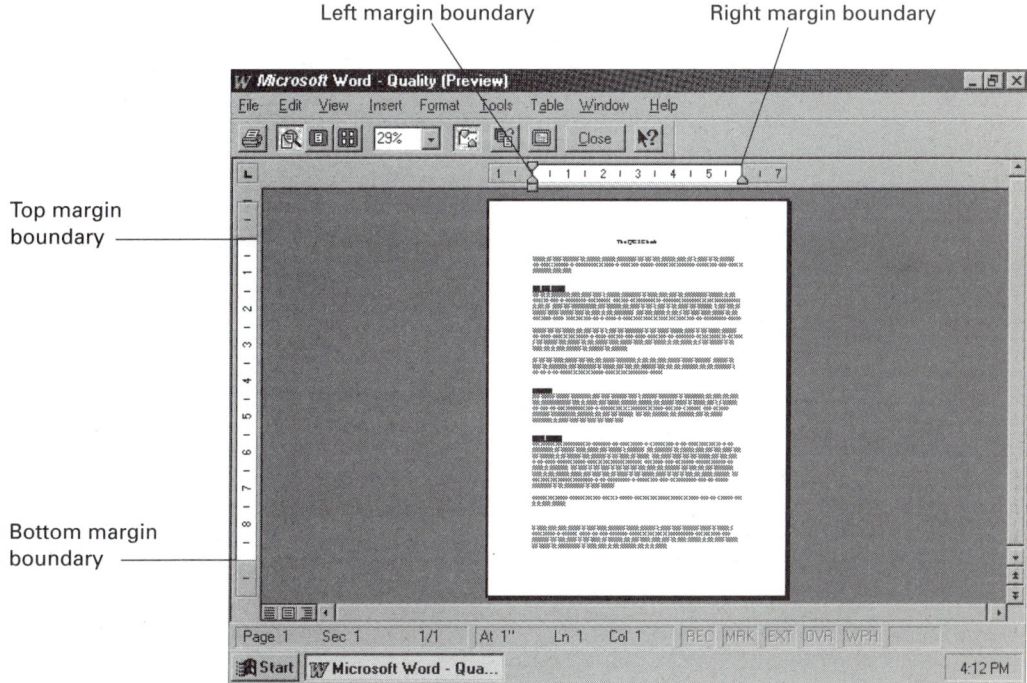

Figure 6.6   **A sample document with custom margins**

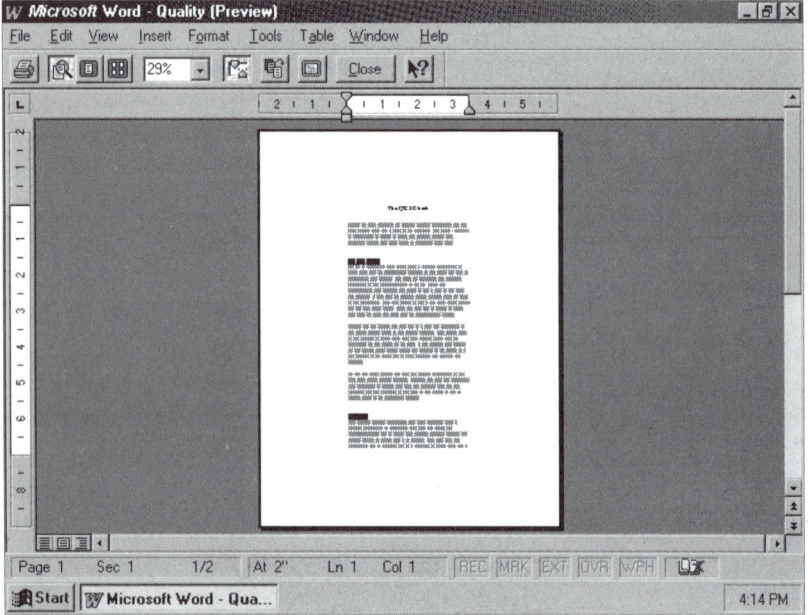

Use the following methods to adjust margins in Print Preview:

- To change the left and right margins, place the mouse pointer over the left margin boundary on the horizontal ruler (between the left-indent and first-line-indent markers) to change the left margin or over the right margin boundary (directly above the right-indent marker) to change the right margin; when the mouse pointer becomes a left- and right-pointing arrow, drag the margin to the desired position.

- To change the top and bottom margins, place the mouse pointer in the vertical ruler, at the top margin boundary to change the top margin, or the bottom boundary to change the bottom margin, until the mouse pointer becomes an up- and down-pointing arrow; then drag the margin to the desired position.

To set margins by using the Page Setup dialog box:

- Choose *File, Page Setup* to open the Page Setup dialog box.

- Display the *Margins* tab, if necessary.

- Enter the new margin settings in the appropriate margin boxes.

- Click on *OK*.

Let's practice changing margins from the Preview window:

1. Observe the margin boundaries in the horizontal and vertical rulers (see Figure 6.5).

2. Position the mouse pointer on the top margin boundary, in the vertical ruler. The arrow changes to an up- and down-pointing arrow.

3. Press and hold the mouse button, and then begin to drag the top margin boundary downward. Notice that the top margin measurement appears above the top margin boundary in the vertical ruler. Drag the handle down until the top-margin measurement reads **1.5"**; then release the mouse button. Note that the new margin boundary line is displayed, and the page is reformatted to reflect this new top margin.

4. Click on the **Multiple Pages** button in the toolbar, and select a **1 × 2** grid to display a single row of two pages (in this case, the first two) of the document. Then click the mouse pointer in **page 2** of the document to select the page. The horizontal and vertical rulers now refer specifically to this page of the document. (The horizontal ruler is now above page 2.) Notice that page 2 also reflects the new margin setting. It's important to note that margin settings apply to the whole document, not only to the selected page.

5. Drag the bottom margin boundary upward until the bottom-margin measurement indicator reads **1.5"**. Release the mouse button, and compare your screen to Figure 6.7. In the status bar, you can see that the margin adjustment has caused the number of pages in the document to increase to 4.

6. Scroll to view pages 3 and 4 of the document (click on the **bottom scroll** arrow). Then click on page 3. The margins have changed on every page. (Pages 3 and 4 contain very little text because manual page breaks have been inserted in the document.)

7. Click on **Close** to close the Preview window.

Now let's change margins by using the Page Setup command:

1. Move to the top of the document, if necessary.

2. Choose **File, Page Setup** to open the Page Setup dialog box, and click on the **Margins** tab, if necessary (see Figure 6.8).

Figure 6.7   **Changing the margins in Print Preview**

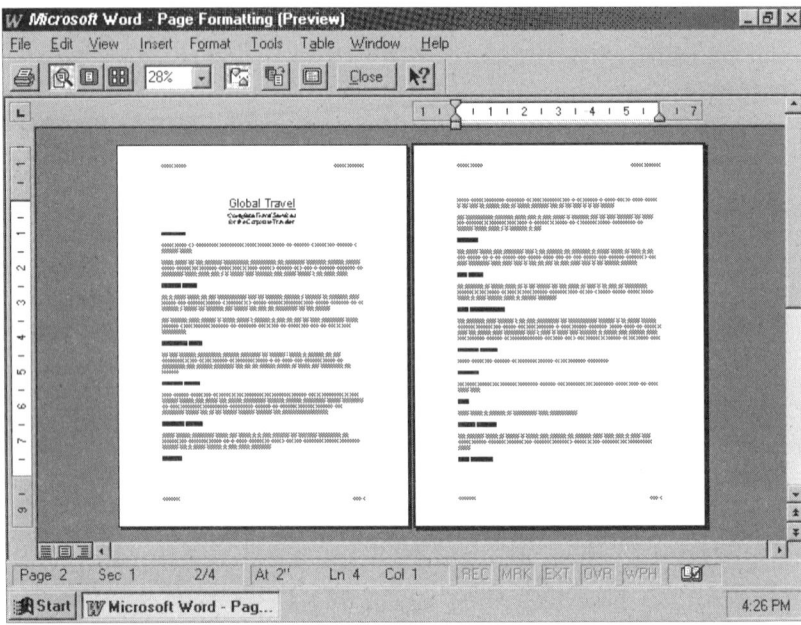

Figure 6.8   **The Margins tab in the Page Setup dialog box**

3. Verify that the top and bottom margins are set to **1.5"**.

4. Double-click in the **Left** box to select the current left margin setting (**1.25"**). Type **1** to change the left margin to 1". You do not have to type the inch symbol (").

5. Press **Tab** to select the current right margin setting (**1.25"**). Type **1** to change the right margin to 1".

6. Press **Enter** (or click on **OK**) to accept your margin changes. Due to the extra 0.5" of text width that you gained (by decreasing the left and right margins by 0.25" each), your text lines now run off the right end of the screen. Note that the screen representation of the left margin has not changed. When you are working in Normal view (as opposed to Print Preview or Page Layout view), Word always displays your left margin in the same place (approximately one-quarter inch to the right of the document window edge), no matter how large or small the margin actually is.

7. Save the disk file as **My Page Formatting**.

Let's use the Zoom Control feature (covered in Chapter 2) to shrink the display, so that the text lines no longer run off the screen:

1. Observe the status bar. The current magnification level is *100%*.

2. Click on the Zoom Control **down arrow** button to open the Zoom Control list box, and select **Page Width**. Observe the text and the Standard toolbar. The magnification level automatically adjusts to fit the entire width (but not the length) of the page on the screen. In the Zoom Control box, you can see that the program has automatically adjusted the magnification level to *92%*.

USING PAGE BREAKS TO PAGINATE A DOCUMENT

Pagination is the process of separating a document's text into pages. The separations between pages are called *page breaks*.

There are two types of page breaks in Word:

- *Automatic* page breaks, which Word automatically inserts into a document. An automatic page break appears as a loosely spaced dotted line across the text area.

- *Manual* page breaks, which you insert into the document. A manual page break appears as a tightly spaced dotted line with the words *Page Break* in the center of the line.

To insert a manual page break:

- Place the insertion point immediately to the left of the first character that you want on the new page.

- Choose *Insert, Break*, verify that *Page Break* is selected, and then click on *OK*; or, simply press *Ctrl+Enter*.

To delete a manual page break:

- Move the mouse pointer into the selection bar.

- Select the page break.

- Press *Del*.

You cannot delete automatic page breaks. However, if you insert a manual page break above an automatic page break, Word will remove the automatic page break.

Let's use the above procedure to insert some manual page breaks in our document:

1. Move to the top of page 2, and scroll up one line. Observe the automatic page break before the paragraph beginning with *Our quality control specialists*. It is displayed as a loosely spaced dotted line (see Figure 6.9).

2. Place the insertion point to the left of the *D* in the heading *Discounts*, near the bottom of page 1. (You'll need to scroll.)

3. Choose **Insert, Break** to open the Break dialog box (see Figure 6.10). Verify that **Page Break** is selected. Point to (but *don't* click on) OK and, while observing the automatic page break between pages 1 and 2, click on **OK**. Word inserts a manual page break (with the words *Page Break*) at your insertion point and then, shortly afterward, deletes the automatic page break. Because you changed the beginning of page 2 to *Discounts*, Word no longer needed to break pages automatically at *Our quality control specialists*.

4. Move to the bottom of page 2. Place the insertion point to the left of the *F* in the heading *Flight Insurance*.

5. Press **Ctrl+Enter** (the keyboard shortcut) to insert a manual page break.

Figure 6.9   **An automatic page break**

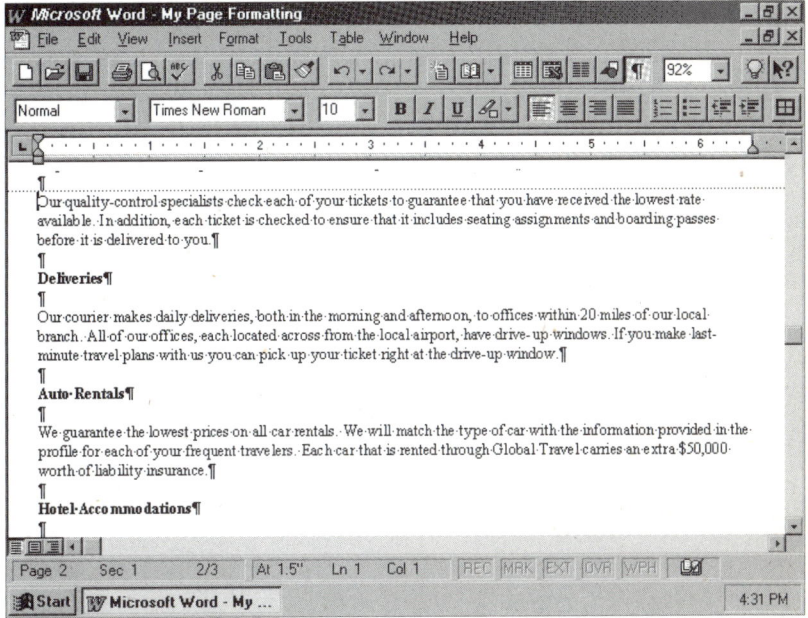

Figure 6.10   **The Break dialog box**

6. Note that the automatic page break after *Flight Insurance* disappears, but that the manual page break before *Fax* remains (see Figure 6.11; you may need to scroll). Automatic page breaks are deleted or repositioned automatically, as necessitated by changes you make to the document (resetting margins, changing font size, inserting new page breaks, and so on). Undesired manual page breaks, however, must be deleted manually.

7. In the selection bar, click on manual page break above *Fax* to select it.

8. Press **Del** to delete the manual page break.

Figure 6.11   **Inserted manual page break**

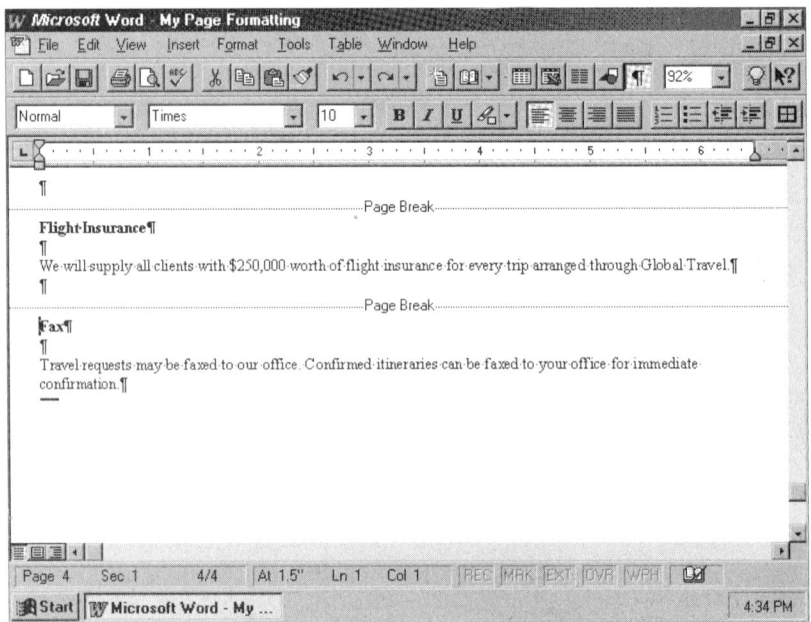

WORKING IN PAGE LAYOUT VIEW

Word's Page Layout view allows you to view all page areas, including headers, footers, and margins. Page Layout view is like a cross between Normal view (where you can edit and format body text, but cannot view headers and footers) and Print Preview (where you can see headers and footers but cannot edit text).

Note: Page Layout view can be useful for applying the finishing touches to your documents. However, you might find that this view significantly slows the operating speed of Word and makes it awkward to move around in the document. For this reason, we recommend that you do most of your work in Normal view.

To enter Page Layout view:

- Choose *View, Page Layout*; or click on the *Page Layout View* button (to the left of the horizontal scroll bar; see Figure 6.12).

To return to Normal view:

- Choose *View, Normal*; or click on the *Normal View* button.

Figure 6.12   **The Normal and Page Layout View buttons**

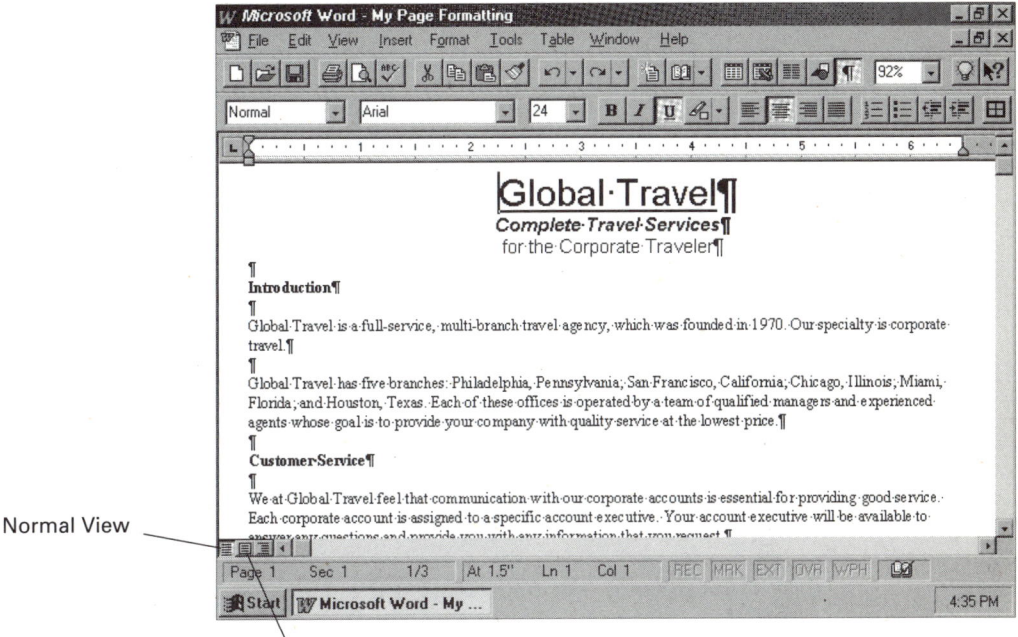

Normal View

Page Layout View

To edit a header or footer in Page Layout view:

- Double-click on the (dimmed) header or footer.

- Edit the header or footer text, as desired.

- Click on *Close*.

Let's edit your header and footer in Page Layout view. But first we'll open the Preview window to observe a page-positioning problem with the header and footer:

1. Move to the top of the document.

2. Open the Preview window (click on the **Print Preview** button). Notice that the header and footer text no longer aligns with the right margin. Why? Because you changed the document's margins in a previous activity, but did not adjust the position of the right-aligned tab stop in the header and footer. This tab stop does not reach the new right margin. (We'll fix the problem in a moment.)

3. Close the Print Preview window (click on **Close**).

4. Click on the **Page Layout View** button (see Figure 6.12) to switch to Page Layout view. Notice that the Zoom Control is set to *100%*, which doesn't allow you to view the right margin.

5. Open the Zoom Control list box, and select **Page Width** to automatically adjust the magnification (see Figure 6.13). In Page Layout view, you can both view and edit headers and footers, even though they are currently dimmed and cannot, therefore, be selected.

Figure 6.13   **My Page Formatting in Page Layout view**

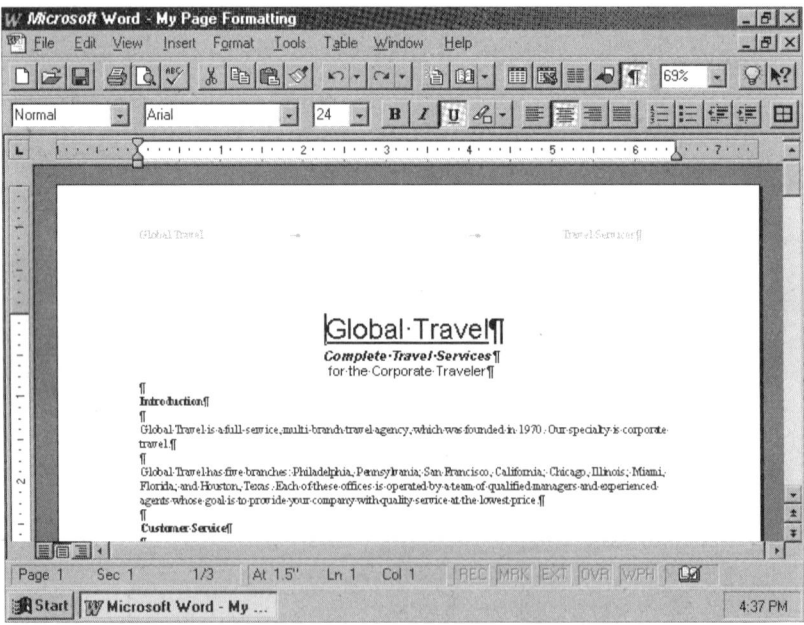

6. Double-click on the dimmed header. Eureka! The Header area is displayed in Page Layout view.

7. Place the insertion point in the header before the *T* in *Travel Services*. Type **Complete** and press the **Spacebar**.

8. Observe the ruler. The right-aligned tab stop at 6" did not automatically adjust when you changed the margins earlier.

9. Drag the right-aligned tab stop at 6" to **6.5"** to set it even with the right margin.

10. Click on the **Switch Between Header and Footer** button (in the Header and Footer toolbar) to view the footer.

11. Drag the right-aligned tab stop at 6" to **6.5"**. Then close the Footer area (click on **Close**).

12. Open the Preview window. Scroll through the document to verify that the headers and footers now align with the right margin on every page. Then close the Preview window.

13. Click on the **Normal View** button (see Figure 6.12) to return to Normal view.

14. Open the Zoom Control drop-down list box, and select **100%** to return to 100% magnification.

15. Update the disk file.

HYPHENATING TEXT

Up to now, we have worked exclusively with unhyphenated text: Each of our documents' lines has ended with a whole word, rather than a *hyphenated* word—a word broken into two parts by a hyphen. You may, at times, wish to hyphenate a document to reduce the raggedness of its right margin (with left-aligned text) or to tighten things up by minimizing the blank space between words (with justified text). Word provides two methods for doing this: *manual hyphenation*, in which you can use either the keyboard or the Tools, Hyphenation command; and *automatic hyphenation*, in which you use the Tools, Hyphenation command.

 MANUAL HYPHENATION

To hyphenate text manually:

• Place the insertion point between the desired letters of the word you wish to hyphenate.

- Insert your desired hyphen, choosing from the three types shown in the following table:

Type of Hyphen	How and When to Use
Regular	Press the *Hyphen* key (-); use when you always want the hyphen to appear, such as in compound words ("left-aligned," "right-aligned," and so on).
Optional	Press *Ctrl+Hyphen*; use when you only want the hyphen to appear if the word is broken at the end of a line (such as "auto-matic").
Hard	Press *Ctrl+Shift+Hyphen*; use when you always want the hyphen to appear, but you never want the word to be broken at the end of a line, such as with names ("Ann-Marie," for instance).

Let's use the Ctrl+Hyphen technique to insert an optional hyphen into a word:

1. Move to the top of the document, if necessary.

2. Use **File, Page Setup** to change the left and right margins to **1.5"**.

3. Click on the **Show/Hide** button to hide nonprinting characters.

4. In the second line of the paragraph beginning with *We at Global Travel* (under the heading *Customer Service*), place the insertion point between the *o* and the *v* of *providing*. Then press **Ctrl+Hyphen** to insert an optional hyphen at the insertion point. Notice that the word *providing* is broken into two parts, *pro-* and *viding* (see Figure 6.14).

5. Place the insertion point to the left of *essential* (in the same sentence). Type **absolutely** and press the **Spacebar** to force the entire word *providing* to move to the next line. Note that the optional hyphen disappears when it is not needed.

6. Click on the **Show/Hide** button to show nonprinting characters. Note that the optional hyphen now appears on-screen as a horizontal line with a slightly downturned right end. (Optional hyphens do not appear when you print a document.)

Figure 6.14   **Inserting an optional hyphen into *providing***

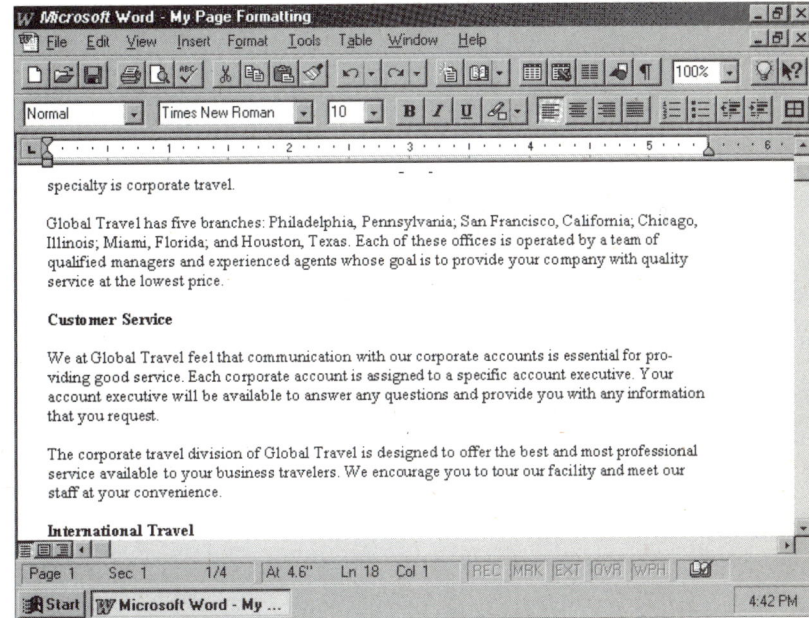

7. Delete **absolutely** (and the trailing space) from the text.

AUTOMATIC HYPHENATION

To hyphenate a document automatically:

• Move the insertion point to the top of the document.

• Choose *Tools, Hyphenation* to open the Hyphenation dialog box.

• Check the *Automatically Hyphenate Document* option.

• Click on *OK* (or press *Enter*) to hyphenate the document.

Now let's use the Tools, Hyphenation command to automatically hyphenate the entire document:

1. Move to the top of the document.

2. Choose **Tools, Hyphenation** to open the Hyphenation dialog box (see Figure 6.15).

Figure 6.15   **The Hyphenation dialog box**

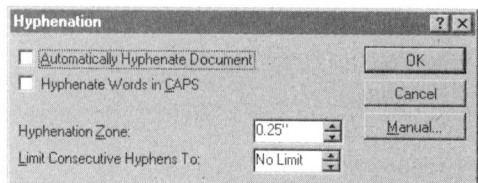

3. Check the **Automatically Hyphenate Document** option. Notice that the Hyphenate Words in CAPS option is unchecked. With this option unchecked, when Word encounters any words that contain all capitals, it will not hyphenate them.

4. Click on **OK** (or press **Enter**) to begin hyphenation. Scroll the document and observe which words have been hyphenated automatically: *dis-count, is-sue, cost-effective* (which was manually hyphenated, but due to the automatic hyphenation has been interrupted by a line break), *assign-ments,* and *infor-mation.* (Your hyphenated words may vary from these, depending on your margins, and so on.)

CONTROLLING THE PRINTING OF YOUR DOCUMENTS

Several times in this book, you've used the File, Print command to print your active document. Let's revisit this very powerful command and learn how to use some of its more advanced features. In addition to printing a single copy of your entire document, File, Print allows you to print the current page, multiple pages, multiple copies, selected text, or nondocument items such as Summary Info.

To use the Print dialog box to control how your documents print:

•   If you wish to print selected text, select that text.

•   Choose *File, Print* to open the Print dialog box.

•   Choose the desired Print options (see Table 6.1).

•   Click on *OK* (or press *Enter*).

PRINT DIALOG BOX OPTIONS

The Print dialog box provides the options shown in Table 6.1.

Table 6.1   **Print Dialog Box Options**

Option	Description
Print What	In this drop-down list box, you choose what you wish to print. The default choice is the current document, but you can also print, for example, summary information (covered later in this section), styles, and AutoText (printing AutoText will be discussed in Chapter 9).
Copies	In this area, you enter the number of copies that you wish to print. The default is 1 copy.
Page Range	In this area of the dialog box, you specify the portion of the document that you wish to print. Choose *All* to print the entire document. Choose *Current Page* to print the page where the insertion point is located. If you selected text in your document before issuing the File, Print command, the Selection button becomes active; choose it to print the selected text. Choose *Pages* and enter page numbers in the Pages text box to print a range of pages; separate page numbers with commas (for nonsequential pages) or dashes (for sequential pages)—for example, enter 3, 6, 10-12 to print pages 3, 6, 10, 11, and 12.
Print	From this drop-down list, you can specify the printing of all the pages in a specified range, only the odd-numbered pages, or only the even-numbered pages.

Let's practice using the print options in the Print dialog box. (If you do not have a printer, please skip this activity.)

1. Move to the top of the document.

2. Choose **File, Print** to open the Print dialog box (see Figure 6.16).

Figure 6.16   **The Print dialog box**

3. In the Page Range area of the box, choose the **Current Page** option (click on the radio button to the left of the option). Click on **OK** to print only the current page (the page on which the insertion point is located), which in this case is page 1. After the page has been sent to the printer, the Print dialog box is automatically closed.

4. Choose **File, Print** to reopen the Print dialog box. Note that Page Range has been reset to its default (*All*). Each time you open the Print dialog box, all of its settings are reset to their default values.

5. In the Page Range area of the box, select the **Pages** option. Type **1-2** in the Pages text box; this informs Word to print only from page 1 through page 2 of the document. Click on **OK** to print these pages.

6. Choose **File, Print** to reopen the Print dialog box. In the Page Range area of the box, notice that the Selection option is currently dimmed, because no text is selected in the document.

7. Select the **Current Page** option. Double-click in the Number of Copies text box to select the current value (**1**); type **2** to tell Word to print two copies of the current page. Click on **OK** to print these copies.

8. Select all text from the heading *Customer Service* up to and including the empty paragraph above *International Travel*.

9. Choose **File, Print** to reopen the Print dialog box. Note that the Copies and Page Range options have been reset to their default values of *1* and *All*, respectively. Note also that the Selection option is now available.

10. Choose the **Selection** option and then click on **OK** to print only your selected text.

11. Press **Ctrl+Home** to deselect and move to the top of the document. Choose **File, Print** to reopen the Print dialog box. Note that the Selection option is once again dimmed (because there is no text selected in the document).

12. Click on the **down arrow** to the right of the Print What list box to display the Print options. Select **Summary Info** to tell Word to print the Summary Info sheet of the current document. Click on **OK** to print this sheet.

 ## USING THE PRINT BUTTON TO PRINT A DOCUMENT

In addition to the File, Print command, Word provides a Print button that you can use to print a single copy of an entire document. To do this, click on the Print button in the toolbar.

Let's end this chapter's activities by using the Print button to print your entire document. (If you do not have a printer, please skip this activity.)

1. Click on the **Print** button to print a single copy of your entire document.

2. Save the disk file and close the document.

SUMMARY

In this chapter, you learned the basics of page formatting. You now know how to create, edit, and view headers and footers; how to use Print Preview to preview a printed document; how to set margins; how to use page breaks to paginate a document; how to work in Page Layout view; how to hyphenate text; and how to control the printing of your documents.

Congratulations on completing your foundation of Word formatting techniques! You now know how to format your documents at the character, paragraph, and page levels. These skills will allow you to create highly professional-looking documents.

Here's a quick reference guide to the Word features introduced in this chapter:

Desired Result	How to Do It
Create header or footer	Choose **View, Header and Footer**; type desired header text, or click on **Switch Between Header and Footer** and type desired footer text; click on **Close**
Delete header or footer	Follow previous procedure to open Header or Footer area; choose **Edit, Select All** to select entire contents of area; press **Del**; click on **Close**
Preview printed document	Click on **Print Preview** button to open Preview window
Set margins in Print Preview	Drag desired margin boundary to desired margin position; repeat previous step until all margin boundary lines are set as desired
Set margins by using Page Setup dialog box	Choose **File, Page Setup**; enter new margin settings in appropriate margin text boxes; click on **OK**
Insert manual page break	Place insertion point immediately to left of first character that you want on new page; choose **Insert, Break**; verify that **Page Break** is selected; click on **OK**; or place insertion point and press **Ctrl+Enter**
Delete manual page break	In selection bar, click to select page break; press **Del**
Enter Page Layout view	Click on **Page Layout View** button

Desired Result	How to Do It
Return to Normal view	Click on **Normal View** button
Hyphenate text manually	Place insertion point where you wish to insert hyphen; insert desired hyphen (regular, optional, or hard)
Hyphenate document automatically	Move insertion point to top of document; choose **Tools, Hyphenation**; check **Automatically Hyphenate Document** option; click on **OK**
Use Print dialog box to control printing	To print selected text, select text; choose **File, Print**; choose desired Print options; click on **OK**
Use Print button to print single copy of entire document	Click on toolbar **Print** button

In the next chapter, we'll explore ways in which Word can help you improve your writing. You'll learn how to check your documents' spelling, how to use the thesaurus to find alternative words, and how to check the grammar, style, and readability of your documents.

CHAPTER 7: PROOFING YOUR DOCUMENTS

Checking the
Spelling of Your
Documents

Using the
Thesaurus to Find
Alternative Words

Checking the
Grammar and
Style of Your
Documents

Misspellings and grammatical mistakes can severely undermine the credibility of your documents. In this chapter, we'll introduce you to tools that allow you to *proof* (check) your documents for potential spelling, grammar, and style errors. Wording is also a critical factor in determining the effectiveness of a document; using inappropriate words may alienate or confuse your readers. We'll explore Word's electronic thesaurus and see how easy it is to find vocabulary alternatives for your documents.

When you're done working through this chapter, you will know

- How to check the spelling of your documents

- How to use the thesaurus to find alternative words

- How to check the grammar, style, and readability of your documents

CHECKING THE SPELLING OF YOUR DOCUMENTS

Word provides a spelling checker that you can use to proof the spelling of your documents. The *spelling checker* checks each word in a document against the words in its own internal dictionary and highlights the words it does not recognize. The spelling checker also checks for such common typing mistakes as repeated words (such as *the the*) and irregular capitalization (such as *tHe*).

Word offers two types of spell-checking: *automatic* and *manual*. Automatic spell-checking is available in Word by default. (You can turn this option on or off by choosing *Tools, Options,* displaying the Spelling tab, and checking or unchecking, respectively, the *Automatic Spell Checking* option.) The way automatic spell-checking works is that, as you enter text, Word will underline any text it does not recognize with a wavy red line. (We briefly pointed this out to you in Chapter 2.)

To correct a misspelling found by the automatic spell-checker:

- Click the right mouse button on the word you wish to correct that has been underlined with the wavy red line. This displays a menu, at the top of which is a list of suggested spellings (if any) for the offending word. Below the list of suggested words are a few menu options: *Ignore All, Add,* and *Spelling.* The Ignore All and Add options are also available through the manual spell-checker; both options are discussed in the list of options following the discussion of manual spell-checking. The Spelling option opens the Spelling dialog box, which is also displayed when you run the manual spell-checker.

- Choose the correct spelling from the menu, or choose one of the menu options.

Here are Word's options for spell-checking documents manually:

- To spell-check a portion of a document, select the text that you wish to check; to check a single word, select that word.

- Choose *Tools, Spelling* or click on the *Spelling* button in the Standard toolbar to open the Spelling dialog box and begin the spelling check. Figure 7.1 illustrates the Spelling dialog box.

Figure 7.1   **The Spelling dialog box**

- Follow the dialog box prompts to spell-check the document or selected text.

When the spelling checker finds a potential spelling error (a word not included in the checker's internal dictionary), this word appears in the Not in Dictionary text box (see Figure 7.1), and a list of suggested spelling corrections appears in the Suggestions list box. The first of these suggested spellings is placed in the Change To text box. At this point, you can choose from the following options:

Option	Action Required
Leave word unchanged	To leave word as is and continue spelling check, click on *Ignore*. To ignore all further occurrences of word, click on *Ignore All*.
Correct spelling	If correction you want is in Change To text box, click on *Change*. If correction you want is in Suggestions list box, click on correction, then click on *Change* (or, as shortcut, simply double-click on desired correction). If correction you want is not suggested, type correction in Change To text box; click on *Change*. To change all occurrences of word throughout document, click on *Change All*.

Option	Action Required
Add word to a dictionary	To build a custom dictionary that contains words not found in spelling checker's dictionary—useful for proper names (*Gillian*), abbreviations (*ACCTDEPT*), and acronyms (*UNICEF*) you use frequently in your documents. To add word to custom dictionary, click on *Add*.
Delete word	To delete highlighted word from document, delete word in Change To text box; click on *Delete* button (appears in place of Change button when you delete contents of Change To text box). To delete all further occurrences of word, delete word in Change To text box; click on *Delete All* (appears in place of Change All button when you delete contents of Change To text box).
Undo last correction	To undo last correction, click on *Undo Last*. Word allows you to undo your most recent corrections, one by one.
Stop spelling check	To cancel spelling check procedure at any point, click on *Cancel* (or *Close*). All changes made up to that point will be preserved. If you used Change All or Delete All options, instances of these words that appear after point where you cancel will not be changed or deleted.

If the error is repeated words (such as *the the*), you can

- Click on *Delete* to delete the second instance of the word.

- Click on *Ignore* to ignore the repeated words and continue the spelling check.

If you are not running Word, please start it now. Let's begin by opening a document and manually spell-checking a selected portion of it:

1. Open **Proofing** from your Word Work folder.

2. Select the heading of the document (the first three lines).

3. Click on the **Spelling** button in the Standard toolbar to open the Spelling dialog box (see Figure 7.1). Note the dialog box

title, *Spelling: English (US)*. By default, United States English is the language against which the words in your document are checked. Word allows you to specify a different language (for example, UK English, French, German, Italian, and so on) by using the *Tools, Language* command.

4. Observe the dialog box. In the Not in Dictionary text box, Word displays the first word it found that was not in its internal dictionary (*Travle*, which appears in the second line of the heading). In the Suggestions list box, Word displays a list of suggested spelling corrections (*Travel*, *Trivial*, and so on). The first of these suggestions (*Travel*) is also placed in the Change To box.

5. Click on **Change** to change *Travle* to *Travel* and to search for the next potential spelling error in your text selection. In this case, no further errors are found. Word prompts

   ```
   Word finished checking the selection. Do you
   want to continue checking the remainder of
   the document?
   ```

6. Click on **No** to end the spelling check and return to the document. Note that *Travle* has been corrected to *Travel* (see Figure 7.2).

Now let's check the spelling of the entire document:

1. Press **Ctrl+Home** to deselect and move the insertion point to the top of the document.

2. Click on the **Spelling** button to open the Spelling dialog box and initiate the spelling check. Word displays the first word it finds that is not in its dictionary (*Filadelphia*).

3. Click on **Change** to replace *Filadelphia* with *Philadelphia* (the entry in the Change To box) and to search for the next potential spelling error. Word displays *lwest*. Note that *lowest* is listed in the Change To text box.

4. Click on **Change** to change *lwest* to *lowest* and to search for the next potential spelling error. Word displays *the* in the uppermost text box, which is now titled *Repeated Word*, instead of *Not in Dictionary* (see Figure 7.3). Although *the* is not misspelled, it appears twice in a row (*the the*) in your document.

Figure 7.2   **A corrected spelling error**

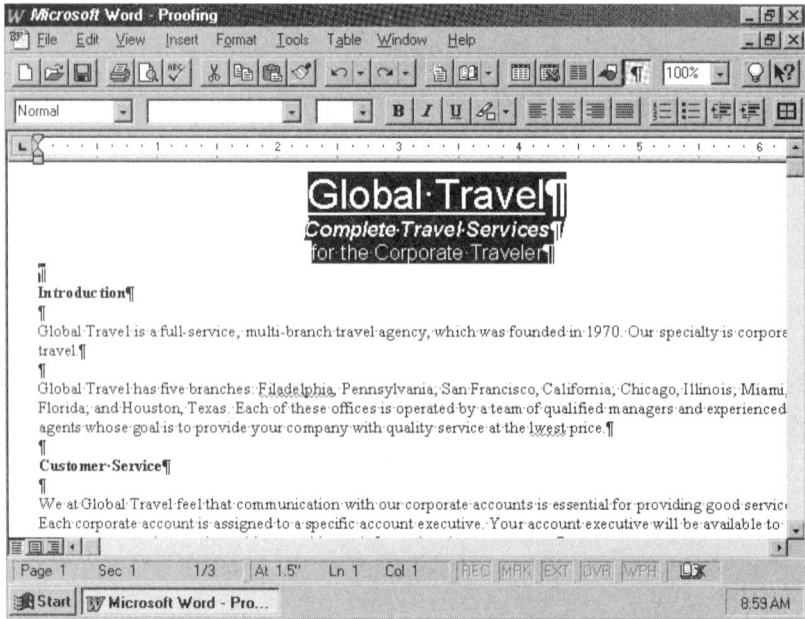

Figure 7.3   **Correcting a repeated word**

5. Click on the **Delete** button to delete the second *the.* Word prompts

   `The spelling check is complete.`

6. Click on **OK** to close the message box.

7. Save the disk file as **My Proofing**.

Now, let's try using the automatic spell-checking feature. (**Note:** If this option is not turned on, do so by following the instructions given earlier in this chapter.) First, we'll have to purposely misspell a word in our newly corrected document:

1. In the second line of the three-line heading, edit the word *Travel* to revert to its original misspelling, *Travle*. Then click on another word or line to move the insertion point away from the word. Notice that *Travle* is once again underlined with a wavy red line.

2. Click the **right mouse button** on **Travle** to open the automatic spell-checking menu (see Figure 7.4). The top portion of this menu lists suggested spellings of the word. Notice that this is exactly the same list of words suggested by the manual spell-checker earlier. The bottom portion of the menu offers three commands: Ignore All, Add (which adds the current spelling to the custom dictionary), and Spelling (which opens the Spelling dialog box).

3. Choose **Travel** from the menu to correct the word's spelling.

Figure 7.4   **The automatic spell-checking menu**

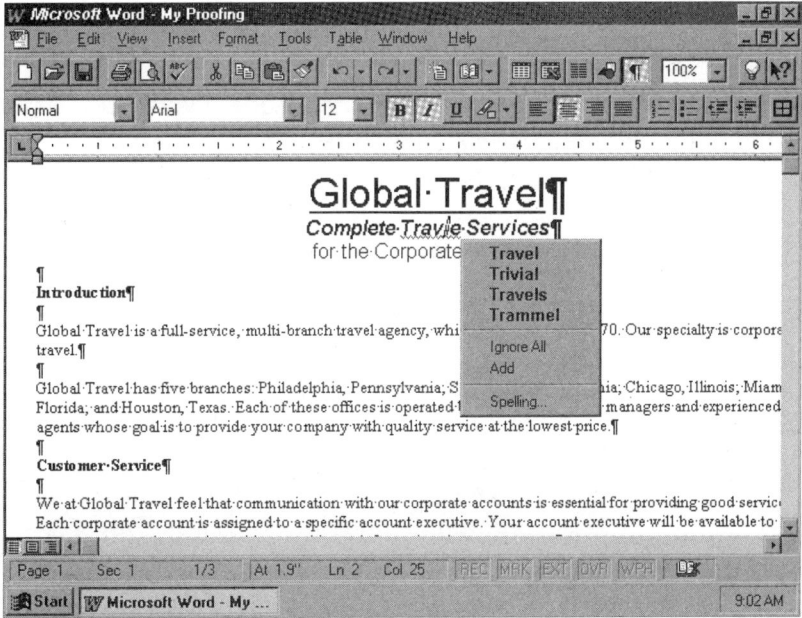

Clearly, the automatic spell-checking feature can be handy, because any spellings unfamiliar to the spell-checker are immediately brought to your attention without your having to run it manually. However, words such as proper names with odd spellings—for example, the word *Lite* in *Travel Lite, Inc.*—would also be identified as potential misspellings. Documents with many such words or names would be littered with distracting, wavy red lines.

Let's turn off the automatic spell-checking feature, so that we won't be distracted by wavy red lines for the remainder of this book:

1. Open the Options dialog box (choose **Tools, Options**), and display the Spelling tab.

2. Uncheck the **Automatic Spell Checking** option.

3. Click on **OK**.

USING THE THESAURUS TO FIND ALTERNATIVE WORDS

You can use Word's internal thesaurus to look up vocabulary alternatives in your documents. The thesaurus provides both *synonyms* (words with similar meanings) and *antonyms* (words with opposite meanings). Having a powerful and lightning-fast electronic thesaurus at your fingertips can greatly enhance the quality of the writing in your documents.

To use the thesaurus to find alternative words:

• Select the desired word in your document, or simply place the insertion point anywhere within the word.

• Choose *Tools, Thesaurus* (or press *Shift+F7*) to open the Thesaurus dialog box; a list of synonyms appears.
  Note: If antonyms are available, an Antonyms option appears in the Meanings list box. If you click on *Antonyms*, a list of antonyms will replace the list of synonyms.

• To replace the selected word, select the desired synonym or antonym and click on *Replace.*

Let's practice using the thesaurus to find synonyms:

1. Select the word **specialty** (located in the first line of the paragraph beginning with *Global Travel is a full-service*).

2. Choose **Tools, Thesaurus** to open the Thesaurus dialog box and display a list of synonyms for *specialty* (see Figure 7.5).

Note the dialog box title, *Thesaurus: English (US)*. As with the spelling checker, you can use the Tools, Language command to change your thesaurus language.

Figure 7.5   **The Thesaurus dialog box**

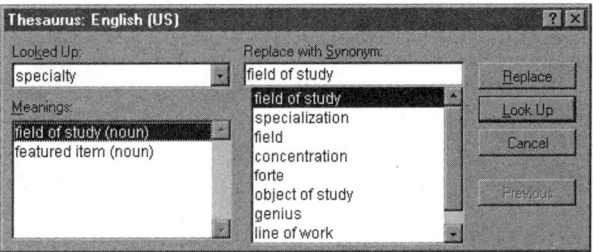

3. Under Replace with Synonym, select **forte** from the list of synonyms. The word *forte* now appears in the Replace with Synonym text box.

4. Click on **Replace** to replace *specialty* with *forte*.

Now let's use the thesaurus to find antonyms:

1. Place the insertion point anywhere in the word *qualified* (located in the paragraph beginning with *Global Travel has five branches*).

2. Press **Shift+F7** to use the shortcut keyboard method for opening the Thesaurus dialog box.

3. In the Meanings list box, select **Antonyms** to display a list of antonyms (opposites) for *qualified*. Notice that what was the *Replace with Synonym* text box is now titled *Replace with Antonym*, and the list of antonyms is displayed below it (see Figure 7.6).

Let's say that you found none of these antonyms appealing and decided to cancel the thesaurus lookup procedure.

4. Click on **Cancel** (or the **Close** button) to close the Thesaurus dialog box and return to your document.

Figure 7.6   **Displaying a list of antonyms**

CHECKING THE GRAMMAR AND STYLE OF YOUR DOCUMENTS

You can use Word's grammar checker to identify and correct sentences in your document that contain grammatical errors and weak writing style.

To check the grammar and style of a document:

- Press *Ctrl+Home* to move the insertion point to the top of the document; to check a portion of a document, select the text that you wish to check.

- Choose *Tools, Grammar* to open the Grammar dialog box and begin the grammar check (see Figure 7.7).

Figure 7.7   **The Grammar dialog box**

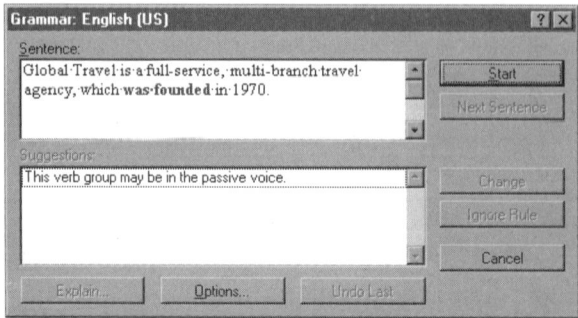

When a potential grammar or style error is found, the dialog box displays the questionable sentence in the Sentence box, with words that are related to the potential error displayed in bold letters. The dialog box might also provide one or more suggested corrections in the Suggestions list box. At this point, you can choose from the following options:

Option	Action Required
Accept suggested correction	Select desired correction in Suggestions list box and click on *Change*; or, as shortcut, simply double-click on desired suggestion.
Leave sentence as is and continue grammar check	Click on *Next Sentence*.
Leave sentence as is and ignore similar potential grammar or style errors	Click on *Ignore Rule*.
Undo recent corrections	Click on *Undo Last*.
Get more information about potential error	Click on *Explain*.
Get help on using grammar checker	Click on *Help*.
Ignore suggested correction	Click on *Ignore*.
Stop grammar check	Click on *Cancel* (or *Close*); all corrections made up to that point will be preserved.

CUSTOMIZING THE GRAMMAR CHECKER

You may disagree with certain rules that the grammar checker uses in assessing the correctness of a sentence. For example, you may find it perfectly acceptable to use the passive voice—a practice that the grammar checker considers to be a potential error. In recognition of the varying grammatical and style preferences of its users, Word allows you to customize the grammar checker to fit your needs. To do this:

- Click on *Options* in the Grammar dialog box.

- Click on *Customize Settings* in the Grammar tab of the Options dialog box.

- Set (check or uncheck) your desired grammar and style rules.

- Click on *OK* (or press *Enter*) to return to the Options dialog box, and then click on *OK* (or press *Enter*) to accept your customized settings and return to the Grammar dialog box.

The changes you made to Word's grammar and style rules will apply to all your grammar checks from this point on.

SPELL-CHECKING WITH THE GRAMMAR CHECKER

By default, Word checks your document for spelling when you run a grammar check. When it finds a spelling error, it opens the Spelling dialog box, allows you to make any necessary changes, and then continues checking for grammar and spelling. For this reason, if you intend to perform both a spelling and grammar check for a document, simply choose Tools, Grammar.

READABILITY STATISTICS

When you complete a grammar check, Word provides character, word, paragraph, and sentence counts for your document. It also provides *readability statistics*—the average number of sentences per paragraph, words per sentence, and characters per word. These readability statistics are calculated into standard *readability indexes*—for example, the Flesch Reading Ease and Coleman-Liau Grade Level indexes. (You'll learn how to display these indexes in the following activity.)

Let's use the grammar checker to check the grammar and writing style of our document:

1. Move the insertion point to the top of the document.

2. Choose **Tools, Grammar** to open the Grammar dialog box and search for the first potential grammar or style error (see Figure 7.7). Word finds *was founded* and informs you that this verb group may be in the passive voice. (By default, Word considers passive-voice verbs to be potential errors.) Let's say we disagree and find passive verbs to be appropriate in this document's context.

3. Click on **Ignore** to leave the sentence unchanged and search for the next potential grammar or style error. Word finds *is operated*, another passive-voice verb. It's clear that Word is going to call our attention to every passive verb group that it finds. Let's stop it from doing this for the remainder of the proofing session.

4. Click on **Ignore Rule** to leave all passive-voice verb groups unchanged (throughout the document) and search for the next potential error. Word finds *You're* and suggests changing it to *Your*. In this case, we'll agree.

5. Click on **Change** to accept the suggested correction (to change *You're* to *Your*) and search for the next potential error. Word finds *ensures*, and suggests that the word might be confused with *assures* and *insures*. Let's leave the word as it is.

6. Click on **Ignore** to let *ensures* stand. The next occurrence of *ensure* is found, and Word provides the same suggestion as in step 5.

7. Click on **Ignore** to let *ensure* stand. The first sentence of the paragraph below *Hotel Accommodations* is selected. Word suggests that this is a run-on sentence; however, we know that it is not.

8. Click on **Ignore** to let the sentence stand. Word finds *provide* and suggests the alternative, *provides*.

9. Click on **Change** to accept the suggested correction and search for the next potential error. Word finds *client* and suggests the alternative *clients*.

10. Click on **Change** to accept the suggested correction and search for the next potential error. Word finds *personal*, and suggests that the word might be confused with *personnel*.

11. Click on **Ignore Rule**. The "word confusion" rule is now no longer in effect. Word finds *travel* and suggests that you change it to *travels*. In this case, we'll disagree; *travel* is what we want.

12. Click on **Ignore** to leave *travel* unchanged and search for the next potential error. A *Readability Statistics* box appears, summarizing the grammar checker's findings for your document (see Figure 7.8), and indicating that the grammar check is complete.

Figure 7.8   **The Readability Statistics box**

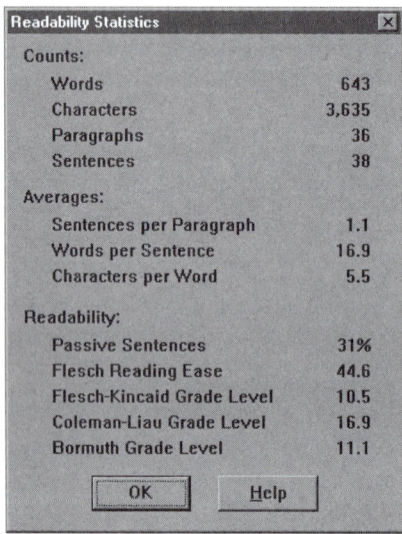

13. Press **F1** to display Word Help on readability statistics. You can read through this topic to learn more about what each of these statistics means.

14. Close the Help window. Take a moment to reexamine the Readability Statistics box in light of your new knowledge. When you are finished, click on **OK** (or press **Enter**) to close the box.

15. Save the disk file and close the document.

SUMMARY

In this chapter, you learned how to proof your documents and improve their quality. Now you know how to check the spelling of your documents, how to use the thesaurus to find alternative words, and how to check the grammar, style, and readability of your documents.

Here's a quick reference guide to the Word features introduced in this chapter:

Desired Result	How to Do It
Spell-check document manually	Move insertion point to top (to spell-check entire document) or select desired text (to spell-check part of document); click on **Spelling** button; follow Spelling dialog box prompts
Spell-check automatically	Click right mouse button on desired word identified by automatic spell-checker; choose desired spelling from list of suggested spellings, or choose other menu option
Use thesaurus to find alternative words	Select desired word or place insertion point anywhere within word; choose **Tools, Thesaurus** or press **Shift+F7**; follow Thesaurus dialog box prompts
Check grammar and style of a document	Move insertion point to top (to check entire document) or select desired text (to check selection); choose **Tools, Grammar**; follow Grammar dialog box prompts
Customize grammar checker	Click on **Options** in Grammar dialog box; click on **Customize Settings** in Grammar tab of Options dialog box; set (check or uncheck) desired grammar and style rules; click on **OK** to return to Options dialog box; click on **OK** to accept customized rule settings and return to Grammar dialog box

In the next chapter, you will build on the basic formatting and editing skills that you have already acquired. You'll learn advanced techniques for moving and copying text, and we'll show you how to copy font formats using the mouse. You'll also learn how to add numbers and bullets to selected text and how to replace and revise font formats.

CHAPTER 8: ADVANCED FORMATTING AND EDITING TECHNIQUES

Moving Text by Dragging

Copying Text from Another Document

Adding and Removing Numbers and Bullets

Using the Mouse to Copy Font Formats

Replacing Font Formats

Revising Font Formats in the Replace Dialog Box

In Chapters 3 and 4, you learned basic techniques for editing and changing font formats of text. In this chapter, you will build on this information by learning more advanced methods of editing and formatting text. For example, you will learn how to copy text from one document to another and how to enhance the readability and visual appeal of your documents by turning selected text into a numbered or bulleted list.

When you're done working through this chapter, you will know

- How to move text using the mouse
- How to copy text from one document to another
- How to add bullets and numbers to selected paragraphs
- How to copy font formats
- How to replace font formats using the Edit, Replace command

MOVING TEXT BY DRAGGING

In Chapter 3, you learned how to copy and move text by using the Cut, Copy, and Paste buttons on the Standard toolbar. In addition to using the toolbar to move text, you can also use the mouse.

To move text (within the same document) using the mouse:

- Select the text you wish to move.
- Point to the selected text.
- Press and hold the mouse button (a small dotted box and dotted insertion point appear attached to the mouse pointer).
- Drag the dotted insertion point to where you want to place the text.
- Release the mouse button.

Let's begin by copying some text. Then we'll use the mouse to move text:

1. Open **Advanced Formatting**.

2. Select the two lines of the *Global Travel* heading and the blank line below them.

3. Click on the **Copy** button in the Standard toolbar. A copy of the selected text is now placed on the Clipboard.

4. Go to the top of page 2.

5. Click on the **Paste** button. The contents of the Clipboard are now placed at the insertion point.

6. Go to the top of page 3.

7. Paste the contents of the Clipboard at the insertion point (click on the **Paste** button). Remember, the contents of the

Clipboard will remain there until another selection is cut or copied.

8. Move the insertion point to the top of the document.

9. Scroll to view the entire Introduction section of the document.

10. Drag to select the entire section, from the *Introduction* heading through the blank line above the *International Travel* heading (see Figure 8.1).

Figure 8.1   **Selected text to be moved**

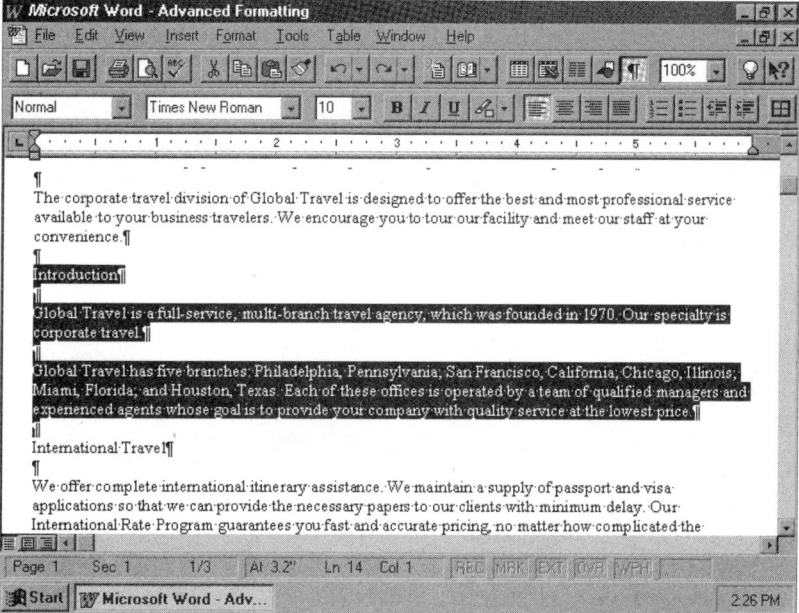

11. Point to the selected text. The mouse pointer becomes an arrow.

12. Press and hold the mouse button. A small, dotted box and a dotted insertion point appear.

13. Drag the dotted insertion point to the left of the *C* in *Customer Service* (toward the top of page 1) to place the Introduction section above the Customer Service section. Notice

that the document scrolls up when you reach the top of the document window.

14. Release the mouse button. The selected text is now displayed in its new location.

15. Save the disk file as **My Advanced Formatting** and compare your screen to Figure 8.2.

Figure 8.2   **The moved text**

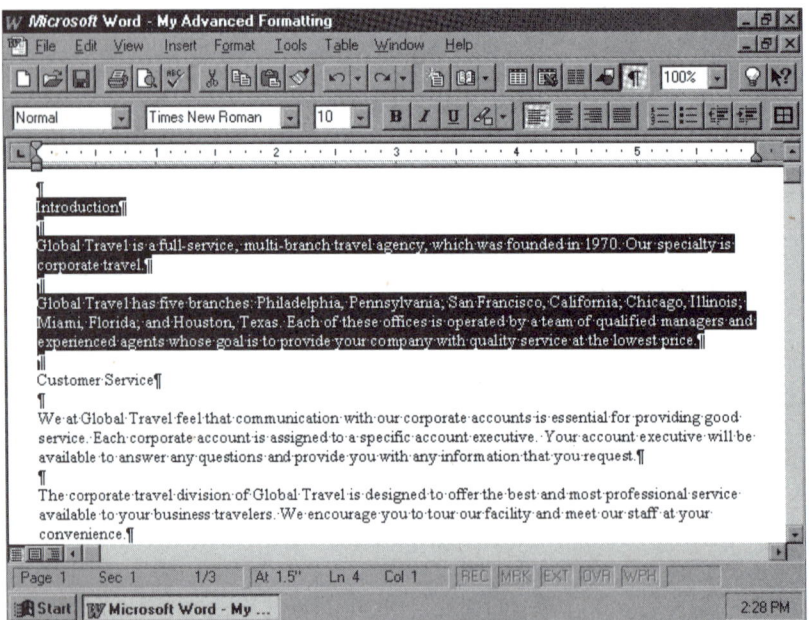

COPYING TEXT FROM ANOTHER DOCUMENT

The first document you open appears in the document window. If you create or open a second document without closing the first one, Word will open the second document on top of the first document, so that both documents are open at the same time. The second document then becomes the active document. You can open several (how many depends on your computer's available memory) documents at one time, but only one document can be active.

The names of the documents appear in the title bars and under the Window menu. To make a document active, either click on the document window, if it is visible, or select the document name from the Window menu.

Tiling is the arrangement of open windows in an equally spaced layout on the screen. To view more than one document window at a time, you can tile the open windows by choosing Window, Arrange All. However, the more windows you have open, the smaller each window will be when it is tiled. You also can use the document Maximize/Restore button to enlarge or reduce the size of each window.

Once you have placed text on the Clipboard, you can move or copy the text from one document to another, in the same way that you would within a document.

Let's open a second document window, and then copy and paste between the two documents:

1. Place the I-beam to the left of the *H* in *Hotel Accommodations*, near the bottom of page 2.

2. Open **Copying and Pasting**. The document consists of a single paragraph, followed by a blank line.

3. Select the paragraph and the blank line below it.

4. Copy the selected text to the Clipboard (click on the **Copy** button).

5. Choose **Window, 2 My Advanced Formatting** (see Figure 8.3) to move to the My Advanced Formatting document window.

6. Paste the contents of the Clipboard at the insertion point (click on the **Paste** button). The paragraph and blank line are now displayed below the *Auto Rentals* heading.

7. Update the disk file.

8. Choose **Window, 1 Copying and Pasting** to move to the Copying and Pasting document window.

9. Close Copying and Pasting.

Figure 8.3   **Switching between documents**

ADDING AND REMOVING NUMBERS AND BULLETS

The longer your document, the more important it is for you to clearly define its major sections and subsections. To achieve this, you can use headings, which you can format differently from the surrounding text. In fact, you've already seen several examples of headings in exercises throughout this book. Furthermore, when your document contains lists of items that you would like to call attention to, such items can be numbered or bulleted. This section focuses on using numbers and bullets to improve your document's organization and appearance.

 ### ADDING NUMBERS AND BULLETS

To add numbers to specific paragraphs, select the desired paragraphs and click on the Numbering button. To add bullets to specific paragraphs, select the desired paragraphs and click on the Bullets button. When you add bullets or numbers to paragraphs, Word automatically formats the paragraphs with hanging indents.

(See "Setting Hanging Indents" in Chapter 5 for details on this feature.)

If you apply numbers to a series of paragraphs and then want to change them to bullets, or vice versa:

- Select the desired paragraphs.
- Click on the *Bullets* or *Numbering* button.

You can also create a numbered or bulleted list before you add the text to the list. To do so:

- Position the insertion point where you wish to place the list.
- Click on the *Numbering* or *Bullets* button.
- Create as many paragraphs as you like.
- Click on the *Numbering* or *Bullets* button again to turn off the feature.

Let's select a list of items, and then add numbers and bullets to the list:

1. Scroll to place the *Newsletter* heading, on page 3, at the top of the screen.
2. Drag to select the paragraphs that begin *Travel costs...*, *Special fares...*, and *Travel basics....*
3. Click on the **Numbering** button in the Formatting toolbar. Numbers appear to the left of the selected paragraphs.

4. Deselect the text to view the numbers. Compare your screen to Figure 8.4.
5. Drag to select the numbered list. Be sure to select all the paragraph marks.
6. Click on the **Bullets** button. Bullets now appear to the left of the selected paragraphs.

7. Deselect the text and compare your screen to Figure 8.5.

Figure 8.4   **The numbered list**

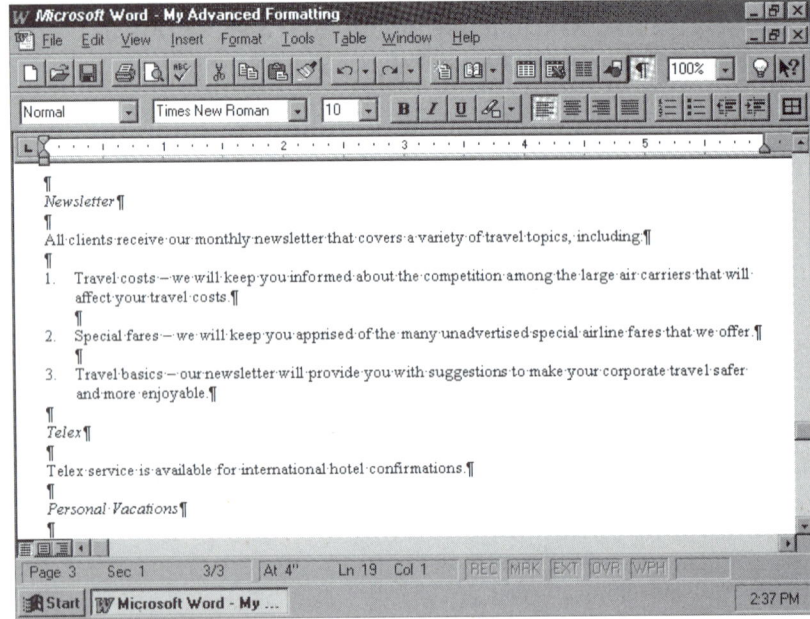

Figure 8.5   **The bulleted list**

REMOVING NUMBERS AND BULLETS

You can remove bullets or numbers from a series of paragraphs. To do so:

• Select the numbered or bulleted list.

• Choose *Format, Bullets and Numbering*.

• Click on *Remove* in the Bullets and Numbering dialog box.

Note: Though the Bullets and Numbering dialog box contains separate Bulleted and Numbered tabs, you do not have to select a particular tab to remove numbers or bullets—just click on Remove. You can also use the Undo command to remove bullets or numbers.

In the Bullets and Numbering dialog box, you can set various options for the type of bullet or number character you want to use, as well as its size (accessible through the Modify option), and you can even remove the hanging indent. There is also a tab for creating multilevel lists.

Let's remove the bullets from our list:

1. Drag to select the bulleted list. Be sure to select all the paragraphs.

2. Choose **Format, Bullets and Numbering** to open the Bullets and Numbering dialog box (see Figure 8.6).

3. Click on **Remove** to remove the bullets from the selected text.

Figure 8.6   **The Bullets and Numbering dialog box**

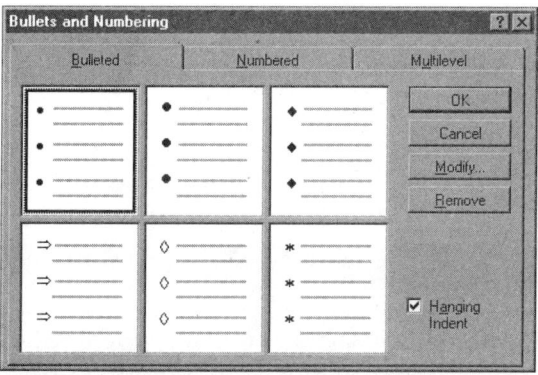

PRACTICE YOUR SKILLS

Make the paragraphs beginning with *Travel costs...*, *Special fares...*, and *Travel basics...* paragraphs with numbers.

USING THE MOUSE TO COPY FONT FORMATS

In Chapter 4, you learned how to apply multiple character, or font, styles using the Format menu. In the same chapter you also learned that you could use the F4 (Repeat) key or choose Edit, Repeat Formatting to repeat the formatting on other text. Remember, however, that when you use either of these methods, only the *last* format applied will be repeated. For example, if you select text and apply first the bold and then the italic formats from the Formatting toolbar, then select different text and press F4, only the italic formatting will be applied.

To copy all of the font formatting from one block of text to another:

* Select or place the insertion point in the text whose formatting you want to copy.

* Click on the *Format Painter* button on the Standard toolbar.

* Select the text to which you wish to copy the formatting.

Let's apply and copy some font formats:

1. Select the **Introduction** heading, near the top of the document.

2. Open the **Font** drop-down list box (in the Formatting toolbar) and select **Arial**.

3. Click on the **Bold**, **Italic**, and **Underline** buttons to apply those font styles to the selected text.

4. Select the **Customer Service** heading, below the Introduction section.

5. Open the Edit menu. Notice the second menu choice, *Repeat Underline*. If you were to choose this option (or press F4), only the underlining would be applied to the selected text.

6. Close the Edit menu. Verify that Customer Service is still selected.

7. Place the insertion point anywhere within the *Introduction* heading to point to the font formats that you will copy.

8. Click on the **Format Painter** button, and move the mouse pointer down into the text area. Notice that it becomes a paintbrush attached to an I-beam.

9. Select the **Customer Service** heading. Notice that as you select the heading, the formatting from the Introduction heading is copied or "painted" onto it. The Format Painter button is no longer depressed, and the mouse pointer returns to normal.

10. With the *Customer Service* heading still selected, scroll down to view the *International Travel* heading.

11. Click on the **Format Painter** button, and then select the **International Travel** heading to copy the formatting from the Customer Service heading.

PRACTICE YOUR SKILLS

1. Apply bold, italic, and underline styles to the *Corporate Profiles* and *Worldwide Services* headings.

2. Deselect the text.

3. Save the disk file and compare your screen to Figure 8.7.

REPLACING FONT FORMATS

You can use the Replace dialog box to search for and replace font formats in a manner that is similar to the way you find and replace text.

To replace font formats:

• Choose *Edit, Replace.*

• Click on *Format.*

• Choose *Font* from the Format pop-up list.

• In the Find Font dialog box, click on the *Font* tab, if necessary, and then select the font formats you want to find.

• Click on *OK* to return to the Replace dialog box.

Figure 8.7   **Copied font formats**

- Press *Tab* to move to the Replace With text box.

- Click on *Format*.

- Choose *Font* to open the Replace Font dialog box, and click on the *Font* tab, if necessary.

- Select the font formats that you want to change to.

- Click on *OK*.

- Click on *Find Next*.

- Click on *Replace* to replace the font formatting, or click on *Find Next* to leave the existing formatting intact.

- Click on *Close* (or *Cancel*) to close the Replace dialog box when you are finished.

In the Find Font dialog box, grayed or unchecked formats under Effects will not change. Clicking in the check box selects the format; clicking twice clears the check box, indicating that you want to remove the format.

Let's replace font formats:

1. Move to the top of the document.

2. Choose **Edit, Replace** to open the Replace dialog box. The insertion point is placed in the Find What text box.

3. Click on **Format** to open the Format pop-up list (see Figure 8.8). Then choose **Font** to open the Find Font dialog box. If necessary, display the Font tab.

Figure 8.8   **The Format pop-up list**

4. In the Font list box, select **Arial** (scroll to display it, if necessary) to search for text with the Arial font.

5. In the Font Style list box, select **Bold Italic** to search for text that is both bold and italic.

6. Open the **Underline** drop-down list box, and select **Single** to search for text with a single underline. Compare your screen to Figure 8.9.

7. Click on **OK** to return to the Replace dialog box.

8. Press **Tab** to move the insertion point to the Replace With text box.

9. Click on the **Format** button and choose **Font** to open the Replace Font dialog box and confirm that the Font tab is still displayed.

Figure 8.9   **Searching for specified font formats**

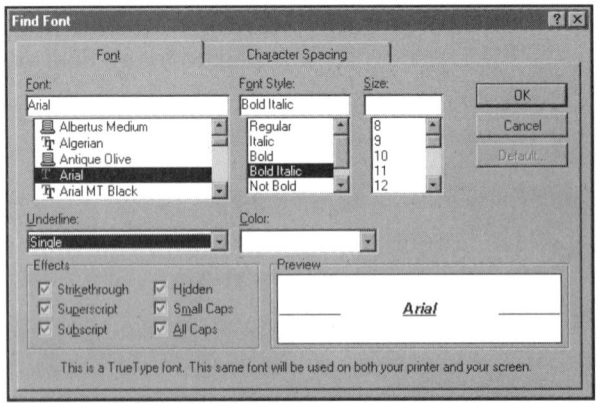

10. In the Font Style list box, check **Italic** to apply the italic font style to selected text.

11. Click on **OK** to return to the Replace dialog box. Notice the font formats listed under the Find What and Replace With boxes, as shown in Figure 8.10.

Figure 8.10   **The specified formats listed in the Replace dialog box**

12. Click on **Find Next** to begin the search and replace procedure. The *Introduction* heading is selected.

13. Click on **Replace** to replace the current format with the italic font style. The *Customer Service* heading is now selected.

PRACTICE YOUR SKILLS

1. Continue replacing font formats until you have found and replaced all of them.

2. Close the Replace dialog box.

3. Save the disk file.

REVISING FONT FORMATS IN THE REPLACE DIALOG BOX

When you select the font formatting you want to find and replace, the formats you choose appear below the Find What and Replace With text boxes. These formats will remain selected until you exit Word or select new formats.

Let's revise font formats in the Replace dialog box, changing the Arial italic text to Arial bold:

1. Choose **Edit, Replace** to open the Replace dialog box. The insertion point is placed in the Find What text box.

2. Observe the text below the Find What text box (see Figure 8.10); the font formats you previously specified remain selected.

3. Open the Find Font dialog box (click on **Format**, and choose **Font** from the pop-up list). You can see that all the previous selections remain selected.

4. Click on **OK** to return to the Replace dialog box.

5. Press **Tab** to move the insertion point to the Replace With text box.

6. Open the Replace Font dialog box (click on **Format**, and choose **Font**).

7. In the Font list box, choose **Arial**, if necessary.

8. In the Font Style list box, choose **Regular** to remove the bold and italic font styles from selected text.

9. Open the Underline drop-down list, and select **(none)** to remove the underline.

10. Click on **OK** to return to the Replace dialog box. Compare your screen to Figure 8.11.

11. Click on **Find Next** to begin to search and replace.

Note: If you know in advance that you want to replace all occurrences of a format, instead of clicking on Find Next, you can click on Replace All.

Figure 8.11 **The revised font formats**

PRACTICE YOUR SKILLS

1. Use the **Replace** button in the Replace dialog box to make the headings bold.

2. Close the Replace dialog box.

3. Save the disk file.

4. Print the disk file and compare your printout to Figure 8.12.

5. Close the document.

PRACTICE YOUR SKILLS

The following instructions lead you through the steps necessary to edit the file Practice 8A to produce the document shown in Figure 8.13.

Follow these steps at your computer:

1. Open **Practice 8A**.

2. Use the mouse to select the *International Travel* section, which is below the *Corporate Profiles* section. Be sure to select the entire section and the blank line following it.

Figure 8.12   **The completed My Advanced Formatting document**

Global Travel
Complete Travel Services

Introduction

Global Travel is a full-service, multi-branch travel agency, which was founded in 1970. Our specialty is corporate travel.

Global Travel has five branches: Philadelphia, Pennsylvania; San Francisco, California; Chicago, Illinois; Miami, Florida; and Houston, Texas. Each of these offices is operated by a team of qualified managers and experienced agents whose goal is to provide your company with quality service at the lowest price.

Customer Service

We at Global Travel feel that communication with our corporate accounts is essential for providing good service. Each corporate account is assigned to a specific account executive. Your account executive will be available to answer any questions and provide you with any information that you request.

The corporate travel division of Global Travel is designed to offer the best and most professional service available to your business travelers. We encourage you to tour our facility and meet our staff at your convenience.

International Travel

We offer complete international itinerary assistance. We maintain a supply of passport and visa applications so that we can provide the necessary papers to our clients with minimum delay. Our International Rate Program guarantees you fast and accurate pricing, no matter how complicated the itinerary.

Corporate Profiles

Your company profile will be stored in our computer, and individual profiles will be maintained on each frequent traveler. Each profile will contain information regarding passport information, seating preference, car rental preference, frequent-flyer membership number, and corporate discount numbers. This information ensures that we can provide frequent travelers, fast, cost-effective itineraries.

Worldwide Services

Global Travel's Reservation Center will handle all of your weekend and after-hour reservations and changes. The reservation center can be dialed toll-free 24 hours a day. The worldwide service emergency numbers will be clearly marked on your travel itineraries.

Figure 8.12   **The completed My Advanced Formatting document (Continued)**

Global Travel
Complete Travel Services

Discounts

Global Travel guarantees the lowest air fares available. Due to the volume of tickets that we issue, several of the large air carriers offer us special discounts that we can pass on to our clients.

Our quality-control specialists check each of your tickets to guarantee that you have received the lowest rate available. In addition, each ticket is checked to ensure that it includes seating assignments and boarding passes before it is delivered to you.

Deliveries

Our courier makes daily deliveries, both in the morning and afternoon, to offices within 20 miles of our local branch. All of our offices, each located across from the local airport, have drive-up windows. If you make last-minute travel plans with us you can pick up your ticket right at the drive-up window.

Auto Rentals

We guarantee the lowest prices on all car rentals. We will match the type of car with the information provided in the profile for each of your frequent travelers. Each car that is rented through Global Travel carries an extra $50,000 worth of liability insurance.

Hotel Accommodations

Our Corporate Hotel Program is the most competitive and comprehensive program in the world, offering corporate travelers cost savings and extra amenities in most business locations. Global Travel has access to more than 10,000 hotels worldwide, with a range of rooms from economy to luxury. This selection offers your corporate travelers the accommodations they want with a cost savings of 10-30% off the regular rates.

Figure 8.12   **The completed My Advanced Formatting document (Continued)**

Global Travel
Complete Travel Services

Additional Services

Global Travel also provides the following services for our corporate customers:

Newsletter

All clients receive our monthly newsletter that covers a variety of travel topics, including:

1. Travel costs – we will keep you informed about the competition among the large air carriers that will affect your travel costs.

2. Special fares – we will keep you apprised of the many unadvertised special airline fares that we offer.

3. Travel basics – our newsletter will provide you with suggestions to make your corporate travel safer and more enjoyable.

Telex

Telex service is available for international hotel confirmations.

Personal Vacations

Our corporate clients are invited to discuss their vacation and personal travel plans with an agent from Global Travel's Vacation Division. Our Vacation Division is skilled in both domestic and international travel.

Flight Insurance

We will supply all clients with $250,000 worth of flight insurance for every trip arranged through Global Travel.

Fax

Travel requests may be faxed to our office. Confirmed itineraries can be faxed to your office for immediate confirmation.

Figure 8.13   **The completed My Practice 8A document**

Global Travel
Complete Travel Services

Introduction

Global Travel is a full-service, multi-branch travel agency, which was founded in 1970. Our specialty is corporate travel.

Global Travel has five branches: Philadelphia, Pennsylvania; San Francisco, California; Chicago, Illinois; Miami, Florida; and Houston, Texas. Each of these offices is operated by a team of qualified managers and experienced agents whose goal is to provide your company with quality service at the lowest price.

Customer Service

We at Global Travel feel that communication with our corporate accounts is essential for providing good service. Each corporate account is assigned to a specific account executive. Your account executive will be available to answer any questions and provide you with any information that you request.

The corporate travel division of Global Travel is designed to offer the best and most professional service available to your business travelers. We encourage you to tour our facility and meet our staff at your convenience.

International Travel

We offer complete international itinerary assistance. We maintain a supply of passport and visa applications so that we can provide the necessary papers to our clients with minimum delay. Our International Rate Program guarantees you fast and accurate pricing, no matter how complicated the itinerary.

Corporate Profiles

Your company profile will be stored in our computer, and individual profiles will be maintained on each frequent traveler. Each profile will contain information regarding passport information, seating preference, car rental preference, frequent-flyer membership number, and corporate discount numbers. This information ensures that we can provide frequent travelers, fast, cost-effective itineraries.

Worldwide Services

Global Travel's Reservation Center will handle all of your weekend and after-hour reservations and changes. The reservation center can be dialed toll-free 24 hours a day. The worldwide service emergency numbers will be clearly marked on your travel itineraries.

Figure 8.13   **The completed My Practice 8A document (Continued)**

Global Travel
Complete Travel Services

Discounts

Global Travel guarantees the lowest air fares available. Due to the volume of tickets that we issue, several of the large air carriers offer us special discounts that we can pass on to our clients.

Our quality-control specialists check each of your tickets to guarantee that you have received the lowest rate available. In addition, each ticket is checked to ensure that it includes seating assignments and boarding passes before it is delivered to you.

Deliveries

Our courier makes daily deliveries, both in the morning and afternoon, to offices within 20 miles of our local branch. All of our offices, each located across from the local airport, have drive-up windows. If you make last-minute travel plans with us you can pick up your ticket right at the drive-up window.

Auto Rentals

We guarantee the lowest prices on all car rentals. We will match the type of car with the information provided in the profile for each of your frequent travelers. Each car that is rented through Global Travel carries an extra $50,000 worth of liability insurance.

Hotel Accommodations

Our Corporate Hotel Program is the most competitive and comprehensive program in the world, offering corporate travelers cost savings and extra amenities in most business locations. Global Travel has access to more than 10,000 hotels worldwide, with a range of rooms from economy to luxury. This selection offers your corporate travelers the accommodations they want with a cost savings of 10-30% off the regular rates.

Figure 8.13   **The completed My Practice 8A document (Continued)**

Global Travel
Complete Travel Services

<u>Additional Services</u>

Global Travel also provides the following services for our corporate customers:

Newsletter

All clients receive our monthly newsletter that covers a variety of travel topics, including:

1. Travel costs – we will keep you informed about the competition among the large air carriers that will affect your travel costs.

2. Special fares – we will keep you apprised of the many unadvertised special airline fares that we offer.

3. Travel basics – our newsletter will provide you with suggestions to make your corporate travel safer and more enjoyable.

Telex

Telex service is available for international hotel confirmations.

Personal Vacations

Our corporate clients are invited to discuss their vacation and personal travel plans with an agent from Global Travel's Vacation Division. Our Vacation Division is skilled in both domestic and international travel.

Flight Insurance

We will supply all clients with $250,000 worth of flight insurance for every trip arranged through Global Travel.

Fax

Travel requests may be faxed to our office. Confirmed itineraries can be faxed to your office for immediate confirmation.

3. Drag the selected text directly *above* the *Corporate Profiles* section.

4. Use the Standard toolbar to copy the two-line heading and the blank line below it at the top of page 1, to the top of pages 2 and 3.

5. Open **Practice 8B**.

6. Use the Standard toolbar to copy all of Practice 8B to the Clipboard.

7. Move to the Practice 8A window.

8. Paste the contents of the Clipboard below the *Deliveries* heading. (**Hint:** Place the insertion point to the left of the *A* in *Auto Rentals* before you paste the contents of the Clipboard.)

9. In the Newsletter section, select the paragraphs that begin *Travel costs...*, *Special fares...*, and *Travel basics....*

10. Add bullets to the selected paragraphs.

11. Change the bulleted list to a numbered list.

12. Change the font formatting of the *Introduction* heading to **Arial**, **Bold**, and **Underline**.

13. Use the mouse to apply the font formats from the *Introduction* heading to the *Customer Service* heading.

14. Apply the font formats from the Customer Service heading to the following headings:

   International Travel

   Corporate Profiles

   Worldwide Services

   Discounts

   Deliveries

   Auto Rentals

   Hotel Accommodations

   Additional Services

15. Save the disk file as **My Practice 8A**.

16. Print the document and compare your printout to Figure 8.13.

17. Close both document windows.

In the next activity you will edit Practice 8C to produce the final document shown in Figure 8.14. You will use the Replace dialog box to replace font formats.

Follow these steps at your computer:

1. Open **Practice 8C**.

2. Use the Replace dialog box to find text that is Arial, 24 point, bold, and replace these formats with **Times New Roman, 14 point, bold**.

3. Use the Replace dialog box to find text that is formatted as Times New Roman, 12 point, bold and italic, and change it to **Arial, 10 point, bold**.

4. Use the Replace dialog box to find text that is formatted as Times New Roman, 14 point, with a single underline. Change the formatting to **Arial, 10 point, bold**, and **no underline**.

5. Use the Replace dialog box to find text that is formatted as Arial, 14 point, italic. Replace these font formats with **Times New Roman, 10 point, italic**.

6. Use the Replace dialog box to find text that is formatted as Arial, 12 point, with a single underline. Replace the formats with **Times New Roman, 10 point** font formats, and **no underline**.

7. Close the Replace dialog box.

8. Save the disk file as **My Practice 8C**.

9. Print the document and compare your printout to Figure 8.14.

10. Close the document.

SUMMARY

In this chapter, you learned a number of advanced formatting and editing techniques that make use of the Standard toolbar and mouse, including copying and moving text within a single document and between documents. You learned how to create numbered lists and bulleted lists by adding numbers or bullets to a contiguous string of paragraphs. You also learned how to change

Figure 8.14 **The completed My Practice 8C document**

Global Travel
Complete Travel Services

Introduction

Global Travel is a full-service, multi-branch travel agency, which was founded in 1970. Our specialty is corporate travel.

Global Travel has five branches: Philadelphia, Pennsylvania; San Francisco, California; Chicago, Illinois; Miami, Florida; and Houston, Texas. Each of these offices is operated by a team of qualified managers and experienced agents whose goal is to provide your company with quality service at the lowest price.

Customer Service

We at Global Travel feel that communication with our corporate accounts is essential for providing good service. Each corporate account is assigned to a specific account executive. Your account executive will be available to answer any questions and provide you with any information that you request.

The corporate travel division of Global Travel is designed to offer the best and most professional service available to your business travelers. We encourage you to tour our facility and meet our staff at your convenience.

International Travel

We offer complete international itinerary assistance. We maintain a supply of passport and visa applications so that we can provide the necessary papers to our clients with minimum delay. Our International Rate Program guarantees you fast and accurate pricing, no matter how complicated the itinerary.

Corporate Profiles

Your company profile will be stored in our computer, and individual profiles will be maintained on each frequent traveler. Each profile will contain information regarding passport information, seating preference, car rental preference, frequent-flyer membership number, and corporate discount numbers. This information ensures that we can provide frequent travelers, fast, cost-effective itineraries.

Worldwide Services

Global Travel's Reservation Center will handle all of your weekend and after-hour reservations and changes. The reservation center can be dialed toll-free 24 hours a day. The worldwide service emergency numbers will be clearly marked on your travel itineraries.

Figure 8.14   **The completed My Practice 8C document (Continued)**

**Global Travel
Complete Travel Services**

Discounts

Global Travel guarantees the lowest air fares available. Due to the volume of tickets that we issue, several of the large air carriers offer us special discounts that we can pass on to our clients.

Our quality-control specialists check each of your tickets to guarantee that you have received the lowest rate available. In addition, each ticket is checked to ensure that it includes seating assignments and boarding passes before it is delivered to you.

Deliveries

Our courier makes daily deliveries, both in the morning and afternoon, to offices within 20 miles of our local branch. All of our offices, each located across from the local airport, have drive-up windows. If you make last-minute travel plans with us you can pick up your ticket right at the drive-up window.

Auto Rentals

We guarantee the lowest prices on all car rentals. We will match the type of car with the information provided in the profile for each of your frequent travelers. Each car that is rented through Global Travel carries an extra $50,000 worth of liability insurance.

Hotel Accommodations

Our Corporate Hotel Program is the most competitive and comprehensive program in the world, offering corporate travelers cost savings and extra amenities in most business locations. Global Travel has access to more than 10,000 hotels worldwide, with a range of rooms from economy to luxury. This selection offers your corporate travelers the accommodations they want with a cost savings of 10-30% off the regular rates.

Figure 8.14   The completed My Practice 8C document (Continued)

Global Travel
Complete Travel Services

Additional Services

Global Travel also provides the following services for our corporate customers:

Newsletter

All clients receive our monthly newsletter that covers a variety of travel topics, including:

- Travel costs – we will keep you informed about the competition among the large air carriers that will affect your travel costs.

- Special fares – we will keep you apprised of the many unadvertised special airline fares that we offer.

- Travel basics – our newsletter will provide you with suggestions to make your corporate travel safer and more enjoyable.

Telex

Telex service is available for international hotel confirmations.

Personal Vacations

Our corporate clients are invited to discuss their vacation and personal travel plans with an agent from Global Travel's Vacation Division. Our Vacation Division is skilled in both domestic and international travel.

Flight Insurance

We will supply all clients with $250,000 worth of flight insurance for every trip arranged through Global Travel.

Fax

Travel requests may be faxed to our office. Confirmed itineraries can be faxed to your office for immediate confirmation.

a numbered list to a bulleted list, and vice versa. Finally, you learned how to copy and replace font formats.

Here is a quick reference guide to the Word features introduced in this chapter:

Desired Result	How to Do It
Move text using mouse	Select desired text; point to selected text; drag selection to desired destination; release mouse button
Copy text from one document to another	Open second document; select desired text; click on **Copy** button; choose **Window** and choose file name of destination document; place insertion point where you wish to place copied text; click on **Paste** button
Add numbers or bullets to existing text	Select desired paragraphs; click on **Numbering** button or **Bullets** button
Change numbers to bullets or vice versa	Select numbered or bulleted list; click on **Bullets** or **Numbering** button, whichever you desire; click on **Yes**
Remove numbers or bullets	Select desired text; choose **Tools, Bullets and Numbering**; click on Remove
Copy font formats	Place insertion point anywhere within text that has formatting that you wish to copy; click on **Format Painter** button; select text to which you wish to copy formats
Replace font formats	Place insertion point at top of document; choose **Edit, Replace**; click on **Format**, and choose **Font**; select settings you want to find; click on **OK**. Press **Tab**; click on **Format**, and choose **Font**; select replacement settings; click on **OK**. Click on **Find Next**; click on **Replace**; continue clicking on **Find Next**, then **Replace**, until you have finished replacing formats

Desired Result	How to Do It
Revise font formats	Place insertion point at top of document; choose **Edit, Replace**; click on **Format**, and choose **Font**; select settings you wish to find; click on **OK**. Press **Tab**; click on **Format**, and choose **Font**; select new replacement settings; click on **OK**. Click on **Find Next**; click on **Replace**; and so on

In the next chapter, you will learn how to create and use the AutoText feature to store frequently used text and graphics.

CHAPTER 9: STORING FREQUENTLY USED TEXT WITH THE AUTOTEXT FEATURE

Creating AutoText Entries

Inserting AutoText Entries

Modifying AutoText Entries

Printing AutoText Entries

Suppose you needed to send out a large number of letters with the same letterhead and closing. It would certainly save you a great deal of time to enter the letterhead and closing only once, and then simply paste them into each document, as needed. You could copy the information to the Clipboard and paste it into each letter. However, you already know that the Clipboard is only a temporary storage area; as soon as you cut or copied other text or exited Windows, the information would be lost.

Word enables you to save such information as an AutoText entry. Word's *AutoText* feature is a kind of shorthand that allows you to save text (or graphics), and then retrieve it whenever you need it. You can insert AutoText entries anywhere in your documents.

When you're done working through this chapter, you will know

- How to create AutoText entries
- How to modify and delete AutoText entries
- How to print AutoText entries

CREATING AUTOTEXT ENTRIES

AutoText entries enable you to store frequently used text and graphics so that you can insert them into your documents quickly and easily. AutoText entries are stored so that they can be used *globally,* in all templates. A *template* is a kind of "model" that determines the general format of the document it is attached to. Templates allow you to custom-tailor your documents. (You'll learn about templates in Chapter 13.) If you do not wish to use AutoText entries globally, you can store them to be used with a specific template.

To create an AutoText entry:

- Select the text or graphics you want in the AutoText entry.
- Choose *Edit, AutoText* to open the AutoText dialog box.
- In the Name text box, type a name for the AutoText entry (or accept the default one).
- Click on *Add.*

AutoText entries can contain any type of formatting. Entry names can have up to 32 characters and can contain spaces. For ease of use, you might want to keep your AutoText entry names brief.

Let's create AutoText entries for a letterhead and closing:

1. Click on the **New** button to open a new document window.
2. Type **Global Travel** and press **Enter**.
3. Type **2345 Industrial Parkway** and press **Enter**.
4. Type **Chicago, Illinois 60603** and press **Enter** three times.

5. Select all of the text. Do *not* select the blank lines below the text.

6. Change the font to **Arial** (use the **Font** drop-down list box).

7. Apply the **Bold** character style to the selected text.

8. Center the selected text, and compare your screen to Figure 9.1.

9. Deselect the text.

10. This time, select all of the text *and* the three blank lines. The heading and blank lines will be included in the AutoText entry.

11. Choose **Edit, AutoText** to open the AutoText dialog box.

12. Observe the Selection box at the bottom of the AutoText dialog box. It allows you to verify the desired selection. Notice that a default name is provided in the Name text box; however, let's change the name.

13. In the Name text box, type **letterhead** to name the AutoText entry. Compare your screen to Figure 9.2.

Figure 9.1   **The completed letterhead**

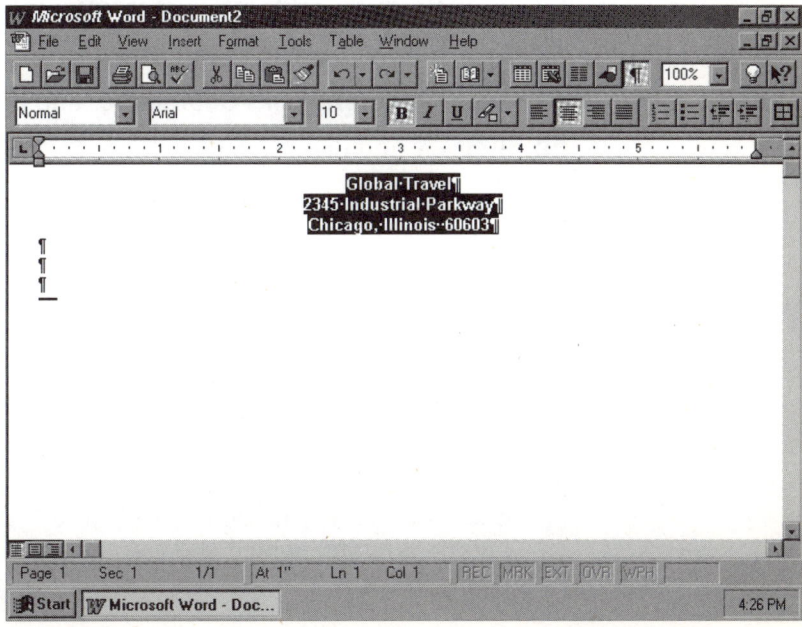

Figure 9.2   **Naming the letterhead AutoText entry**

14. Click on **Add** to add the AutoText entry to the list.

15. Close the document without saving it; saving is not necessary because the document's text has already been saved as an AutoText entry.

16. Click on the **New** button to open a new document window.

17. Type **Cordially,** and press **Enter** four times.

18. Type your name and press **Enter.**

19. Type **Corporate Sales Coordinator** and press **Enter** twice.

20. Type **cc:** and press **Tab** to move to the first tab stop.

21. Type **N. Rorem** and press **Enter.**

22. Press **Tab**, type **J. Coltrane** and compare your screen to Figure 9.3.

23. Select all of the text and paragraph marks. The selected text will be included in the AutoText entry.

24. Choose **Edit, AutoText** to open the AutoText dialog box again.

25. In the Name text box, type **cordially** to name the AutoText entry. Compare your screen to Figure 9.4. Notice that the letterhead entry, which you created earlier, is listed in the Name list box.

Figure 9.3   **Completed letter closing**

Figure 9.4   **Naming the letter-closing AutoText entry**

26. Click on **Add** to add the AutoText entry to the list.

27. Close the document without saving it.

INSERTING AUTOTEXT ENTRIES

To insert an AutoText entry in a document:

- Place the insertion point where you want to insert the Auto-Text entry.

- Choose *Edit, AutoText*.

- Select the name of the AutoText entry you want to insert.

- Click on *Insert*.

Directly below the Name text box is the Insert As portion of the AutoText dialog box. Under Insert As, two choices are provided:

- *Formatted Text*, which will retain the formatting of the Auto-Text entry as it was originally created

- *Plain Text*, which tells Word to apply the formatting of the surrounding text to the AutoText entry

To insert an AutoText entry using the keyboard:

- Place the insertion point where you want to insert the Auto-Text entry.

- Type the name of the AutoText entry.

- Press *F3*.

If you want to insert the AutoText entry quickly, retaining its original formatting, we recommend using the keyboard. However, if you don't remember the name of the entry, wish to insert it as plain text (without its original formatting), or simply wish to preview its contents, use the Edit, AutoText command.

Note: If you type the AutoText entry name in front of text, be sure to type a space after the AutoText name, and if you type an entry after text, make sure there is a space before the name. Otherwise, Word will beep to let you know that it can't determine which portion of the text is the AutoText name. Also remember that the AutoText name must be typed exactly the way you typed it when you named it (although the case of the name doesn't matter).

Let's insert the AutoText entries in a document:

1. Open **AutoText**. This letter contains no letterhead or closing.

2. Verify that the insertion point is at the top of the document.

3. Choose **Edit, AutoText** to open the AutoText dialog box.

4. In the Name list box, select **letterhead** (see Figure 9.5).

Figure 9.5   **Inserting an AutoText entry**

5. Click on **Insert** to insert the letterhead AutoText entry in the document. Compare your screen to Figure 9.6.

6. Move the insertion point to the end of the document.

7. Open the AutoText dialog box (choose **Edit, AutoText**).

8. In the Name list box, select **cordially** (if necessary).

9. Click on **Insert** to insert the AutoText entry in the document. Compare your screen to Figure 9.7.

Note: The "extra" paragraph mark (¶) after the closing was produced by inserting the AutoText entry before an existing paragraph mark.

10. Save the disk file as **My AutoText**.

MODIFYING AUTOTEXT ENTRIES

After you have created an AutoText entry, you can go back and edit the text of the entry, in much the same way as you would a normal document.

Figure 9.6   **The inserted *letterhead* AutoText entry**

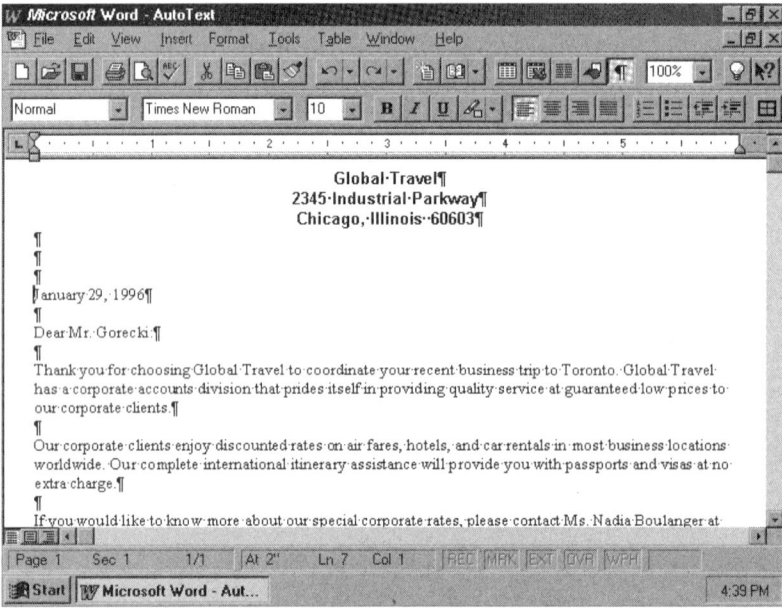

Figure 9.7   **Inserted closing AutoText entry**

EDITING AUTOTEXT ENTRIES

To edit an AutoText entry:

- Insert the AutoText entry that you want to edit into your document.

- Make the desired changes.

- Select the text and/or graphics you want in the AutoText entry.

- Choose *Edit, AutoText*.

- Select the original name of the AutoText entry. (If you wish to keep the original entry intact, type a new name for the entry.)

- Click on *Add*; a message box displays, asking if you want to redefine the AutoText entry. (If you used a new name for the revised entry, no message box will be displayed.)

- Click on *Yes*.

Let's edit one of our AutoText entries:

1. Verify that the insertion point is at the end of the document.

2. Press **Tab**, then type **K. Stockhausen**, and press **Enter** (to add more names to the list).

3. Press **Tab**, then type **A. Berg**, and press **Enter**.

4. Select the entire closing, from *Cordially* through *A. Berg*. Do *not* select the last paragraph mark.

5. Open the AutoText dialog box.

6. In the Name list box, select **cordially**.

7. Click on **Add**. A message box displays, asking if you wish to redefine the AutoText entry (see Figure 9.8).

8. Click on **Yes** to redefine the *cordially* AutoText entry under the same name.

Figure 9.8   **Editing an AutoText entry**

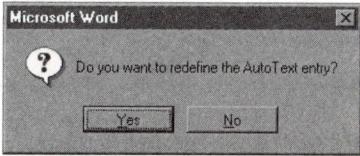

PRACTICE YOUR SKILLS

1. Delete the selected text. Do *not* move the insertion point.

2. Insert the new *cordially* AutoText entry.

 DELETING AUTOTEXT ENTRIES

To remove an AutoText entry:

* Choose *Edit, AutoText*.

* In the Name list box, select the name of the AutoText entry that you want to delete.

* Click on *Delete*.

* Click on *Close*.

Let's edit the AutoText entry, give it a new name, and then delete the old entry:

1. Select **Cordially,** and type **Sincerely,**

2. Select the entire closing, from *Sincerely* through *A. Berg*. Do not select the last paragraph mark.

3. Open the AutoText dialog box.

4. In the Name text box, type sincerely to name the AutoText entry.

5. Click on **Add** to add the AutoText entry to the list.

6. Delete the selected text. Do *not* move the insertion point.

7. Type **sincerely** and press **F3** to insert the AutoText entry using the keyboard. Notice that the AutoText entry replaced the word *sincerely*.

8. Save the disk file.

9. Open the AutoText dialog box.

10. Select **cordially** (if necessary).

11. Click on **Delete** to delete the selected AutoText entry.

12. Click on **Close** to close the AutoText dialog box.

PRACTICE YOUR SKILLS

Delete the *letterhead* AutoText entry.

PRINTING AUTOTEXT ENTRIES

You can print your AutoText entries so that you can see the contents of each entry. To print AutoText entries:

- Choose *File, Print*.

- In the Print What drop-down list box, select *AutoText Entries*.

- Click on *OK*.

All AutoText entries available to the active document are printed in alphabetical order. The formatting appears as it would if it were inserted in a document.

Let's print our AutoText entries:

1. Choose **File, Print**.

2. In the Print What drop-down list box, select **AutoText Entries** to print only AutoText entries (see Figure 9.9). Notice that under Page Range, all options are dimmed.

3. Click on **OK**.

Figure 9.9   **Printing AutoText entries**

4. At least one AutoText entry should have printed.

5. Close the document.

SUMMARY

In this chapter, you learned how to create AutoText entries and insert them in your documents. You also learned how to edit, delete, save, and print your AutoText entries.

Here is a quick reference guide to the Word features introduced in this chapter:

Desired Result	How to Do It
Create AutoText entry	Select desired text and/or graphics to be placed in entry; choose **Edit, AutoText**; name entry in Name text box; click on **Add**
Insert AutoText entry in document using mouse	Place insertion point at desired destination for AutoText entry; choose **Edit, AutoText**; select desired entry; click on **Insert**
Insert AutoText entry using keyboard	Place insertion point at desired destination for AutoText entry; type name of entry; press **F3**
Edit AutoText entry	Insert AutoText entry to be edited in document; make desired changes; select contents of entry; choose **Edit, AutoText**; select original name of entry; click on **Add**; click on **Yes**
Delete AutoText entry	Choose **Edit, AutoText**; select name of entry to be deleted; click on **Delete**; click on **Close**
Save AutoText entry globally	Choose **File, Save All**
Print all AutoText entries	Choose **File, Print**; under Print What, select **AutoText Entries**; click on **OK**

In the next chapter, you will learn how to create, modify, and enhance tables.

CHAPTER 10: WORKING WITH TABLES

Creating Tables

Modifying Tables

Enhancing Tables

Converting Tabbed
Text to a Table

If you want to arrange information in a table, you can do so by setting tabs. However, creating tabbed tables is a slow and tricky process; you must figure out exactly how the table should look, measure the width of each column, and then set tabs that correspond to each measurement. (You've already seen an example of a tabbed table in Chapter 5.) You can also run into problems if your text does not fit between your tabs.

Word's Table feature allows you to create rows and columns of information without having to set tabs. You can even convert tabbed text to a table. A table can be useful for enhancing the presentation of data in your document, for creating side-by-side paragraphs, and for organizing information used in form letters.

When you're done working through this chapter, you will know

- How to create a table

- How to modify a table

- How to enhance a table

- How to convert tabbed text to a table

CREATING TABLES

To insert a table into your document:

- Place the insertion point where you want to insert the table.

- Choose *Table, Insert Table*, or click on the *Insert Table* button in the Standard toolbar.

When you create tables by using the menu command, you specify the number of columns and rows in the Insert Table dialog box. You can also specify the width of the columns. When you use the Insert Table button to create tables, you drag on the Insert Table button grid to specify the number of columns and rows. This is analogous to the technique you used to print-preview multiple pages in Chapter 6. (You'll use the Insert Table button grid later in this section.)

Word creates a table that fills the area inside the margins. The width of the columns adjusts automatically according to the amount of space available between the left and right margins.

A table consists of vertical *columns* and horizontal *rows* (see Figure 10.1). The intersection of a column and a row is called a *cell*. Dotted lines called *gridlines* are displayed between the cells. You can hide the gridlines by choosing Table, Gridlines. Dotted lines called *column boundaries* are displayed between the columns. The gridlines and column boundaries are for visual reference only; they do not appear when you print the document.

If you display nonprinting characters, *end-of-cell* marks appear in each cell and *end-of-row* marks appear at the end of each row. You can use these marks to select and edit the table. Squares are displayed in the ruler above the column boundaries; these are called *column markers*. You can use these column markers to adjust the width of the columns by dragging them left or right. When you place the insertion point in a column, indent markers for that column are displayed in the ruler, enabling you to indent selected text as you desire.

Figure 10.1   **Table components**

Note: When you Print Preview the table, the gridlines, end-of-cell marks, and end-of-row marks are not displayed.

Let's create and examine a table:

1. Open **Tables**.

2. Go to page 2 and scroll to place the paragraph that begins *Global Travel guarantees* near the top of the document window. Place the insertion point in the blank line directly above the paragraph that begins *Our quality control.*

3. Choose **Table, Insert Table** to open the Insert Table dialog box, shown in Figure 10.2.

Figure 10.2   **The Insert Table dialog box**

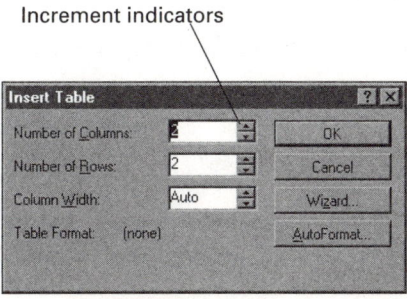

4. Observe the *Number of Columns* text box. You can change the number of columns by typing a number in the text box or by clicking on the increment indicators (see Figure 10.2).

5. Observe the *Number of Rows* text box. You can change the number of rows by typing a number in the text box or by clicking on the increment indicators.

6. Click on **Cancel**.

7. Click on the **Insert Table** button in the Standard toolbar to display the Insert Table button grid.

8. Point to the upper-left corner of the Insert Table button grid.

9. Press and hold the mouse button and drag down to select four rows of the grid. Then drag to the right to select two columns of the grid. The bottom of the grid displays *4 x 2 Table* (see Figure 10.3).

10. Release the mouse button to display the table at the insertion point. Observe the following features (see Figure 10.1):

    • The *columns* are displayed vertically on the page.

    • The *rows* are displayed horizontally on the page.

    • The *cells* are the intersections of columns and rows.

    • The *gridlines* are the dotted lines between the cells.

    • The *column boundaries* are the vertical dotted lines between the columns.

    • The *end-of-cell marks* are the small circles inside the cells.

    • The *end-of-row marks* appear at the end of each row.

    • The *column markers* in the ruler (not shown in Figure 10.1) are the square buttons placed above the column boundaries.

Figure 10.3   Specifying table size in the Insert Table button grid

MOVING IN A TABLE

You can use the mouse to move to a table cell, or you can use the keyboard. To move to a specific cell using the mouse, simply place the I-beam on (or to the right of) the end-of-cell mark in the desired cell, and click. Table 10.1 lists the keystrokes used for moving within a table.

If the insertion point is in the last cell of a row when you press Tab, the insertion point will move to the first cell in the next row (although if you press Tab while the insertion point is in the last cell of the last row, Word will add a new row to your table). Likewise, if the insertion point is in the first cell of a row when you press Shift+Tab, it will move to the last cell in the previous row.

Table 10.1   **Moving in a Table Using the Keyboard**

Desired Result	How to Do It
Move one cell to right	Press *Tab*.
Move one cell to left	Press *Shift+Tab*.
Move up one row	Press *Up Arrow*.
Move down one row	Press *Down Arrow*.

Note: If you use the arrow keys on the numeric keypad, Num Lock must be turned off.

Let's practice moving in the table we've created:

1. Press **Tab** to move the insertion point to the second column of the first row.

2. Press **Tab** to move the insertion point to the first column in the second row.

3. Press **Shift+Tab** to move back to the second column of the first row.

4. Press **Down Arrow** to move down one row.

5. Press **Up Arrow** to move up one row.

6. Place the I-beam in the last cell of the table on (or to the right of) the end-of-cell mark, and click the mouse button to place the insertion point in the last cell.

PRACTICE YOUR SKILLS

Place the insertion point in the first cell of the table.

SELECTING TABLE COMPONENTS

You can select a cell, a row, a column, or the entire table. Table 10.2 lists the methods used for making these selections.

Table 10.2   **Selecting in a Table**

Desired Selection	How to Do It
Cell	Click in cell's selection bar (area to left of text, if any, and end-of-cell mark)
Row	Place insertion point anywhere within desired row; choose *Table, Select Row*; click in selection bar to left of row; or double-click in selection bar of any cell within row
Column	Place I-beam on top border of desired column until it becomes downward-pointing arrow; click mouse button; or place insertion point anywhere in column and choose *Table, Select Column*
Entire table	Place the insertion point anywhere within the table and choose *Table, Select Table*

Let's try various selection techniques within our table:

1. Point to the left of the end-of-cell mark in the first cell until the mouse pointer becomes an arrow. (Make sure that the mouse pointer is still located within the cell.)

2. Click to select the cell. Compare your screen to Figure 10.4.

3. In the selection bar, point to the left of the first row.

4. Click the mouse button to select the entire row (see Figure 10.5).

5. Point to the top border of the second column, until the mouse pointer becomes a downward-pointing arrow. Then click to select the entire column (see Figure 10.6).

6. Choose **Table, Select Table** to select the entire table. Compare your screen to Figure 10.7.

Figure 10.4   **The selected cell**

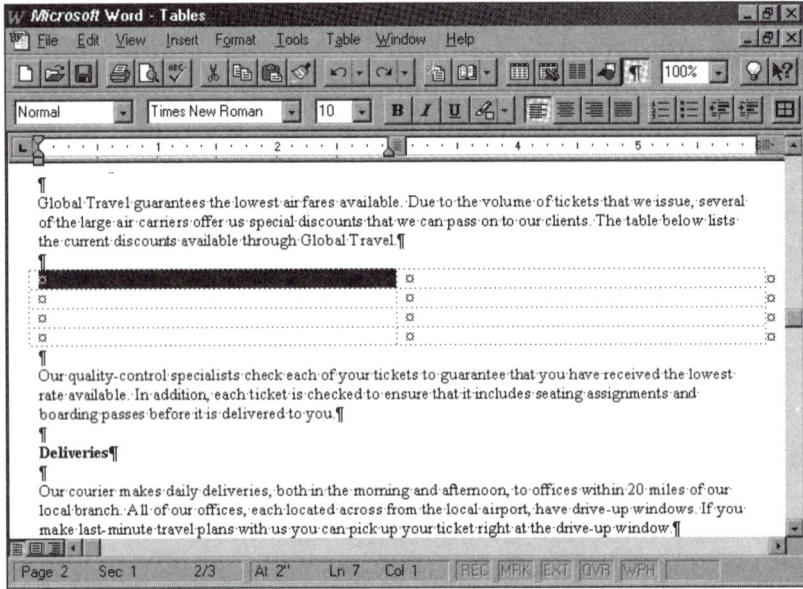

Figure 10.5   **The selected row**

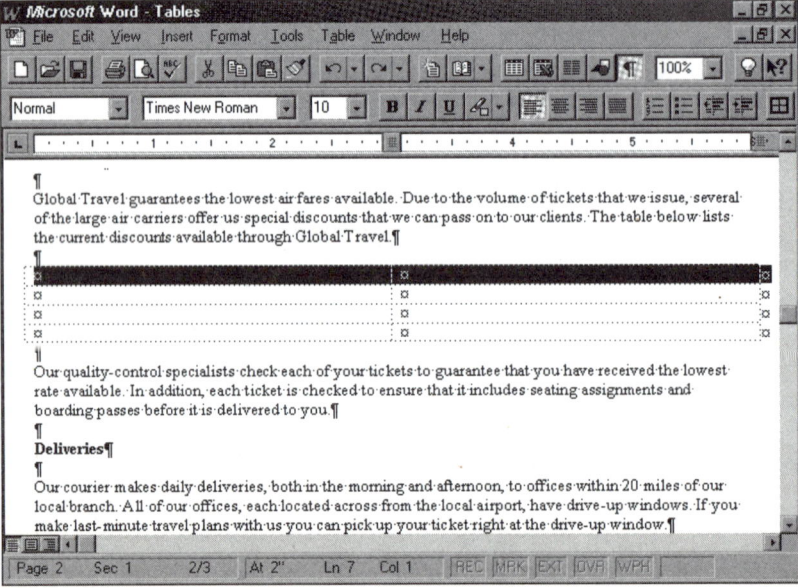

Figure 10.6 **The selected column**

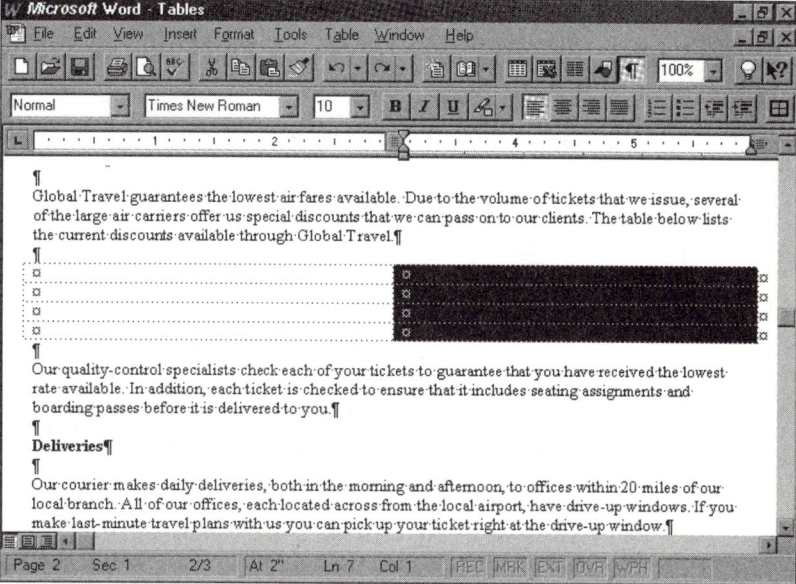

Figure 10.7 **The selected table**

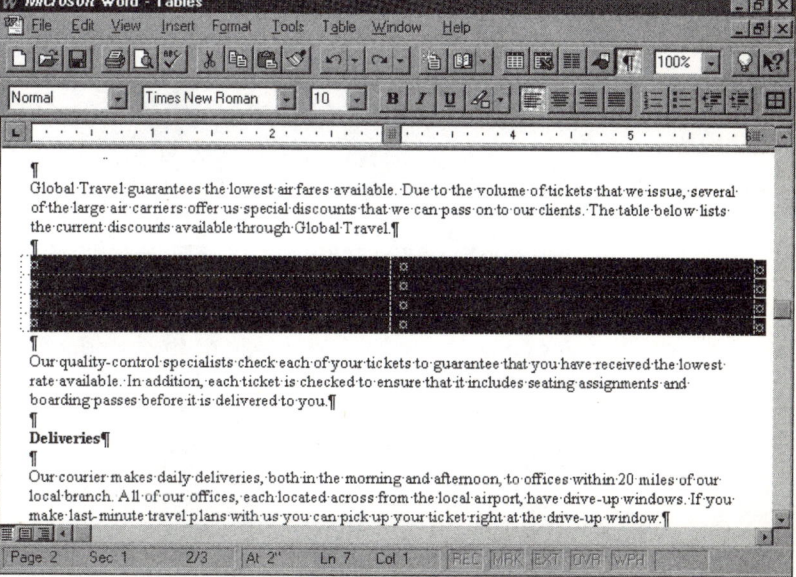

7. Deselect the table (click above or below the table) and choose **Table**. Notice that when the insertion point is not in the table, only four Table menu commands are available. Close the Table menu.

ENTERING TEXT IN A TABLE

To enter text in a table, either select a cell or place the insertion point in the cell; then begin typing.

Let's enter text in our table:

1. Place the I-beam on the end-of-cell mark in the first cell and click.

2. Type **Destination**.

3. Press **Tab** to move to the next cell.

4. Type **Your Price** and press **Tab**.

PRACTICE YOUR SKILLS

1. Complete the table as shown in Figure 10.8.

2. Print Preview the table. (Don't expect much; the table is currently fairly nondescript. We'll spice up its appearance as the chapter progresses.)

3. Save the disk file as **MyTables**.

MODIFYING TABLES

After you have created your table—even after you have entered all the desired data—you can still change its structure. You can insert rows and columns within the table, add rows to the bottom or columns to the right side of the table, change the width of the columns, and delete rows and columns.

Figure 10.8   **The completed table**

INSERTING ROWS AND COLUMNS

To insert a row at the end of a table, place the insertion point in the last cell of the table and press the Tab key. To insert a row *within* a table, select the row where you want to insert the new row (the new row will be inserted above the selected row) and choose *Table, Insert Rows*, or click on the *Insert Rows* button (the erstwhile *Insert Table* button). To insert more than one row in a table, select as many rows as you want to insert (the new rows will be inserted above the selected rows) and choose *Table, Insert Rows*, or click on the *Insert Rows* button. The number of rows that you select is the number of rows that will be inserted.

To insert a column at the end of a table, select all of the end-of-row marks (by placing the I-beam directly above the marks until it becomes a downward-pointing arrow and clicking once); then choose *Table, Insert Columns* or click on the *Insert Columns* button (you guessed it—the same button as Insert Table and Insert Rows). To insert a column within a table, select the column where you want to insert a new column (the new column will be inserted to the left of the selected column) and choose *Table, Insert Columns* or click on the *Insert Columns* button. To insert more than one column within a table, select as many columns as you want to insert (the new columns will be inserted to the left of the selected columns) and choose *Table, Insert Columns* or click on the *Insert Columns* button. The number of columns that you select is the number of columns that will be inserted.

Let's insert rows and columns in our table:

1. Verify that the insertion point is in the last cell of the table.

2. Press the **Tab** key. Voilà! A new row is inserted at the end of the table.

3. Type **Hong Kong** and press **Tab**.

4. Type **2,100.00**.

5. In the selection bar, point to the left of the second row. Press and hold the mouse button, and drag to select the second and third rows (to tell Word to insert two rows); then release the mouse button.

6. Place the mouse pointer (but do *not* click) on the Insert Table button. Notice that its name has changed to *Insert Rows*. Let's use the menu to insert our rows.

7. Choose **Table, Insert Rows** to insert two rows above the selected rows. Compare your screen to Figure 10.9.

8. Select the entire second column (click on the top border of the second column).

9. Open the Table menu. Notice (but do *not* choose) the first menu option: *Insert Columns*. This time, let's use the Standard toolbar. Click on **Table** to close the menu.

10. Place the mouse pointer on what was the Insert Rows button in step 6. The name *Insert Columns* is displayed.

11. Click on the **Insert Columns** button, and then compare your screen to Figure 10.10.

12. Scroll right to view the end-of-row marks.

13. Place the I-beam directly above the end-of-row mark at the end of the first row, and click once to select all the end-of-row marks.

Figure 10.9   **The inserted rows**

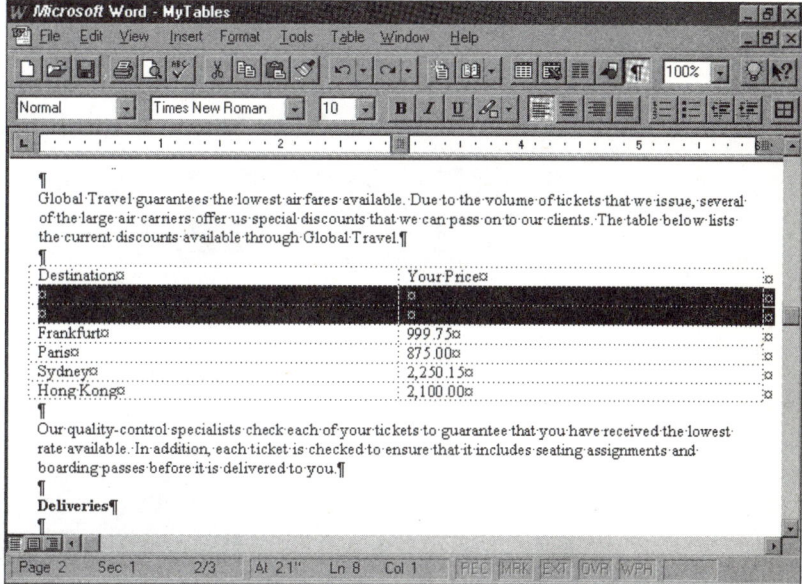

Figure 10.10   **The inserted column**

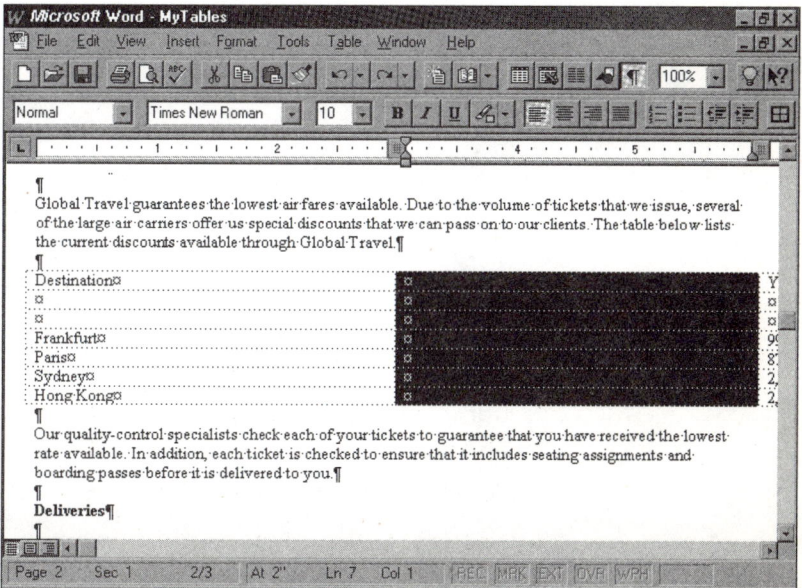

14. Click on the **Insert Columns** button to insert a column at the end of the table.

15. Scroll right to view the entire inserted column, and compare your screen to Figure 10.11.

Figure 10.11 **The column added to the end of the table**

PRACTICE YOUR SKILLS

1. In the first row of the second column, enter the heading **Standard Price**.

2. Complete the second column as shown in Figure 10.12.

3. In the first row of the fourth column, enter the heading **Savings**.

4. Complete the fourth column as shown in Figure 10.13.

5. Save the disk file.

Figure 10.12 **The data entered in the second column**

DELETING ROWS, COLUMNS, AND ENTIRE TABLES

To delete one or more contiguous rows in a table, select the row or rows that you want to delete; then choose *Table, Delete Rows*.

To delete one or more contiguous columns, select the column or columns that you want to delete; then choose *Table, Delete Columns*.

To delete an entire table, select the table; then choose *Table, Delete Rows*.

Let's delete a row in our table:

1. Select the second row (click in the selection bar, to the left of the second row).

2. Choose **Table, Delete Rows** to delete the selected row (see Figure 10.14).

Figure 10.13   **The data entered in the fourth column**

CHANGING COLUMN WIDTH

To change column width by dragging column boundaries:

- Point to the column boundary that you want to move; the mouse pointer will become a horizontal, double-headed arrow.

- Press and hold the mouse button.

- Drag the column boundary to the desired location.

- Release the mouse button.

To change column width by using the ruler:

- On the ruler, point to the column marker that you want to move; the mouse pointer will become a horizontal, double-headed arrow.

- Press and hold the mouse button.

- Drag the column marker to the desired location.

Figure 10.14   **The table after deleting a row**

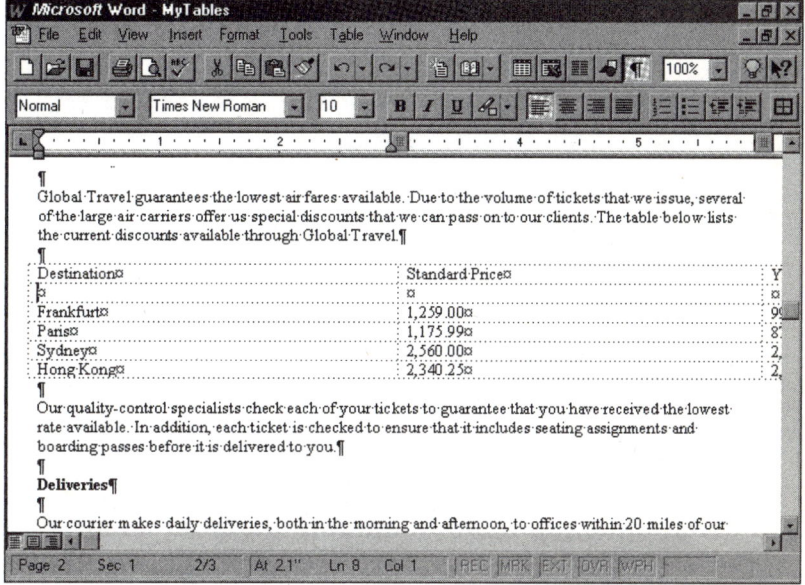

- Release the mouse button.

To change column width by using the menu:

- Select the desired column (or the entire table).

- Choose *Table, Cell Height and Width*.

- Click on the *Column* tab.

- Type the desired width in the Width of Column text box.

- Click on *OK*.

When you change the column width using the first two of these techniques (dragging column boundaries and column markers), all columns to the right are proportionally resized, and the width of the entire table does not change. If you change column width using the third technique (the Cell Height and Width menu command), the width of the table changes to accommodate the adjusted width of its columns. If you decrease the width of the columns, the width of the entire table decreases. If you increase the width of the columns, the width of the entire table increases.

Note: Before you print a document that contains a table, use Print Preview to make sure that the entire table fits on the page.

To automatically adjust column width so that the table fits on the page:

- Choose *Table, Cell Height and Width.*

- Click on the *Column* tab.

- Click on *AutoFit.*

Let's try using all three manual methods to change the width of columns in our table:

1. Point to the column boundary between the *Destination* and *Standard Price* headings. The mouse becomes a double-headed arrow.

2. Press and hold the mouse button, and drag the column border to the left until it is just to the right of the end-of-cell mark in the *Hong Kong* cell. This decreases the width of the first column. Release the mouse button. The second column is now considerably wider.

3. In the ruler, point to the column marker near the 5" mark. Drag the column marker to decrease the width of the second column to approximately 1.75" on the ruler.

4. Select the entire table (choose **Table, Select Table**).

5. Choose **Table, Cell Height and Width** to open the Cell Height and Width dialog box, and click on the **Column** tab (if necessary).

6. In the Width of Columns 1-4 text box, click to place the insertion point, and type **1.25** to set the width of all columns in the table to 1.25" (see Figure 10.15).

7. Click on **OK** to close the dialog box, and deselect the table. Notice that all four columns are now equal in width. Compare your screen to Figure 10.16.

Figure 10.15   **Setting column width**

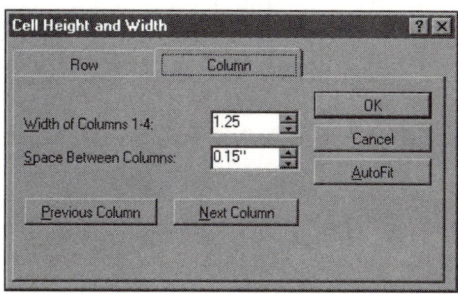

Figure 10.16   **The table with columns of equal width**

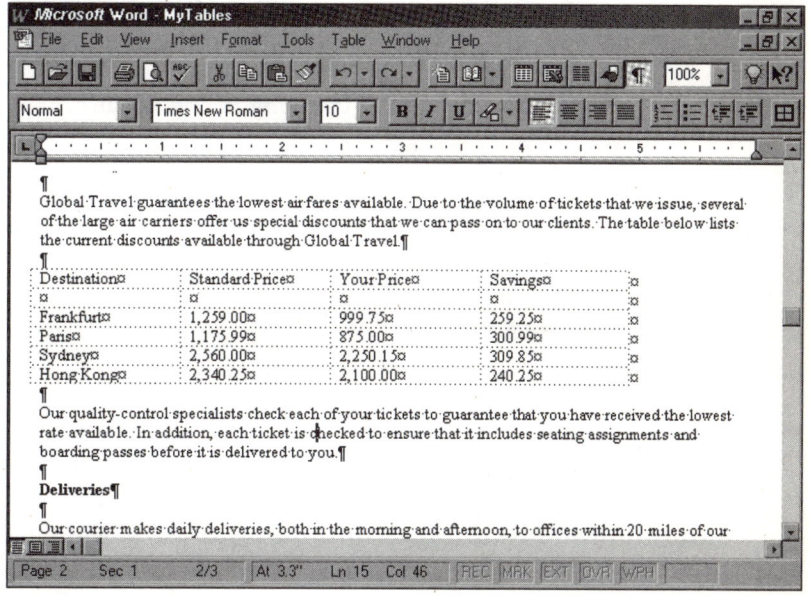

ENHANCING TABLES

You already know how to enhance text in your document; doing so can improve its appearance and often its readability. Accentuating important text helps the eye to locate these reference points. The same text enhancements that are available in standard document text are also available when working in tables, including, for example, bold and italic font styles, changes in font and font size, and text alignment within a cell. In addition, you can alter the alignment of the entire table relative to the margins you're using. You can apply any font formats to text within a table. You can also enhance a table by adding a border or gridlines that will appear when the document is printed.

 ## ALIGNING A TABLE

To align a table between the left and right margins:

- Select the entire table.
- Choose *Table, Cell Height and Width*.
- Click on the *Row* tab, if necessary.
- Under Alignment, select the desired alignment.
- Click on *OK*.

Let's format and align text in our table, and then center the table between the left and right margins:

1. Select the first row, which contains the column headings.

2. Make all of the text in the first row bold.

3. Select the entire second column without releasing the mouse button, and then drag (within the table) to select the third and fourth columns. The second through fourth columns are now selected. Release the mouse button.

4. Right-align the text in the selected columns.

5. Click on the **Show/Hide** button to hide the end-of-cell marks. Now you can view the table without all the extraneous marks.

6. Click on the **Show/Hide** button to display the end-of-cell marks.

7. Print Preview page 2. The table is currently aligned along the left margin.

8. Close Print Preview.

9. Select the entire table. Then choose **Table, Cell Height and Width** to open the Cell Height and Width dialog box. Click on the **Row** tab, if necessary.

10. Under Alignment, click on **Center** to center the table between the left and right margins (see Figure 10.17).

Figure 10.17   **Centering the table**

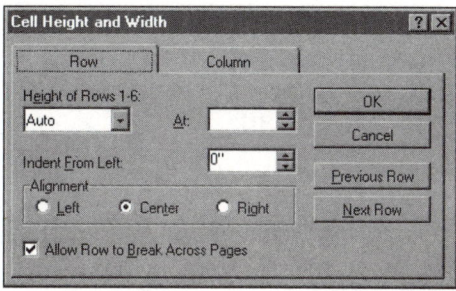

11. Click on **OK**. Then deselect the table.

12. Print Preview the document. The table is centered between the left and right margins.

13. Close Print Preview.

14. Save the disk file.

ADDING BORDERS

To add a border to a table:

- Select the table, column, row, or cell around which you want to add a border.

- Choose *Format, Borders and Shading* and click on the *Borders* tab.

- Under Presets, click on the desired border type.

- Under Line, select a line style from the Style list box.

- Click on *OK*.

Before closing the dialog box, you can observe the sample diagram in the Border portion of the dialog box to see the effect of the border and line type that you selected.

Let's add borders to our table:

1. Select the entire table.

2. Choose **Format, Borders and Shading** to open the Table Borders and Shading dialog box, and click on the **Borders** tab (if necessary).

3. Under Presets (in the top-left corner of the dialog box), click on **Box** to specify a box-type border for the table.

4. Under Line, in the Style list box, select the **3/4 pt** thin double lines (approximately halfway down the list). Compare your screen to Figure 10.18.

Figure 10.18   Selecting a table border

5. Observe the Border box. The double line is displayed around the sample diagram.

6. Click on **OK**. Deselect the table. Notice that the selected border is now displayed around the table.

7. Select the entire table. (Remember to click inside the table first.)

8. Choose **Format, Borders and Shading** to open the Table Borders and Shading dialog box.

9. Under Presets, click on the **Grid** option to place a grid around the cells. Unlike the dotted gridlines that currently appear in our document, this grid will display when the document is printed. (Selecting the Grid option will also place a border around the table if it doesn't already have one.)

10. Click on **OK**. Deselect the table. Notice the change in the table. The dotted gridlines are replaced with solid ones (see Figure 10.19).

Figure 10.19   The completed table with border and gridlines

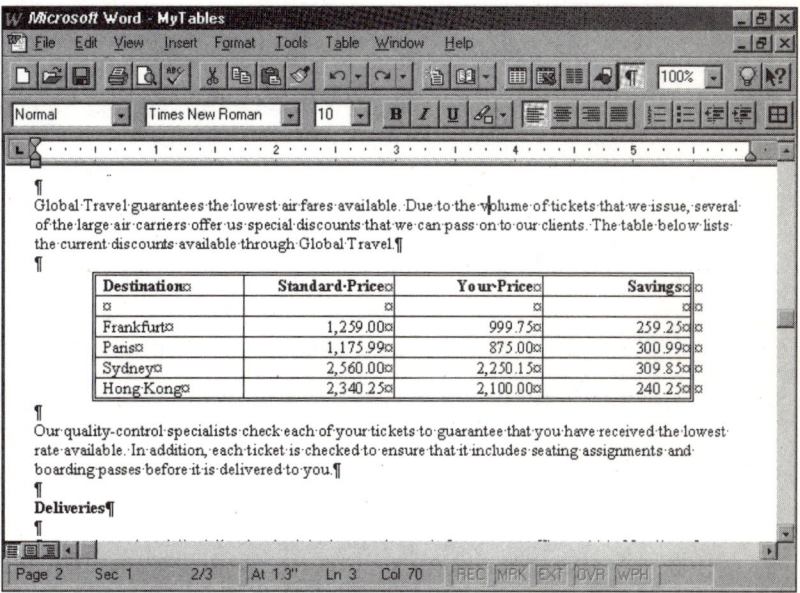

CONVERTING TABBED TEXT TO A TABLE

Word enables you to convert a tabbed table created by inserting tabs between columns of text into an actual table consisting of cells, rows, and columns. To convert tabbed text to a table:

• Select the text that you want to convert to a table.

- Choose *Table, Convert Text to Table*.

- In the Number of Columns text box, enter the desired number of columns.

- Click on *OK*.

Note: In addition to converting text separated by tabs, you can convert text that is separated by paragraph marks, commas, or other characters. To indicate the type of character you want to use to separate the text, select the character under *Separate Text At* in the *Convert Text to Table* dialog box.

You can also convert table text into ordinary text.

Let's convert tabbed text to a table:

1. Scroll to place the *Hotel Accommodations* heading, near the bottom of page 2, at the top of the screen.

2. Observe the tabbed text at the bottom of page 2.

3. Select all of the lines in the tabbed table, from *Location* to *Hong Kong*, that will be placed in the table. Notice that our tabbed table consists of three columns of information in six rows. We'll retain this structure.

4. Choose **Table, Convert Text to Table**. The Convert Text to Table dialog box is displayed. Word knows how many rows we want in our table (determined by the paragraph marks), but we need to supply the number of columns.

5. In the Number of Columns text box, type **3** to specify three columns.

6. Under Separate Text At, click on **Tabs** to tell Word that tab marks currently indicate column boundaries. Compare your screen to Figure 10.20.

Figure 10.20   Converting tabbed text to a table

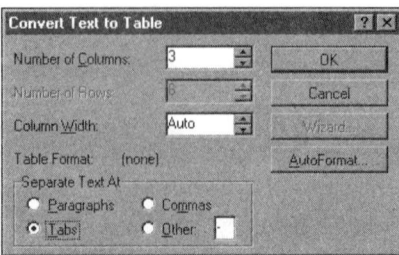

7. Click on **OK**. The selected text appears in a table. Notice that the column widths need some adjustment.

8. Verify that the entire table is selected. Then choose **Table, Cell Height and Width** to open the Cell Height and Width dialog box, and display the Column tab.

9. In the Width of Columns 1-3 text box, type **1.5** to set the width of all of the columns to 1.5", and click on **OK**. The table now consists of three equally spaced columns.

PRACTICE YOUR SKILLS

1. Place a grid border around the table and between all the cells. (**Hint**: Use the **Grid** option under Presets in the Table Borders and Shading dialog box.) Accept the default line style.

2. Center all the information in column 2.

3. Right-align all the information in column 3.

4. Center the table between the left and right margins.

5. Deselect the table.

6. Save the disk file and compare your screen to Figure 10.21.

7. Close the document.

PRACTICE YOUR SKILLS

This exercise gives you the opportunity to practice the skills you just learned. The following instructions lead you through the steps necessary to edit the disk file Practice 10A to produce the document in Figure 10.22.

Follow these steps at your computer:

1. Open **Practice 10A** (Chapter 2).

2. Type the following information into the table titled *Projected Quarterly Sales Table:*

Row 3:	**Trader Tom's**	2300	1.49
Row 4:	**Aunt Emily's Market**	4900	1.29
Row 5:	**Hamlet Farms**	6500	1.29

Figure 10.21   The converted table

Figure 10.22   The completed My Practice 10A document

3. Delete the row that contains information for *Price Farms*.

4. Right-align the second and third columns.

5. Change the column width for the *Boxes Sold* column to **1"**.

6. Change the column width for *Profit (per box)* to **1.25"**.

7. Center the table on the page.

8. Save the disk file as **My Practice 10A** (Chapter 2).

9. Print preview the document and compare it to Figure 10.22 (Chapter 2).

10. Close the document (Chapter 2).

If you have finished the activity, you might like to try a more challenging one requiring similar skills. In the next activity you will edit Practice 10B to create the document shown in Figure 10.23.

Figure 10.23   The completed My Practice 10B document

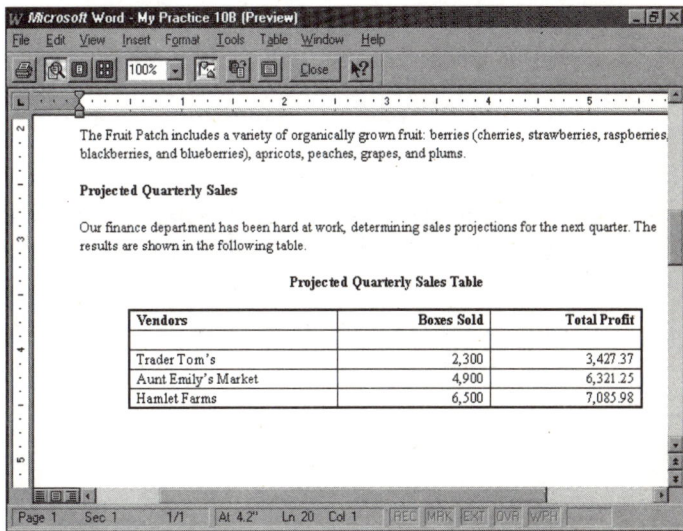

Follow these steps at your computer:

1. Open **Practice 10B** (Chapter 2).

2. Below the *Projected Quarterly Sales Table* heading, create a table that contains three columns and five rows.

3. Enter the data as shown in Figure 10.23.

4. Make the column headings in the first row bold.

5. Right-align the second and third columns.

6. Decrease the column width for the second and third columns to **1.5"**.

7. Center the table on the page.

8. Place a grid border on the table.

9. Save the disk file as **My Practice 10B** (Chapter 2).

10. Print preview the document and compare it to Figure 10.23 (Chapter 2).

11. Close the document (Chapter 2).

SUMMARY

In this chapter, you learned how to create tables using the Insert Table button in the Standard toolbar, or the Table, Insert Table command from the menu. You learned how to move within a table; how to select cells, rows, columns, and the entire table; and how to enter data in a table. You also learned how to insert and delete rows and columns, how to change column width, how to change the alignment of a table between the left and right margins, and how to enhance the appearance of a table by creating various types of borders. Finally, you learned how to convert tabbed text to a table.

Here is a quick reference guide to the Word features introduced in this chapter:

Desired Result	How to Do It
Create table using menu	Choose **Table, Insert Table**; type desired number of columns in Number of Columns text box; type number of rows in Number of Rows text box; click on **OK**

Desired Result	How to Do It
Create table using Standard toolbar	Click on **Insert Table** button; drag to select boxes of grid corresponding to desired number of rows and columns; release mouse button
Move within table using mouse	Place I-beam on (or to right of) end-of-cell mark of desired cell; click
Move within table using keyboard	(See Table 10.1)
Select portion of or entire table	(See Table 10.2)
Add row at end of table	Place insertion point in last cell of table; press **Tab**
Insert row within table	Select row above which you want to insert new row; choose **Table, Insert Rows**, or click on **Insert Rows** button
Insert multiple rows in table	Select as many rows as you want to insert; choose **Table, Insert Rows**, or click on **Insert Rows** button
Add column to right side of table	Select all end-of-row marks; choose **Table, Insert Columns** or click on **Insert Columns** button
Insert column within table	Select column to left of where you want to insert new column; choose **Table, Insert Columns** or click on **Insert Columns** button
Insert multiple columns within table	Select as many columns as you want to insert; choose **Table, Insert Columns** or click on **Insert Columns** button

Desired Result	How to Do It
Delete one or more rows	Select row(s) you want to delete; choose **Table, Delete Rows**
Delete one or more columns	Select the column(s) you want to delete; choose **Table, Delete Columns**
Delete entire table	Select table; choose **Table, Delete Rows**
Change column width by dragging column boundaries	Point to column boundary that you want to move until mouse pointer becomes horizontal, double-headed arrow; drag column boundary to desired location; release mouse button
Change column width by using ruler	On ruler, drag column marker that you want to move to desired location; release mouse button
Change column width by using menu	Select desired column (or entire table); choose **Table, Cell Height and Width**; click on **Column** tab (if necessary); type desired width in Width of Column text box; click on **OK**
Align table between left and right margins	Select entire table; choose **Table, Cell Height and Width**; click on **Row** tab (if necessary); under Alignment, select desired alignment; click on **OK**
Create table border	Select table, column, row, or cell around which you want to add border; choose **Format, Borders and Shading**; click on **Borders** tab (if necessary); under Presets, select border type; under Line, select line style in Style list box; click on **OK**

Desired Result	How to Do It
Convert tabbed text to table	Select tabbed text that you want to convert to table; choose **Table, Convert Text to Table;** enter desired number of columns; under Separate Text At, select desired separation character (if necessary); click on **OK**

In the next chapter, you will learn how to create newspaper-style columns and add graphics to your documents.

CHAPTER 11: NEWSPAPER-STYLE COLUMNS AND GRAPHICS

Creating Multicolumn Text

Modifying Multicolumn Text Formats

Using Graphics

This chapter introduces ways to format text into *newspaper-style columns* (two or more columns running side-by-side down the page). Newspaper-style columns are useful in creating documents such as newsletters, brochures, and reports. In newspaper columns, the document text "snakes," or flows, down the length of one column, then continues at the top of the next column, and so on. If all of the columns on the page become filled, any additional text continues onto the first column of the next page.

Word also provides you with powerful tools for incorporating graphic images, or *graphics,* into your documents.

When you're done working through this chapter, you will know

- How to format text into newspaper-style columns

- How to insert a graphic into your document

- How to size and move a graphic

- How to create a border around a graphic

CREATING MULTICOLUMN TEXT

You can define your columns before typing the text, or you can reformat existing text into newspaper-style columns.

To create newspaper-style columns using the Format, Columns command:

- Place the insertion point where you want the columns to begin.

- Choose *Format, Columns* to open the Columns dialog box.

- Specify the desired number of columns in the *Number of Columns* text box, or click on one of the predefined column formats under Presets.

- In the *Apply To* drop-down list box, select *This Point Forward*, *Whole Document*, or *This Section* (as explained shortly).

- Click on *OK*.

Note: There is a limit to the number of columns you can specify, based on your document's margins and the default tab stops. Each column must be at least as wide as the distance between the default tab stops (0.5").

When you select *This Point Forward* in the Apply To drop-down list box, Word applies your specified multicolumn format from the insertion point to the end of the document. Word then inserts a *section break* directly before the insertion point; the section break is displayed as a double dotted-line marked *End of Section*. Compare this to a page break, which is displayed as a single dotted-line marked *Page Break*. Dividing a document into sections—each of which consists of one or more pages—allows you to apply different page-formatting options to each section. The status bar displays the section number in which the insertion point is placed.

When you select *Whole Document* in the Apply To drop-down list box, Word sets your specified multicolumn format for the entire document, regardless of where the insertion point is placed.

When you select *This Section* in the Apply To drop-down list box, Word sets your specified multicolumn format for the entire section in which the insertion point is placed. (This option will only be available if your document already contains section breaks.)

To create newspaper-style columns using the Columns button:

- Place the insertion point anywhere in the section of the document where you want to create your newspaper-style columns.

- Click on the *Columns* button in the Standard toolbar to open a miniature four-column window.

- Click on the first (leftmost) miniature column to specify a single-column format; click on the second column to specify two columns; click on the third column to specify three columns; or click on the fourth (rightmost) column to specify four columns.

Note: When you use the Columns button to create newspaper-style columns, Word automatically applies your specified number of columns (1, 2, 3, or 4) to the entire section in which the insertion point is placed.

Columns will not appear in the document window in Normal view. To display the text in columns, you must either Print Preview the document or change to Page Layout view.

Let's open a new document and create a newspaper-style column format:

1. Open **Columns and Graphics**.

2. Preview the document (click on the **Print Preview** button). Notice that all of the text is currently in a standard, single-column format.

3. Close Print Preview (click on the **Close** button) to return to Normal view.

4. Place the insertion point to the left of the *I* in the *Introduction* heading, near the top of the page.

5. Choose **Format, Columns** to open the Columns dialog box.

6. In the Presets box, click on **2**. The Preview box displays a sample of the two-column format.

7. Open the **Apply To** drop-down list box. Select **This Point Forward** to format the text as two columns from the insertion point to the end of the document. Again, observe the Preview box, as shown in Figure 11.1.

Figure 11.1   **Changing to two-column format**

8. Click on **OK**.

9. Observe the section break, the double dotted-line marked *End of Section* above the *Introduction* heading. All of the text from the section break to the end of the document is formatted as two columns. Note that *Sec 2* appears in the status bar, because the insertion point is in the second (newly formatted) section. Note also that the side-by-side columns are not visible in Normal view.

10. Switch to Page Layout view (choose **View Page Layout**). The side-by-side columns are now visible.

11. Scroll to view the document.

MODIFYING MULTICOLUMN TEXT FORMATS

When you create multiple (newspaper-style) columns, Word automatically apportions even amounts of space within each column and between columns, based on your document's margins. However, you can modify these values. For example, by default, Word places one-half inch of space between each column. Depending on the effect you desire, as well as how many columns appear on the page, you might want to increase or reduce this amount.

To change the space between columns:

- Place the insertion point in the section containing the columns.
- Choose *Format, Columns* to open the Columns dialog box.
- In the *Spacing* box, specify the desired width between columns.
- Click on *OK.*

You can also insert a vertical dividing line between adjacent columns, which can produce a visually pleasing effect and help the eye separate the columns. This is particularly true of columns that are by necessity spaced closely together.

To add a vertical line between columns:

- Place the insertion point in the section containing the columns.
- Choose *Format, Columns* to open the Columns dialog box.
- Check the *Line Between* option.
- Click on *OK.*

Let's change the space between our columns, and then add a vertical line to highlight their readability:

1. Check the status bar to verify that the insertion point is in the second section of the document.

2. Observe the space between the columns. It is large enough to be reduced slightly to make more room within the columns for text. Notice also that one or more lines of text (or blank lines) have wrapped up to the second column, above the *Worldwide Services* heading. (This may or may not be true, depending on what printer you are using.)

3. Choose **Format, Columns** to open the Columns dialog box.

4. Under Width and Spacing, click twice on the Spacing **down increment indicator** to decrease the amount of space between the columns of text to 0.3" or as close to this value as your configuration will allow.

5. Click on **OK**. The text columns now appear closer together. Notice that the text that earlier wrapped to the second

column (if any) has now moved to the bottom of the first column, placing the *Worldwide Services* heading near the top of the second column. (Again, this may or may not be true, depending on your printer.)

6. Delete the paragraph mark between the *End of Section* line and the *Worldwide Services* heading to move the heading to the top of the column.

7. Verify that the insertion point is still in the second section.

8. Choose **Format, Columns**.

9. Check the **Line Between** option. Compare your screen to Figure 11.2.

10. Click on **OK**.

11. Print Preview the document to see how it will look printed (see Figure 11.3).

12. Close Print Preview.

13. Save the document as **My Columns and Graphics**.

Figure 11.2   **Inserting a vertical line between columns**

USING GRAPHICS

You can place graphics in any Word document, as well as in headers and footers. Graphics can be imported into a document from

Figure 11.3   **Print Previewing the column modifications**

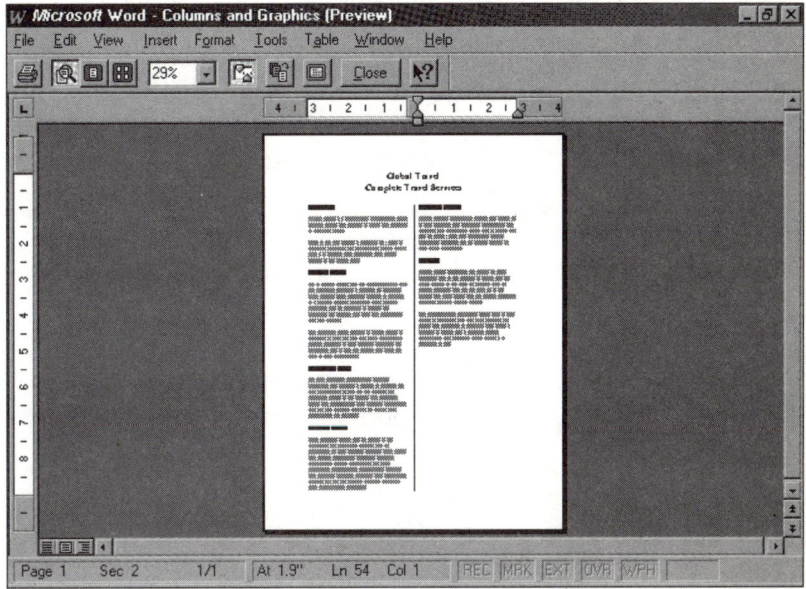

many draw or paint software programs or from *clip art* (sources of digitized images). Word also comes with a number of graphics files, which you can use in your documents and even edit.

To insert a graphic in your document:

*   Switch to Page Layout view. This view is most effective for working with graphics.

*   Place the insertion point where you want to insert the graphic.

*   Choose *Insert, Picture* to open the Insert Picture dialog box.

*   Select the drive and directory where the graphic is stored.

*   Select the file name of the desired graphic.

*   If you want to preview your selected graphic, check the Preview Picture option and observe the Preview box.

*   Click on *OK.*

Let's insert a graphic in our document:

1. Verify that you are still in Page Layout view.

2. If necessary, place the insertion point to the left of the *W* in the *Worldwide Services* heading at the top of the second column. Doing so will place the graphic above the heading.

3. Choose **Insert, Picture** to open the Insert Picture dialog box.

4. If you did not install Office 95, display the contents of the Clipart subdirectory of the Winword directory. If you installed Office 95, display the Clipart subdirectory of the Office 95 directory.

5. In the Insert Picture dialog box, click on the **Preview** button (if necessary). This button enables you to display a file's contents without first having to open it.

6. Select different file names and observe the previewed image of each, until you arrive at one that you think might be relevant to our newsletter. If you have installed Office 95, select the Legal file in the Clipart subdirectory. The previewed image of the Legal file is shown in Figure 11.4.

7. When you have arrived at an appropriate image (if different than the one shown in Figure 11.4), click on **OK** to place the graphic in your document. Observe the results. The graphic is inserted to the left of the *Worldwide Services* heading.

8. Press **Enter** three times to move *Worldwide Services* a bit further below the image.

INSERTING A FRAME AROUND A GRAPHIC

If you insert a graphic in a document and the graphic is not wide enough to fill the column of text, the text will "flow" around the graphic. However, it will flow around the graphic unevenly, following the graphic's shape. You can make the text flow evenly around the graphic by placing a frame around it.

To place a frame around a graphic, you must first select the graphic by clicking on it with the mouse. When the graphic is selected, you

Figure 11.4   **Previewing a graphic**

will notice small black *selection handles* on each side and in each corner of the graphic. Once the graphic is selected, you choose the Insert, Frame command.

Let's insert a frame around our graphic:

1. Point to the middle of the graphic and click the mouse button to select it.

2. Observe the selection handles around the graphic.

3. Choose **Insert, Frame** to insert a frame around the graphic. Observe the results. The frame enables you to move and size the graphic; however, it will not print. Compare your screen to Figure 11.5. Notice that the Worldwide Services heading and some of the text below it has filled in the space to the right of, or "wrapped around," the graphic. The anchor symbol to the right of the graphic indicates that the graphic has been automatically "anchored" to its closest paragraph.

SIZING A GRAPHIC

The simplest way to size a graphic is by using the mouse to drag one of the selection handles. When you drag a handle on the side of the graphic, only the width of the graphic changes. When you drag a handle on the top or bottom of the graphic, only the height

Figure 11.5   **Framing the graphic**

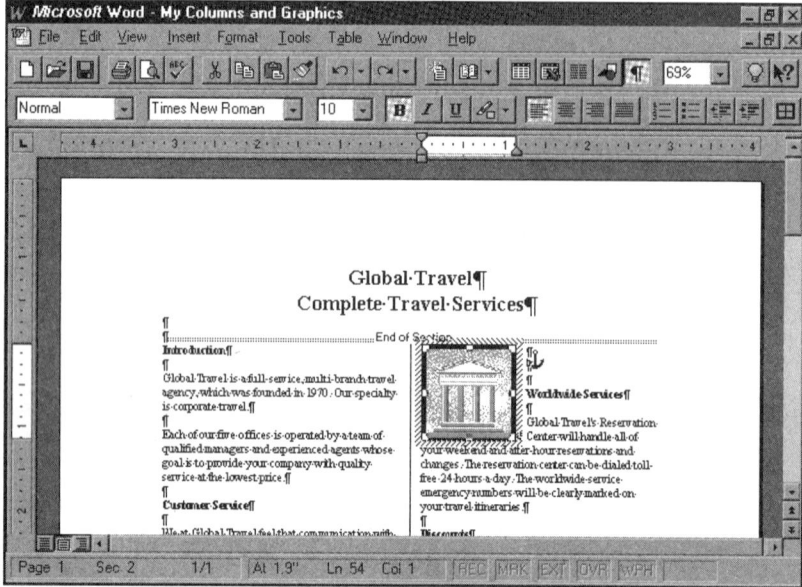

of the graphic changes. When you drag a corner handle, the width *and* height of the graphic change proportionately.

If you have sized the graphic and it appears distorted, you can restore it to its original size by choosing Format, Picture; clicking on Reset; and then clicking on OK; or you can press Ctrl and double-click on the graphic.

Let's experiment with sizing our graphic:

1. Place the mouse pointer on the selection handle in the middle of the right side of the graphic frame. The mouse pointer becomes a horizontal, two-headed arrow.

2. Press and hold the mouse button. Drag the handle rightward to the end of the *End of Section* line above it. Note that a *dotted frame* is displayed as you drag the handle.

3. Release the mouse button. The graphic is now wider (not taller). The Worldwide Services heading has been "pushed" below the graphic.

4. Place the mouse pointer on the handle in the middle of the bottom of the graphic. The pointer becomes a vertical, two-headed arrow.

5. Drag the handle down to the first line of the paragraph following the *Worldwide Services* heading. (If you need to drag below the bottom edge of the document window to reach this line, simply move the mouse pointer down into the horizontal scroll bar and wait for the screen to scroll.)

6. Release the mouse button. The graphic is taller (see Figure 11.6).

Figure 11.6   **Enlarging the graphic**

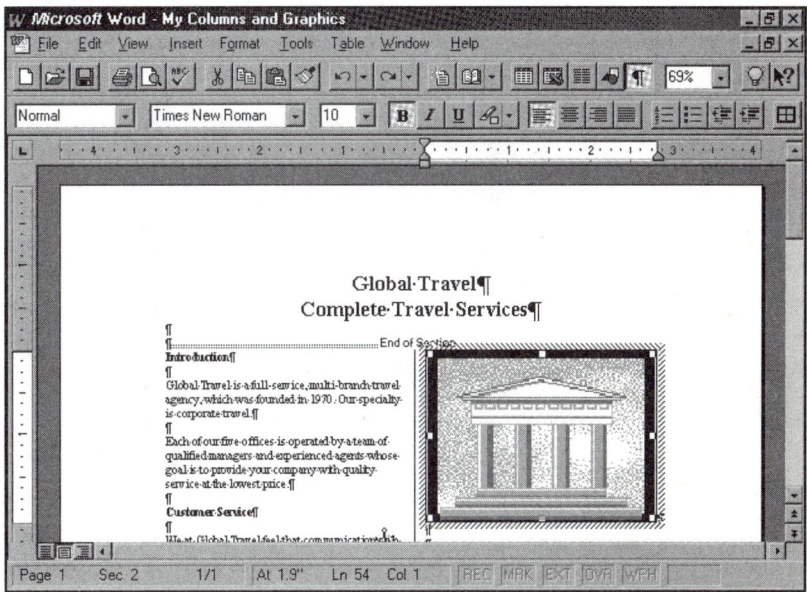

7. With the graphic still selected, choose **Format, Picture** to open the Picture dialog box. Observe the *Scaling* box. The percentages of Width and Height are not equal. Once you've used the mouse to size the graphic, its width and height may no longer be proportionate.

8. Click on **Reset** to restore the compass to its original size. Observe the Scaling box. The Width and Height are once again displayed as *100%*, meaning that the graphic's original size has been restored (see Figure 11.7).

9. Click on **OK**. The graphic is displayed at its original size.

10. With the graphic still selected,scroll, if necessary, to display the graphic and the *End of Section* line above it.

11. Place the mouse pointer on the handle in the bottom-right corner of the graphic. The mouse pointer becomes a diagonal, two-headed arrow.

12. Drag the handle down and to the right until the right border of the graphic is even with the end of the *End of Section* line above it. Release the mouse button, scroll to view the entire graphic, and compare your screen to Figure 11.8. The width and height of the graphic have changed proportionately.

Figure 11.7   **Restoring the graphic to its original size**

13. Choose **Format, Picture**. Observe the Scaling box. The Width and Height percentages are similar (to within 1%).

14. Click on **Cancel** to close the Picture dialog box.

MOVING A GRAPHIC

Suppose that you insert a graphic, and perhaps even size it, and then decide that you don't like its placement in your document. After you have inserted a graphic in your document, you do have the option of moving it.

To move a graphic:

Figure 11.8   **Resizing the graphic proportionately**

- Select the graphic.
- Point to the graphic and press and hold the mouse button.
- Drag the dotted frame to the desired location.
- Release the mouse button.

We have decided that our graphic would be more appropriate above the *Discounts* heading. Let's move it there:

1. Use the Zoom Control box in the Standard toolbar to set the magnification to **50%,** and then scroll your window until you can see the graphic and the heading *Discounts* below it. When moving large graphics, you'll find it much easier to work at a lower magnification.

2. Verify that the graphic is selected, and point to it so that the positioning pointer (a four-headed arrow) is visible.

3. Drag the graphic downward (taking care not to jiggle it to the left or right) until the bottom of its dotted frame slices right through the paragraph mark above *Discounts.* Release

the mouse button. The graphic is displayed above the *Discounts* heading (see Figure 11.9).

Figure 11.9   **Moving the graphic**

ADDING A BORDER TO A GRAPHIC

To add a border around a graphic:

- Select the graphic.

- Choose *Format, Borders and Shading* to open the Picture Borders and Shading dialog box.

- Click on the *Borders* tab, if necessary, to display the Borders settings.

- Select the desired line style from the Style list box.

- In the Presets box, click on your desired border (*None, Box,* or *Shadow*).

- Click on *OK.*

Let's add a shadow border to our graphic:

1. With the graphic selected, choose **Format, Borders and Shading** to open the Picture Borders and Shading dialog box.

2. Click on the **Borders** tab, if necessary, to display the Borders settings.

3. In the Presets box, select **Shadow** (see Figure 11.10). Observe the Border box; it shows a sample of your selected border.

Figure 11.10   **Selecting a shadow border**

4. Verify that the *3/4 pt* line is selected under Style, and click on **OK**.

5. Deselect the graphic. A shadow (slightly thicker line) is displayed at the right and bottom borders of the graphic frame. Change the magnification to **100%** to see this more clearly. Compare your screen to Figure 11.11.

Figure 11.11   **Adding a shadow border**

MODIFYING A GRAPHIC BORDER

After you have applied a border to a graphic, you can change its thickness and style (or remove it altogether).

To modify the border:

- Select the graphic.

- Choose *Format, Borders and Shading* to open the Picture Borders and Shading dialog box.

- Click on the *Borders* tab, if necessary, to display the Borders settings.

- In the Border box, click on the desired border line to select it.

- In the Style box, click on the desired style.

- To apply this same style to another border line, simply click on it (in the Border box); to apply a different style, click on the border line and then click on the desired style.

- Click on *OK*.

Let's modify our graphic's border to increase the thickness of the shadow:

1. Select the graphic.

2. Choose **Format, Borders and Shading** to open the Picture Borders and Shading dialog box.

3. In the Border box, click on the right (vertical) border line to select it. Note that the border line disappears when selected.

4. In the Style box, click on the **6 pt** line to apply a thicker line to the right border. Observe the change in the Border box.

5. In the Border box, click on the bottom border line to apply the same **6 pt** thick line to the bottom border. Compare your screen to Figure 11.12.

Figure 11.12   Modifying the shadow border

6. Click on **OK**.

7. Deselect the graphic and compare your screen to Figure 11.13. Observe the thicker frame shadow.

Now let's make a few final adjustments to our document, and then print it:

Figure 11.13   **The completed graphic border**

1. Change back to **50%** magnification.

2. If there are any blank paragraphs between the *End of Section* line and the *Worldwide Services* heading, delete them now.

3. If your graphic is no longer above the *Discounts* heading, move it there now.

4. Print Preview the completed document, shown in Figure 11.14.

5. Close Print Preview, if necessary.

6. Save the document and then close it.

Figure 11.14   **Previewing the completed My Columns and Graphics document**

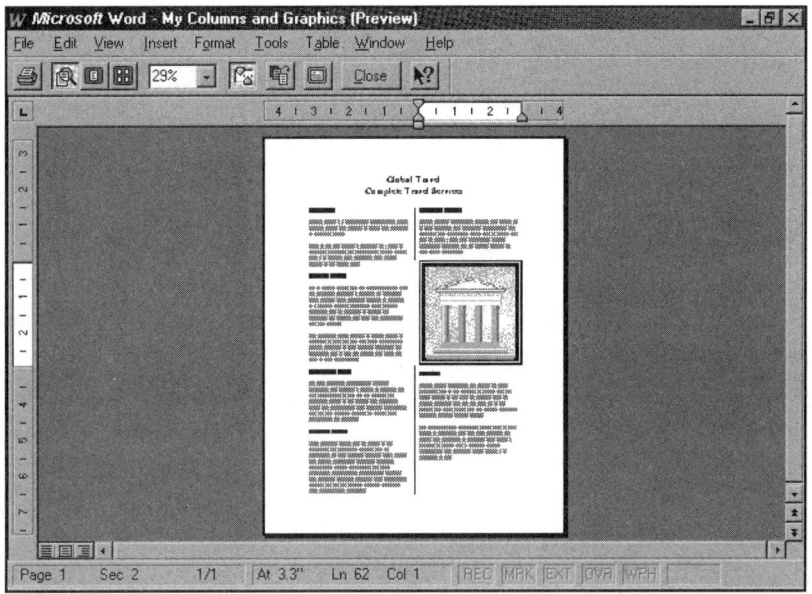

SUMMARY

In this chapter, you learned how to create newspaper-style columns of text, how to import a graphic image into your document, how to move and size the graphic, and how to change the style of its border.

Here is a quick reference guide to the Word features introduced in this chapter:

Desired Result	How to Do It
Create newspaper-style columns	Place insertion point where you want the columns to begin; choose **Format, Columns**; in Number of Columns text box, specify desired number of columns or click on desired column format under Presets; in Apply To drop-down list box, select portion of document you wish to affect; click on **OK**

Desired Result	How to Do It
Display multicolumn text	Click on **Print Preview** button or **Page Layout** button
Change space between columns	Place insertion point in section containing columns to be affected; choose **Format, Columns**; in Spacing box, type desired value, or use increment arrows; click on **OK**
Insert line between columns	Place insertion point in desired section; choose **Format, Columns**; check **Line Between**; click on **OK**
Insert graphic	Place insertion point where you want to insert graphic; choose Insert, Picture; select drive and directory where graphic is stored; select file name of desired graphic; click on **OK**
Size graphic	Select graphic; drag middle handle on left or right edge of graphic frame to affect width; drag middle handle on top or bottom edge to affect height; or drag corner handle to increase or decrease width and height proportionally
Restore graphic to its original size	Select graphic; choose **Format, Picture**; click on **Reset**; click on **OK**
Move graphic	Select graphic; drag it to desired location, using dotted rectangle as reference; release mouse button
Add graphic border	Select graphic; choose **Format, Borders and Shading**; click on **Borders** tab, if necessary; in Preset box, select desired type of border (**None, Box,** or **Shadow**); click on **OK**

Desired Result	How to Do It
Modify graphic border	Select graphic; choose **Format, Borders and Shading**; click on **Borders** tab, if necessary; in Border box, select desired border line; in Style box, click on desired style; to apply same style to another border line, click on it; to apply a different style, click on border line and then click on desired style; click on **OK**

In the next chapter, you will learn how to create form letters.

CHAPTER 12: CREATING FORM LETTERS

Components of a
Form Letter

Attaching the
Data File to the
Main Document

Generating Your
Form Letters

Sorting the
Information in a
Data File

Sorting Records
in the Main
Document

In word processing, *merging* or *mail-merge* is the process of transferring selected information from one document to another document. For example, you can write a form letter and instantly merge it with your mailing list to produce a customized letter for everyone on the mailing list. Other common mail-merge documents include mailing labels, interoffice memos, and reports.

Word's Tools, Mail Merge command enables you to take information from two documents—for example, a form letter and a list of names and addresses—and combine them into a single document. Of equal importance, perhaps, is the ability to sort the information in the mailing list, say, in alphabetical order by last name.

When you're done working through this chapter, you will know

- How to create and attach the components of form letters
- How to generate form letters
- How to sort data

COMPONENTS OF A FORM LETTER

Before using Word's Mail Merge feature, you should be familiar with three important terms that correspond to the three main components of the merge process: the main document, the data file, and the merged document.

THE MAIN DOCUMENT

The *main document* contains normal text plus *field names,* which contain the instructions for carrying out the merge. The basic information in the main document remains the same. For example, suppose a form letter of invitation were to serve as the main document. The main document would contain the invitation text and various field names that would cause Word to retrieve names and addresses from a data file (discussed after the next section). Word would then insert the names and addresses in specific places in the merged document. Before you can instruct Word to merge documents, you must have inserted field names in your main document.

FIELD NAMES

In the main document, field names are used to indicate where variable information is to be inserted. In the data file (discussed next), field names indicate the category of information in each column. The field names inserted in the main document must match the field names in the data file. You can insert field names in your main document before the data file is attached; however, then you would have to enter field names twice. Thus, it is easier to insert the field names *after* the two files have been attached (you'll learn how to attach files later in this chapter).

THE DATA FILE

The *data file* stores information to be brought into the main document. You can think of the data file as a name-and-address list from which the program gets what you want to include in the main document. However, not only can you store names and addresses in the data file, you can also use it to store sentences, whole paragraphs, as well as any text or data you expect to use repeatedly. You can set up your data file as ordinary paragraphs or as a table. In this chapter, we use a table to compile data file information. In Chapter 10, you saw how compiling data in a table is an efficient way to keep the data organized. For this reason, when you create a data file using the Mail Merge Helper dialog box, Word automatically sets up the data as a table.

The *data-file table* contains a column for each category of information, or *data field*, in the data file. The *header row* is the first row of the table; it contains field names, which indicate the type of information in each column. Except for the header row, each additional row of the table contains a set of related information, known as a *data record*. Each record includes all of the information for one person in the name-and-address list. The various types of information in each record are known as *fields*, which are the equivalent of cells in a standard table.

There are several important guidelines for naming fields in data files:

- Each field name must be unique.

- It must begin with a letter.

- It can contain up to 40 characters.

- It can contain letters, numbers, and underscore characters; however, it cannot contain spaces.

Let's open a data file with missing records and then complete it:

1. Open **Data Source**.

2. Observe the header row, the top row of the table.

3. Observe the data records, located in the rows below the header row.

4. Place the insertion point in the first field of the last row.

5. Type **Dudley** and press **Tab**.

6. Type **Long** and press **Tab**.

7. Type **Unique Rugs** and press **Tab**.

8. Type **125 North Road** and press **Enter**. Then type **Suite 3904**. Notice that you can press Enter to force information to a separate line in the record. The second line of information remains within the same record, and the insertion point remains in the same field.

PRACTICE YOUR SKILLS

1. Complete the table with the following information:

   Yuma   AZ   85365   Beijing

2. Save the disk file as **My Data Source** and compare your screen to Figure 12.1.

3. Close the document.

Figure 12.1   The completed My Data Source document

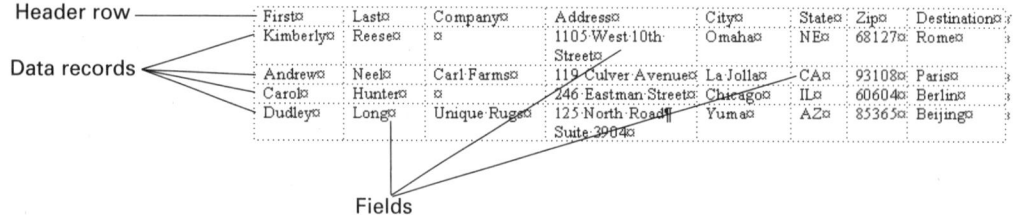

ATTACHING THE DATA FILE TO THE MAIN DOCUMENT

Attaching the data file to the main document identifies the data file as the one to be used for the variable information when the two documents are merged. Make sure that the main document is open when you attach the data file.

To attach a data file to a main document:

• Make the main document the active window.

- Choose *Tools, Mail Merge* to open the Mail Merge Helper dialog box.

- Click on *Create*, and choose the desired type of main document; for example, Form Letters.

- Click on *Active Window*.

- Click on the *Get Data* button.

- Click on *Open Data Source*.

- Specify the location and the name of the data file.

- Click on *OK*.

- Click on *Close* to close the Mail Merge Helper dialog box.

When you attach the data file, the *Mail Merge* toolbar is displayed above the ruler (see the following exercise). The Mail Merge toolbar enables you to quickly and accurately insert the field names and perform the merge.

To insert field names in the main document by using the Mail Merge toolbar:

- Place the insertion point where you want to add a field name.

- Click on the *Insert Merge Field* button.

- From the Insert Merge Field drop-down list, choose the desired field name.

Once the field name is inserted in the main document, it is enclosed by chevrons—for example, *<<First>>*, which represents the first-name field.

To enter a field name in the main document without using the Mail Merge toolbar, press Ctrl+F9 and type the field name between the braces ({ }) that appear. Be sure to use the identical field names used in the data file. If you are unsure of the field names, you can click on the Edit Data Source button in the Mail Merge toolbar to display the data file.

Let's view the main document, attach the data file, and then complete the main document:

1. Open **Main Document**. You can see that this document is a form letter.

2. Observe the field names in the document.

3. Choose **Tools, Mail Merge** to open the Mail Merge Helper dialog box. Notice that the dialog box conveniently places the three steps of the mail-merge process in a numbered list. As you can see, only the Create button is not dimmed. This tells us that we first need to create the main document. However, in this case, we want the current document to serve as our main document, so we must first instruct Word to use Main Document as the main document.

4. Click on **Create**. Notice the various choices for a main document available in the drop-down list box (see Figure 12.2).

Figure 12.2   **The Create options in the Mail Merge Helper dialog box**

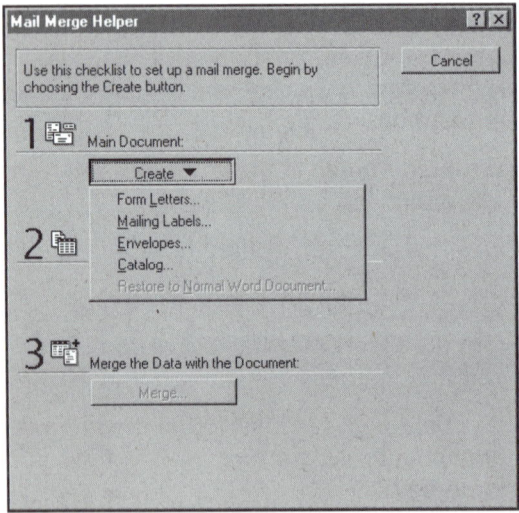

5. Choose **Form Letters**. A message box is displayed telling you that you can use the Main Document file in the active window as the main document or select another one.

6. Click on the **Active Window** button to select Main Document as the main document and return to the Mail Merge Helper dialog box. Notice that under the Create button, the selected type of merge is displayed, as well as the name and location of the main document. Next to the Create button, an Edit button has appeared, allowing you to edit data in the main document.

7. Click on the **Get Data** button, and choose **Open Data Source** from the drop-down list (see Figure 12.3). The Open Data Source dialog box is displayed, along with the contents of the Word Work folder.

Figure 12.3   **The Get Data drop-down list**

8. From the list of files, select **My Data Source**, the data file you saved earlier.

9. Click on **Open** to attach the data file to the main document and return to the Mail Merge Helper dialog box. The selected data file is now listed below the Get Data button, and next to it is displayed another Edit button, this one for editing data in the data file.

10. Click on **Close** to close the Mail Merge Helper dialog box. (Before we perform the merge, we'll insert some fields in our document.) The Mail Merge toolbar is now displayed above the ruler in the main document window (see Figure 12.4).

11. Place the insertion point on the first blank line below the *<<Company>>* field. Then click on the **Insert Merge Field** button. A drop-down list of fields is displayed (see Figure 12.5).

Figure 12.4   **The Mail Merge toolbar**

12. Choose **Address** from the list box to tell Word to place the information from the Address column of the data file in the completed form letter. The *<<Address>>* merge field is inserted in the document.

13. Press **Enter** so that three blank lines will remain between the address and the greeting.

14. Click on the **Insert Merge Field** button, and click on **City** to place the information from the City column of the data file in the completed form letter.

15. Type **,** and press the **spacebar** to place a comma and space after the city name.

PRACTICE YOUR SKILLS

1. Complete the form letter contained in the Main Document file, using Figure 12.6 as a guide. Be sure to include the *Destination* merge field at the end of the first sentence of the letter (before the period) and to insert any spaces where necessary.

2. Save the disk file as **My Main Document**.

Figure 12.5   **The Insert Merge Field drop-down list**

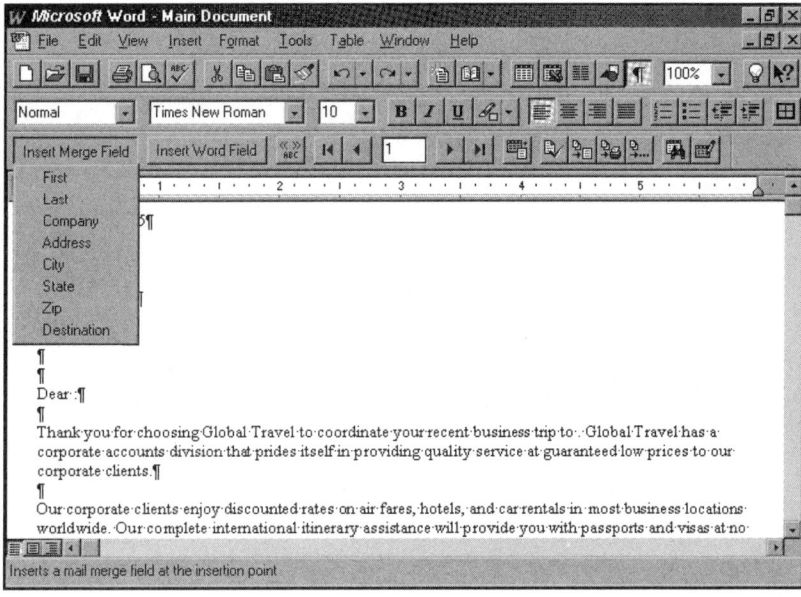

GENERATING YOUR FORM LETTERS

After you have completed and attached the data file and the main document, you can then merge the two documents. However, before you do so, you can preview your merged data in the main document window. This allows you to make any last-minute changes before committing the merge to a separate document or printing its results.

To preview the merge results, click on the View Merged Data button in the Mail Merge toolbar (see Figure 12.4). This switch is a toggle, which allows you to turn the feature on or off. With the View Merged Data feature turned on, you can

- Select specific merged records for viewing by entering a record number in the Go to Record box on the Mail Merge toolbar

- Cycle through contiguous records by using the Previous Record and Next Record buttons

- View the first or last record by clicking on the First Record or Last Record button, respectively

Figure 12.6   **The form letter with inserted fields**

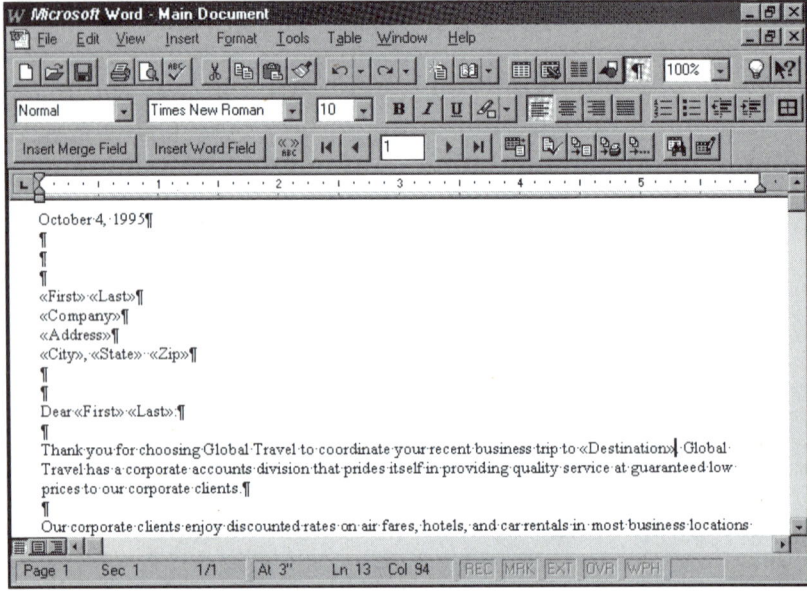

There are three ways to merge the documents in Word using the Mail Merge toolbar:

- Click on the *Merge to New Document* button to save the merged files in a single, new file.

- Click on the *Merge to Printer* button to print the resulting merged documents.

- Click on the *Mail Merge* button to specify a range of data records to be merged or to choose other options in the Merge dialog box.

When you click on the Merge to New Document button to merge documents, a new document is created with the name Form Letters1 (if the type of merge you've selected is Form Letters). If you merge another document before you exit Word, the new document's name will be Form Letters2, and so on. A form letter is created for each record in the data file. You can print all the form letters by clicking on the Merge to Printer button, or you can print individual form letters by merging the documents first using the

Merge to New Document or Mail Merge button, and then by displaying the desired merged form letter and choosing File, Print from the menu.

Note: By default, Word deletes any blank lines in the merged document that are created by empty fields in the data file. For this reason, records should not be left blank.

Let's merge the main document and the data file to create our form letters:

1. Observe the name of the current document, *My Main Document.*

2. Click on the **View Merged Data** button in the Mail Merge toolbar (see Figure 12.4). The merged data is displayed for the first record listed in the data file, that of Kimberly Reese (see Figure 12.7). Notice how the various fields have been "filled-in" with their corresponding information.

3. Click on the **Next Record** button in the Mail Merge toolbar to advance to the next record of information. Kimberly Reese's information is replaced with that of Andrew Neel.

4. This time, double-click in the **Go to Record** box to select the current record number (*2*); then type **3** and press **Enter** to advance to the third record of information contained in the data file. The data for Carol Hunter is displayed.

5. Click on the **Last Record** button in the Mail Merge toolbar to go to the last record, that of Dudley Long.

6. Click on the **First Record** button to return to Kimberly Reese's data.

7. Click on the **View Merged Data** button to turn off the feature. Notice that the button is no longer depressed. The field codes are once again displayed in the document instead of actual merged data.

8. Click on the **Merge to New Document** button in the Mail Merge toolbar. My Data Source and My Main Document are now merged. Notice that the new document is named *Form Letters1*. Each letter is placed in a separate section within the document.

9. Scroll through the document to view the three remaining form letters. Notice the section breaks inserted between

Figure 12.7   **Viewing the merged data**

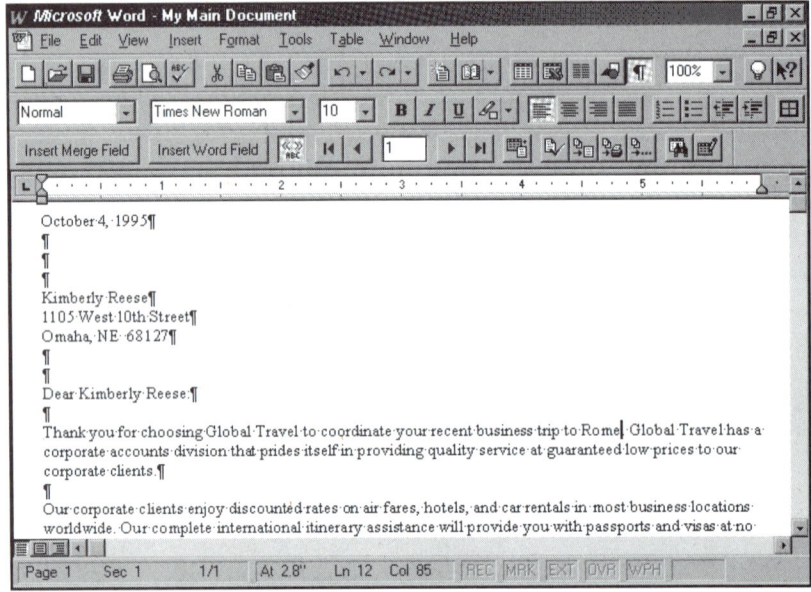

them. A letter has been created for every data record in the My Data Source file. Notice that the first and third letters do not have a company name, and the fourth letter has a two-line address.

10. Close all of the documents *without* saving them as disk files.

SORTING THE INFORMATION IN A DATA FILE

There will probably come a time when you will need to arrange a list of data, such as an address list, in alphabetical or numerical order. For example, you might want your data file records to appear in ascending alphabetical order by last name, or in descending numerical order by zip code.

You can use the Table, Sort command to sort columns of text in tables alphabetically, numerically, or by date. If you want to sort by a column other than the first one, you need to specify the column number. Columns are numbered from left to right. (For more information about tables, see Chapter 10.)

To sort data in a table:

- Select all of the text in the column that you want to sort; do not select headings or blank lines.

- Choose *Table, Sort*.

- Under Sort By, select the desired column number from the drop-down list box.

- In the Type drop-down list box, select the type of sort: *Text, Number,* or *Date.*

- Select a sort order: *Ascending* or *Descending.*

- Click on *OK.*

Note: You can select the header row of a table before performing a sort. However, if you do so, be sure to click on the *Header Row* option under *My List Has* in the Sort dialog box. If you do not select the Header Row before sorting, or if your table truly has no header row and you'd like the *entire* table sorted, the *No Header Row* option should be selected.

Let's experiment with sorting the records in a data file a couple of ways:

1. Open **Records**. Observe the second column, which contains last names. The last names are not arranged alphabetically.

2. Select all of the rows except the header row (see Figure 12.8).

Figure 12.8   **Selected records to be sorted**

First¤	Last¤	Company¤	Address¤	City¤	State¤	Zip¤	Destination¤
Kimberly¤	Reese¤	¤	1105 West 10th Street¤	Omaha¤	NE¤	68127¤	Rome¤
Andrew¤	Neel¤	Carl Farms¤	119 Culver Avenue¤	La Jolla¤	CA¤	93108¤	Paris¤
Carol¤	Hunter¤	¤	246 Eastman Street¤	Chicago¤	IL¤	60604¤	Berlin¤
Dudley¤	Long¤	Unique Rugs¤	125 North Road¶ Suite 3904¤	Yuma¤	AZ¤	85365¤	Beijing¤

3. Choose **Table, Sort** to open the Sort dialog box.

4. Under Sort By, select **Column 2** from the column-number drop-down list box to instruct Word to sort by the second column of the table.

5. In the Type drop-down list box, verify that **Text** is selected.

6. Verify that **Ascending** order is selected, in order to sort the last names from A to Z. Compare your screen to Figure 12.9.

Figure 12.9   **The specified sort criteria**

7. Click on **OK** to perform the sort.

8. Deselect the records and observe that they have been sorted, and that the last names in column 2 are listed in ascending alphabetical order (see Figure 12.10). Observe that the zip-code data is not sorted in any particular order.

Figure 12.10   **The records sorted by last name**

First¤	Last¤	Company¤	Address¤	City¤	State¤	Zip¤	Destination¤	¤
Carol¤	Hunter¤	¤	246·Eastman·Street¤	Chicago¤	IL¤	60604¤	Berlin¤	¤
Dudley¤	Long¤	Unique·Rugs¤	125·North·Road¶ Suite·3904¤	Yuma¤	AZ¤	85365¤	Beijing¤	¤
Andrew¤	Neel¤	Carl·Farms¤	119·Culver·Avenue¤	La·Jolla¤	CA¤	93108¤	Paris¤	¤
Kimberly¤	Reese¤	¤	1105·West·10th Street¤	Omaha¤	NE¤	68127¤	Rome¤	¤

9. Select all of the rows of the table except for the header row, and choose **Table, Sort** to open the Sort dialog box.

10. Under Sort by, select **Column 7,** and select **Descending** order, to sort the zip codes from 9 to 0. Notice that *Number* is already selected in the Type box; because we selected Column 7 for sorting, Word has detected that we want to sort by number.

11. Click on **OK** to perform the sort.

12. Deselect the data and observe that the zip-code data is sorted in descending numeric order (see Figure 12.11).

Figure 12.11   **The records sorted in descending order by zip code**

First¤	Last¤	Company¤	Address¤	City¤	State¤	Zip¤	Destination¤
Andrew¤	Neel¤	Carl·Farms¤	119·Culver·Avenue¤	La·Jolla¤	CA¤	93108¤	Paris¤
Dudley¤	Long¤	Unique·Rugs¤	125·North·Road¶ Suite·3904¤	Yuma¤	AZ¤	85365¤	Beijing¤
Kimberly¤	Reese¤	¤	1105·West·10th· Street¤	Omaha¤	NE¤	68127¤	Rome¤
Carol¤	Hunter¤	¤	246·Eastman·Street¤	Chicago¤	IL¤	60604¤	Berlin¤

PRACTICE YOUR SKILLS

1. Sort the records by zip code in ascending order.

2. Save the disk file as **My Records**.

3. Close the document.

SORTING RECORDS IN THE MAIN DOCUMENT

In the previous section, you learned how to sort records in a data file. However, you can also sort the records from the main document window, even after you've already attached the data file to the main document.

To sort records in the main document:

- Activate the main document window.

- Choose *Tools, Mail Merge*.

- Under step 3—Merge the Data with the Document—click on the *Query Options* button to open the Query Options dialog box.

- Display the *Sort Records* tab.

- Under Sort By, select the field you wish to sort by from the drop-down list box.

- Select the desired sort order.

- Click on *OK*.

Let's sort the records in a main document:

1. Open **New Main Document**. This is a copy of My Main Document, which we created earlier in this chapter. Notice that the Mail Merge toolbar is automatically displayed, since Word knows this is a main document.

2. Open the Mail Merge Helper dialog box (choose **Tools, Mail Merge**, or click on the **Mail Merge Helper** button on the Mail Merge toolbar). Notice that **New Main Document** is listed as the main document. The data file remains *My Data Source*. Notice the Query Options button next to the Merge button under step 3.

3. Click on the **Query Options** button to open the Query Options dialog box, and display the Sort Records tab.

4. Under Sort By, select **State** from the drop-down list, and retain the Ascending order. Compare your screen to Figure 12.12.

Figure 12.12   **Specifying sort criteria in the Query Options dialog box**

5. Click on **OK** to accept the sort criteria and return to the Mail Merge Helper dialog box. Under Options in Effect, near the bottom of the dialog box, notice the statement

   `Query Options have been set`

6. Close the Mail Merge Helper dialog box to return to the main document.

7. Preview the merge results (click on the **View Merged Data** button in the Mail Merge toolbar). Then view each record. Notice that the form letters are now displayed in ascending

order by state. Dudley Long's data is displayed first, because his address is in Arizona (see Figure 12.13).

Figure 12.13   **Previewing the results of the sort in the main document**

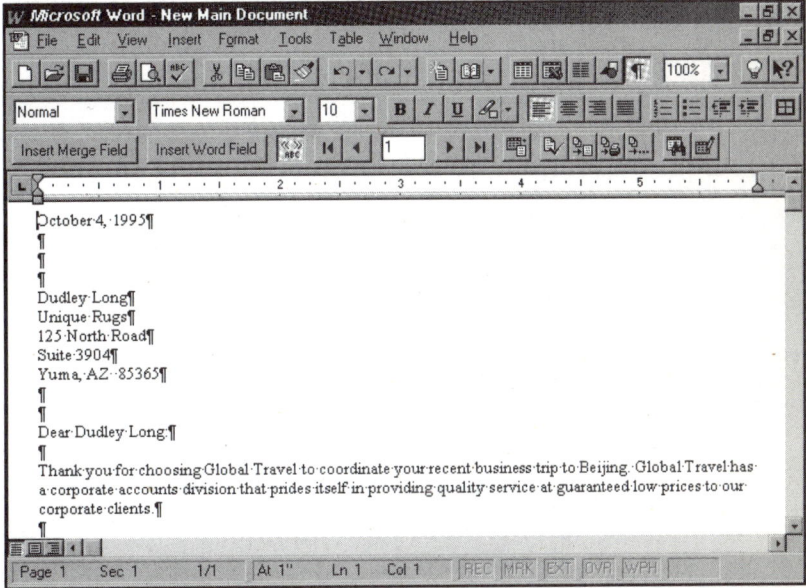

8. Close the file without saving your changes.

PRACTICE YOUR SKILLS

This exercise gives you the opportunity to practice the skills you just learned. The following instructions lead you through the steps necessary to complete and attach the components of a form letter.

Follow these steps at your computer:

1. Open **Practice 12A Data** (Chapter 2).

2. Enter the data shown in Figure 12.14 (Chapter 10, this chapter).

3. Save the disk file as **My Practice 12A Data** (Chapter 2).

4. Open the disk file **Practice 12A Main** (Chapter 2).

5. Create the form letter and attach the data file **My Practice 12A Data**. (**Hint:** When the message box is displayed, click

Figure 12.14   The completed data file

First¤	Last¤	Address¤	City¤	State¤	Zip¤	¤
Joy¤	Stevens¤	49 March Street¤	Chicago¤	IL¤	60606¤	¤
Andrew¤	Neel¤	2730 South Carl Street¤	Yuma¤	AZ¤	85365¤	¤
Patty¤	Morse¤	558 Charleston Avenue¤	New York¤	NY¤	10051¤	¤
Joe¤	Glenn¤	3948 East Avenue¤	Pittsburgh¤	PA¤	15222¤	¤
Pat¤	Fisk¤	213 Driscoll Road¤	Torrence¤	CA¤	90504¤	¤

on the **Edit Main Document** button as suggested. Word displays this message only if you haven't yet inserted field names into your main document.)

6. Enter the field names shown in Figure 12.15. (**Hint**: Use the **Insert Merge Field** button on the Mail Merge toolbar.)

Figure 12.15   The entered fields

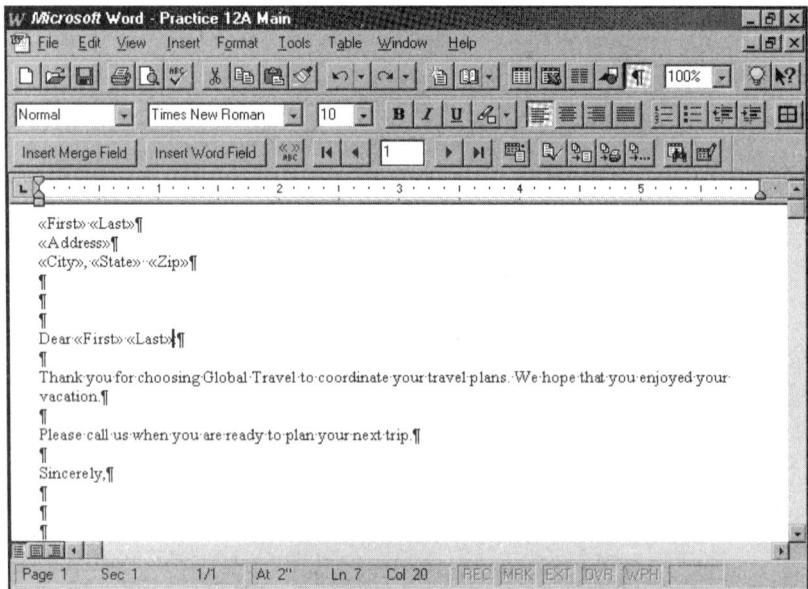

7. Save the disk file as **My Practice 12A Main** (Chapter 2).

8. Merge the files to create a new document.

9. Print the merged form letters and compare them to Figure 12.16.

Figure 12.16   The merged form letters

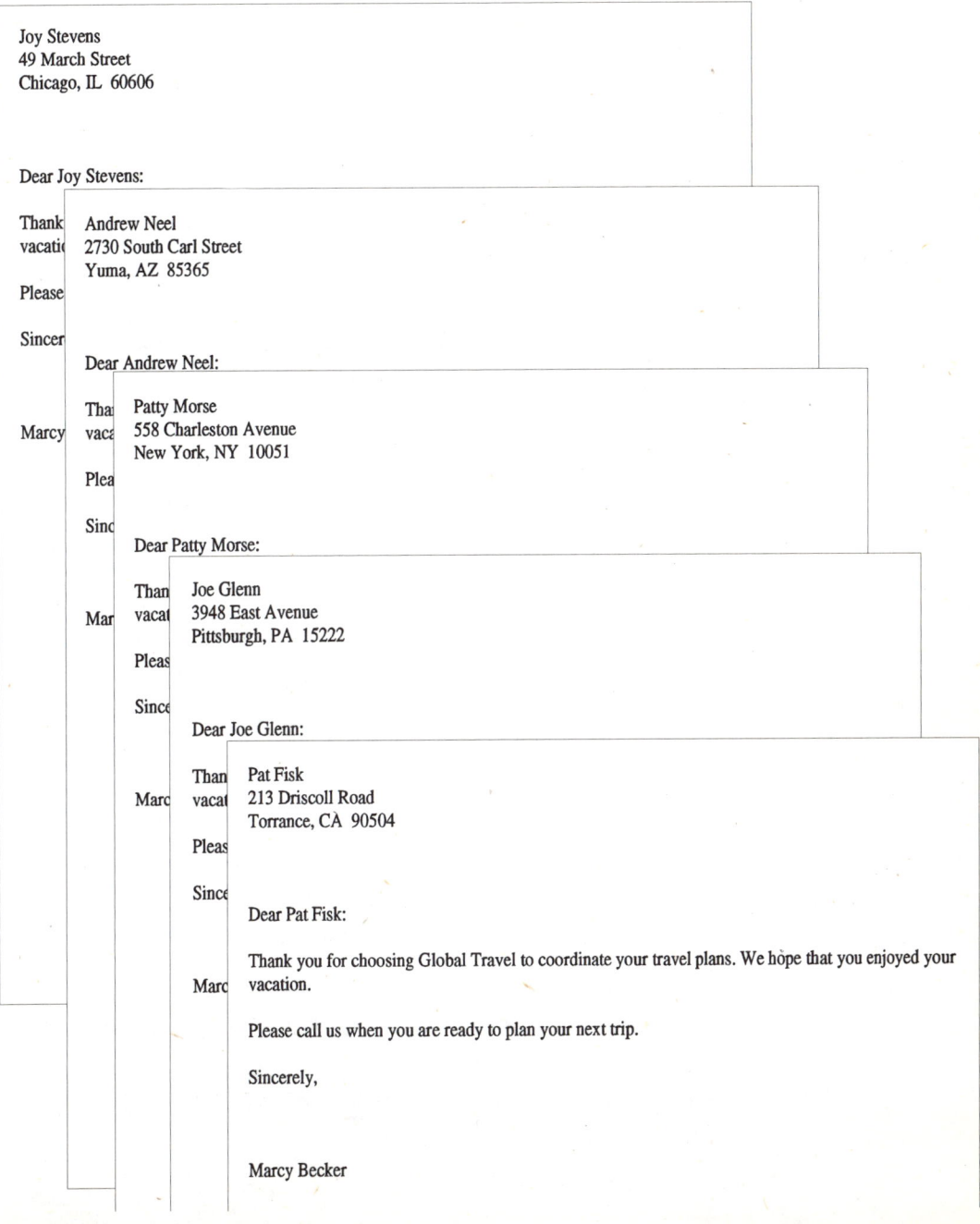

Joy Stevens
49 March Street
Chicago, IL 60606

Dear Joy Stevens:

Thank
vacati

Please

Sincer

Marcy

Andrew Neel
2730 South Carl Street
Yuma, AZ 85365

Dear Andrew Neel:

Tha
vaca

Plea

Sinc

Mar

Patty Morse
558 Charleston Avenue
New York, NY 10051

Dear Patty Morse:

Than
vaca

Pleas

Since

Mar

Joe Glenn
3948 East Avenue
Pittsburgh, PA 15222

Dear Joe Glenn:

Than
vaca

Pleas

Since

Marc

Pat Fisk
213 Driscoll Road
Torrance, CA 90504

Dear Pat Fisk:

Thank you for choosing Global Travel to coordinate your travel plans. We hope that you enjoyed your
vacation.

Please call us when you are ready to plan your next trip.

Sincerely,

Marcy Becker

10. Close all of the documents (Chapter 2) without saving them as disk files.

If you have finished the activity, you might like to try a more challenging one requiring similar skills. In this activity, you will create a data file, complete a main document, and merge the files to create form letters.

Follow these steps at your computer:

1. Open a new document (Chapter 2).

2. Create a table with six columns and four rows (Chapter 10).

3. Enter the data shown in Figure 12.17.

4. Save the disk file as **My Practice 12B Data** (Chapter 2).

5. Open the document **Practice 12B Main** (Chapter 2).

6. Attach the data file **My Practice 12B Data**.

7. In line 6, enter the following field names:
<<First>> <<Last>>

Figure 12.17   **The completed data file**

First¤	Last¤	Address¤	City¤	State¤	Zip¤	¤
Kimberly¤	Kreboplowitz¤	96 Haven Drive¤	Lee's Summit¤	MO¤	64063¤	¤
Ashweta¤	Chandrasekhar¤	318 Acapulco Trail¤	Thousand Palms¤	CA¤	92276¤	¤
Androcles¤	Threadbare¤	2350 Southern Way¤	Mesa¤	AZ¤	85210¤	¤

8. In line 8, enter the following fields:
<<City>>, <<State>>

9. Save the disk file as **Practice 12B Main** (Chapter 2).

10. Merge the files to create a new document.

11. Print the merged form letters and observe the results.

12. Close all of the documents without saving them as disk files (Chapter 2).

SUMMARY

In this chapter, you learned how to create form letters by merging the main document and the data file. You learned how to insert merge fields in a main document, and then attach the corresponding data file. You also learned how to sort a data file in alphabetical and numerical order.

Here is a quick reference guide to the Word features introduced in this chapter:

Desired Result	How to Do It
Attach data file to main document	Activate main document window; choose **Tools, Mail Merge**; click on **Create**; click on **Active Window**; click on **Get Data**; click on **Open Data Source**; select desired data file; click on **Open**
Insert field names in main document	Place insertion point in desired location; click on **Insert Merge Field** button; select desired field name
Merge documents	Attach data file; activate main document window; click on **Merge to New Document** button
Sort data in data file table	Select all data to be sorted; choose **Table, Sort**; under Sort By, select desired sort criteria; click on **OK**
Sort records in main document	Activate main document window; choose **Tools, Mail Merge**; click on **Query Options**, and display **Sort Records** tab; under Sort By, select desired sort criteria; click on **OK**

In Chapter 13, you will work with templates and styles.

CHAPTER 13:
USING TEMPLATES
AND STYLES TO
AUTOMATE YOUR
WORK

Using the Normal Template

Creating a Memo with Memo Wizard

Using Styles

Each time you instruct Word to create a document, the program does so according to a template. A *template* is a stored file that contains boilerplate text and/or special formatting information. It serves as a kind of skeleton or blueprint, providing your documents with an underlying structure. Templates also include styles, which contain special character and paragraph formats. (You were introduced to character and paragraph formats in Chapters 4 and 5, respectively.) Each style is stored under a specific name—for example, *Heading 1*.

Word comes with a number of useful templates, each designed for a specific kind of document. For example, the Normal template is used to create a standard document, while the Invoice template can be used to create a business invoice. Word also comes with several *wizards*, whch are specialized templates that walk you through the steps required to create a specific type of document. For example, the Memo Wizard leads you through the process of creating a business memo.

The primary benefit of using a template or a wizard is that all, or at least some, of the document's characteristics have been defined in advance. This enables you to create documents that have similar character and paragraph formats, as well as similar page setups, without having to specify each parameter for each document.

When you're done working through this chapter, you will know

- How to create a document using the Normal template
- How to create a document using the Memo Wizard
- How to use styles
- How to create and modify styles

USING THE NORMAL TEMPLATE

Every document that you create in Word uses a template. By default, Word uses the Normal template for each new document. You can select a different template for a new document by choosing File, New to open the New dialog box and selecting a template from the general tab.

To attach a different template to a document:

- Choose *File, Templates* to open the Templates And Add-ins dialog box.
- Click on *Attach* to open the Attach Template dialog box.
- In the File Name list box, select the desired template.
- Click on *OK* once to close the Attach Template dialog box and again to close the Templates And Add-ins dialog box.

Let's create a memo using the Normal template:

1. Choose **File, New** to open the New dialog box, and display the General tab, shown in Figure 13.1. The Blank Document template is selected by default.
2. Click on **OK**.
3. Type **Interoffice Memo** and press **Enter** twice.
4. Type **To:** and press **Tab**.
5. Type **Ruth Allen** and press **Enter**.
6. Type **From:** and press **Tab**.

Figure 13.1   **The New dialog box**

7. Type **Nancy Wright** and press **Enter**.

8. Type **Date:** and press **Tab**. We'll insert the date in the next exercise.

INSERTING THE CURRENT DATE

Rather than typing the current date in every document that you create, you can have Word enter your computer's current system date.

To insert the current date:

- Place the insertion point where you want to add the date.

- Choose *Insert, Date and Time*.

- In the Available Formats list box, select the desired format.

- Click on *OK*.

Let's insert your computer's current system date:

1. Choose **Insert, Date and Time** to open the Date And Time dialog box.

2. In the Available Formats list box, select the fourth option (see Figure 13.2), which gives the full month, followed by the

day, followed by the full year. (The date displayed is the current date.)

Figure 13.2   **Selecting a date format**

3. Click on **OK**. The system date is displayed in the document.

4. Press **Enter**.

5. Type **Subject:** and press **Tab**.

6. Type **Change in Additional Services** and press **Enter** twice.

INSERTING A FILE

In Chapter 8 you learned how to use the Copy and Paste commands to copy and move selected text from one document to another document. However, the easiest way to insert the entire contents of one document in another document is to use the Insert, File command.

To insert an entire file:

• Place the insertion point where you want the document to appear.

• Choose *Insert, File*.

• Select the desired folder, if necessary.

• Select the desired disk file.

• Click on *OK*.

Note: If you have more than one window open, remember to activate the window of the document receiving the inserted disk file before you choose Insert, File. The inserted file is always placed in the active window.

Let's insert the contents of the Memo Text A disk file in our memo:

1. Choose **Insert, File** to open the File dialog box.

2. Double-click on **Memo Text A** in the Word Work folder to place the contents of the file in the current document.

3. Verify that the insertion point is at the end of the document.

4. Press **Enter** twice.

5. Type **cc:** and press **Tab**.

6. Type **Grace Berg, Keith Donnelly**.

7. Save the disk file as **My Memo A**.

8. At the top of the document, select *Interoffice Memo,* apply the bold font style, and change the point size to **12**.

9. Select the four paragraphs beginning with *To:* and ending with *Subject:.* Then set a left-aligned tab at the 1" mark.

10. Deselect the text.

11. Select *To:* (do *not* select the entire line) and apply the bold font style.

12. Apply the bold font style to *From:, Date:,* and *Subject:.*

13. Select *Additional Services,* below the *Subject* line, and apply the bold font style. Change the point size to **11**.

14. Select the *Newsletter* heading, and apply the bold font style. Then select *Telex* and repeat the character formatting. Deselect the text, and compare your screen to Figure 13.3.

PRACTICE YOUR SKILLS

1. Apply the bold font style to the *Personal Vacations, Flight Insurance,* and *Fax* headings.

2. Print Preview the document.

3. Save the disk file and close the document.

Figure 13.3   **Formatting the memo**

CREATING A MEMO WITH MEMO WIZARD

Word's wizards provide you with a fast way to create letters, memos, newsletters, resumes, calendars, faxes, and other common types of documents. For example, earlier you learned how to create a memo using the Normal template. However, you can also create a business-style memo by using Word's Memo Wizard.

To create a document using a wizard:

- Choose *File, New.*

- Click on the tab corresponding to the type of document you wish to create.

- Select the desired wizard; for example, Memo Wizard.

- Click on *OK.*

- In the wizard dialog box, answer the question or prompt provided.

- Click on *Next* to move to the next prompt, and answer it.

- Repeat the previous step until the Next button is dimmed (meaning that you have responded to the last prompt).

- To change a setting, click on *Back* until that prompt is displayed; then change the setting.

- Click on *Finish*.

Note: If you do not wish to change any settings in the Memo Wizard dialog box, simply click on Finish when the first prompt (or any thereafter) is displayed.

Let's create a memo using the Memo Wizard:

1. Choose **File, New,** and click on the **Memos** tab. (Remember, clicking on the New button in the Standard toolbar does *not* open the New dialog box.)

2. Select **Memo Wizard** (see Figure 13.4; the files in your list box may differ from those shown). A typical memo is displayed in the Preview box.

Figure 13.4   **Choosing the Memo Wizard**

3. Click on **OK**. After some furious hard-disk activity, the first prompt in the Memo Wizard dialog box is displayed (see Figure 13.5). In the left side of the box, a preview of the

memo's current structure is displayed. Notice the first prompt:

Do you want to include a heading?

Under the Yes option, the heading box suggests *Interoffice Memo*. The heading text will be inserted as a first-page header in the memo. Click on **Next** to accept the suggested heading. (It is possible to alter the suggested heading: Simply click in the heading box, and edit the existing heading as desired. An example of why you might choose No would be that you were going to print the memo on stationery that already contains a heading.)

Figure 13.5   **The first prompt in the Memo Wizard dialog box**

4. At the prompt

   Do you want a separate page for your distribution list?

   verify that *No* is selected, and click on **Next** to accept the option and display the next prompt.

5. At the prompt

   Which items do you want to include in your memo?

   verify that *Date, To, CC, From,* and *Subject* are checked. Click on **Next**.

6. At the prompt

   ```
   Which of these items would you like?
   ```

   verify that all the options are unchecked, and click on **Next**. Two prompts are now displayed in the dialog box.

7. Under the prompt

   ```
   Which items would you like in the header
   after the first page?
   ```

   verify that *Topic* is checked and that *Interoffice Memo* is displayed in the Topic box. (This selection will actually be moot because our memo will only consist of a single page.)

8. Under the prompt

   ```
   Which items would you like in the footer for
   all of the pages?
   ```

   verify that *Confidential, Date,* and *Page Number* are checked.

9. Click on **Next** to display the next prompt:

   ```
   Which style would you like?
   ```

10. Click on **Contemporary**, and click on **Next**. The final prompt (and quite a snazzy one it is!) is displayed (see Figure 13.6):

   ```
   These are all the answers the Wizard needs
   to create your memo!
   ```

   Notice that the Next button is now dimmed.

Figure 13.6   **The final Memo Wizard prompt**

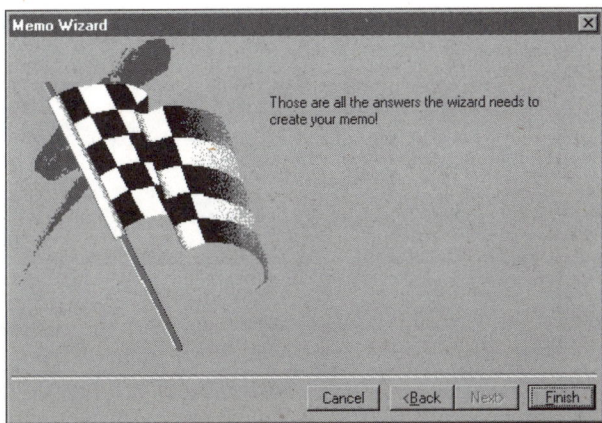

11. Click on **Finish**. After another considerable bout of hard-disk activity, the memo template is inserted in a new document in Page Layout view.

12. Scroll down in the memo, and verify that the placeholder provided for body text is selected. Then choose **Insert, File** to open the File dialog box, and double-click on **Memo Text B**. The body of the memo is inserted in the document.

13. Save the disk file as **My memo B**.

14. Move to the top of the document. Notice that the current date is displayed in the Date field, and your name is displayed in the From field. Placeholders are provided for the To, CC, and RE fields.

15. Switch to Normal view. Select the placeholder in the To field. Then type **Ruth Allen**.

16. In the CC (carbon copy) field, select the placeholder, and type **N. Boulanger, J. Coltrane, H. Gorecki, A. Berg**.

17. Select the RE placeholder, and type **Change in Additional Services**. Then compare your screen to Figure 13.7.

Figure 13.7 **The memo with completed fields**

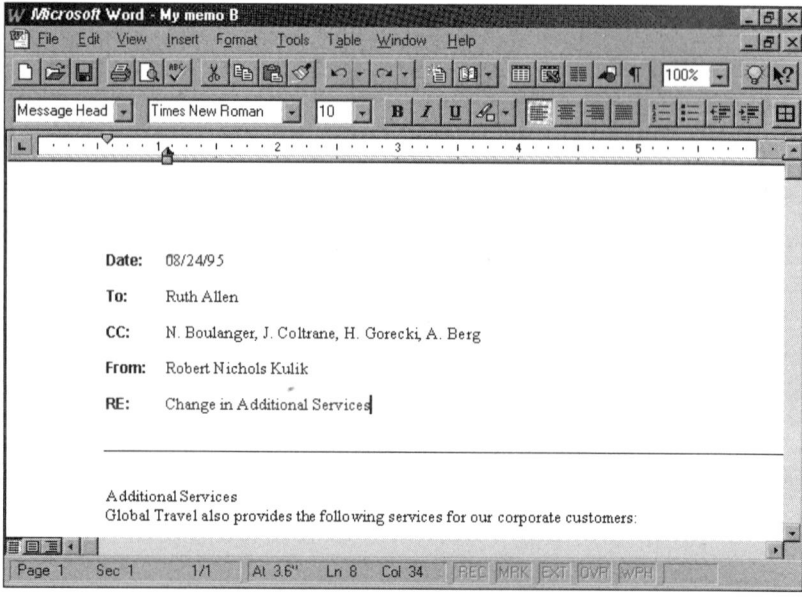

18. Save the disk file, and display the document in Page Layout view. Scroll to view the footer at the bottom of the page. Notice that it is dimmed, indicating that it can't be edited.

19. Return to Normal view.

USING STYLES

Templates contain styles, which are named sets of formatting instructions. Styles enable you to quickly and easily format the paragraphs in a document. You can use the styles included in the templates, or you can create your own.

Note: These styles differ from the ones you learned about in Chapter 4—here each style might contain a set of instructions, as opposed to a single instruction. For example, in Chapter 4 you saw how a word can have the bold font style applied to it. As it is used here, a style might refer to bold, 10 point, Times Roman, *and* underline. Furthermore, these styles are applied to whole paragraphs. All of the paragraphs using the same style will contain the same formatting.

The Style drop-down list box, at the left end of the Formatting toolbar, lists all of the styles included in the template of the current document.

To apply a style to one or more paragraphs:

- Select (or place the insertion point in) the appropriate paragraph, or, for more than one paragraph, select the paragraphs.

- Open the Style drop-down list box.

- Select the desired style.

Let's examine styles that have already been applied, and then apply some of our own:

1. Select the memo title, *interoffice memo*. Observe the Style list box (in the Formatting toolbar). The style applied to the header is named *Document Label*.

2. Observe the font and font size. The Document Label style applies the Times New Roman font and 30-point type size.

3. Place the insertion point anywhere in the name *Allen* (the last name of the addressee). Notice that the current style name applied to Allen is *Message Head*. Observe the font

style and size: The Message Head style applies the Times New Roman 10-point font to the text.

4. Place the insertion point in *Global Travel*, below *Additional Services*. Notice that the current style applied to Global Travel is *Normal*. Observe the font style and size. Because we chose the Contemporary style for our memo, the Normal style applies the Times New Roman 10-point font to the text. Had we applied another style to our memo, the body text would have been different.

5. Place the insertion point in the *Additional Services* heading.

6. Open the Style drop-down list box and select the **Heading 1** style. The Heading 1 style applies the Arial 11-point font size and bold formatting to text.

7. Place the insertion point in the *Newsletter* heading. Open the Style drop-down list box, and select the **Heading 3** style. This style makes text italic.

8. Place the insertion point in the *Telex* heading and apply the Heading 3 style to it (press **F4**). Do *not* use the Format Painter button; doing so will copy only the font formatting and not the heading style. Compare your screen to Figure 13.8.

PRACTICE YOUR SKILLS

1. Apply the Heading 3 style to the *Personal Vacations*, *Flight Insurance*, and *Fax* headings.

2. Print Preview the document.

3. Save the disk file and close the document.

 ## CREATING STYLES

You now know how to select an existing style from the Style list box. You can also create customized styles. The first step is to apply the desired formatting to text, or place the insertion point in text that already has the desired formatting applied to it. Then, either choose Format, Style from the menu or use the Style list box in the Formatting toolbar. We recommend using the Style list box, as it is simpler and faster.

To create a style based on a formatted paragraph:

Figure 13.8   **The applied heading styles**

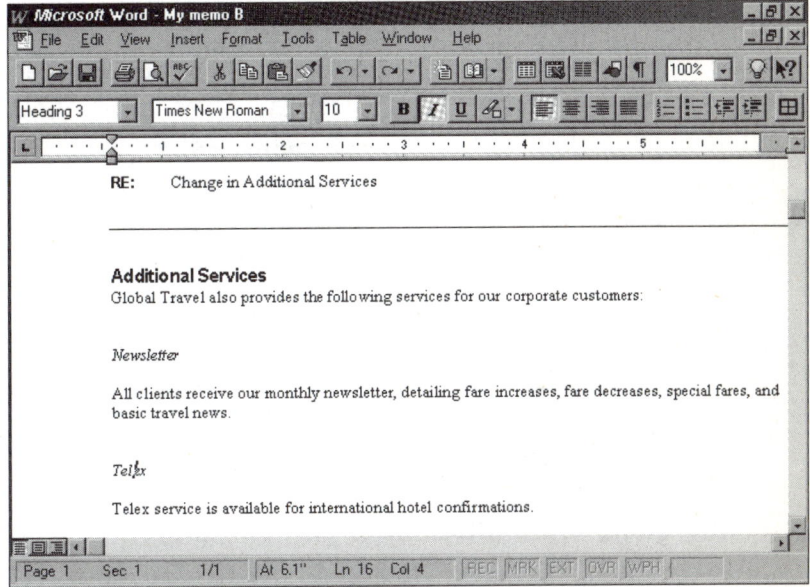

- Select the formatted paragraph.

- Select the style name in the Style list box (or press *Ctrl+Shift+S*).

- Type the new style name.

- Press *Enter*.

Style names can contain up to 253 characters, though we recommend keeping them as short as possible. They can include any combination of characters and spaces, except the backslash (\), braces ({}), and semicolon (;). Of course, style names should be as descriptive as possible, and they must be unique; you can't have two styles with the same name. However, as you saw in the previous section, styles with names such as "Heading 1," "Heading 2," and so on, are perfectly acceptable.

When you create a new style for a document, it is saved whenever you save the disk file. The styles created in a document can be used only in that document. If you create a style in a template, it can be used in any new documents that are based on that template.

Let's examine the styles in the Normal template and then create our own style:

1. Open **Styles**.

2. Select the **Introduction** heading, near the top of the document.

3. Observe the Formatting toolbar. The Normal style applies the Times New Roman font and the 10-point size to the paragraph.

4. Apply the **Heading 1** style (or any heading style that your printer can support). The Heading 1 style applies the Arial 14-point font and bold formatting to the paragraph.

5. Apply the **Heading 2** style. This style applies the Arial 12-point font, and bold and italic formatting.

6. Apply the **Heading 3** style. This style applies the Times New Roman 12-point font, and bold formatting.

7. Apply the **Normal** style.

8. Verify that the *Introduction* heading is selected (or that the insertion point is placed there).

9. Use the Formatting toolbar to change the font size to **12** and make the heading bold and italic. These formats will be used in our new style.

10. Click on **Normal** in the Style box to select it.

11. Type **Subhead** to name the new style (see Figure 13.9).

12. Press **Enter**.

13. Open the Style list box and observe the list of styles. The Subhead style is included at the bottom of the list.

14. Close the Style list box.

15. Apply the Subhead style to the *Customer Service* heading.

PRACTICE YOUR SKILLS

Apply the Subhead style to the following headings:

International Travel

Corporate Profiles

Worldwide Services

Figure 13.9   **Naming a style**

MODIFYING STYLES

Using styles to format a document is an easy way to make formatting changes. For example, if you format the Subhead style (see the previous section) to include bold and italics, and then want to remove the italic font style and add underlining, all you have to do is redefine, or modify, the style. When you modify the style, all of the paragraphs that have the Subhead style applied to them will be updated with the new formatting.

To modify a style:

- Apply the formatting changes to a paragraph containing the desired style.

- Select or place the insertion point in the paragraph.

- Choose *Format, Style*.

- Click on *Modify*.

- To modify the style's font, click on *Format*, and choose *Font*.

- Make the desired modifications in the Font dialog box.

- Click on *OK.*

- Click on *OK.*

- Click on *Apply.*

Let's modify our Subhead style:

1. Place the insertion point in the *Introduction* heading.

2. Use the Formatting toolbar to remove the italic font style and apply the underline font style.

3. Choose **Format, Style** to open the Style dialog box (see Figure 13.10). In the Styles list box, notice that the *Subhead* style is currently selected. The Paragraph Preview box displays a sample of the text. The Description box describes the characteristics of the style. Notice that the Subhead style is defined as based on the Normal style, which we indeed used to create it.

Figure 13.10   The Style dialog box

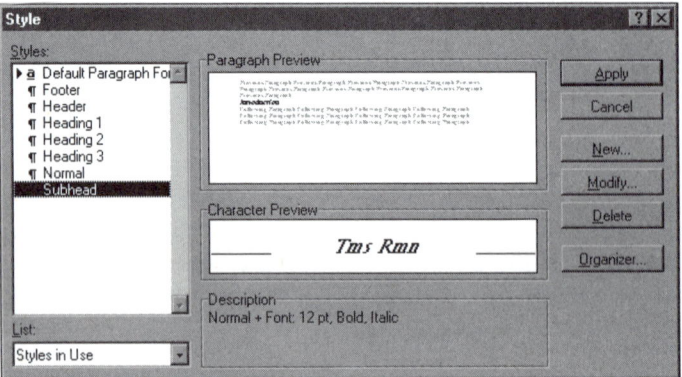

4. Click on **Modify** to open the Modify Style dialog box, and click on **Format** to open the Format drop-down menu (see Figure 13.11).

5. In the Format drop-down menu, choose **Font** to open the Font dialog box (the same one you first encountered in Chapter 4). Click on the **Font** tab, if necessary. In the Font Style list

Figure 13.11 **The Format drop-down menu in the Modify Style dialog box**

box, select **Bold** (to remove the italic formatting), and choose **Single** from the Underline drop-down list box. Notice the sample text displayed in the Preview box.

6. Click on **OK** to close the Font dialog box and return to the Modify Style dialog box.

7. Click on **OK** to return to the Style dialog box. Notice the difference in the sample text displayed in the Character Preview box. In the Description box, *Underline* replaces *Italic* (see Figure 13.12).

8. Click on **Apply** to apply the modified style. Notice that all text with the Subhead style now reflects the changes. Scroll to view all the headings. All of the headings are updated.

9. Save the disk file as **My Styles**.

10. Print the document and compare your printout to Figure 13.13.

11. Close the document.

SUMMARY

In this chapter you learned how to create documents using the templates provided with Word. You also learned how to use existing styles, as well as how to create your own styles and apply them to your documents. Finally, you learned how to modify styles.

Figure 13.12   **Previewing the modified style**

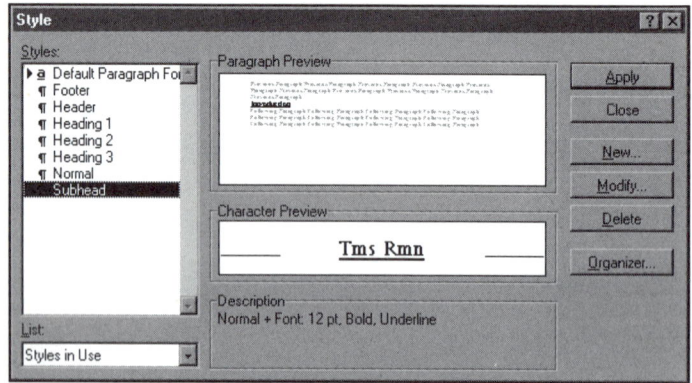

Here is a quick reference guide to the Word features introduced in this chapter:

Desired Result	How to Do It
Attach Normal template to file	Click on **New** button in Standard toolbar
Insert current date	Position insertion point where you want date to appear; choose **Insert, Date and Time;** select desired date format; click on **OK**
Insert file	Activate destination document window; place insertion point at desired destination; choose **Insert, File;** select name of file to be inserted; click on **OK**
Attach Memo Wizard to document	Choose F**ile, New;** select **Memo Wizard;** click on **OK;** answer each prompt as desired in Memo Wizard dialog box, and click on **Next;** after answering last prompt, click on **Finish**
Apply style	Place insertion point in or select desired paragraph; open Style drop-down list and select desired style

Figure 13.13   The completed MY Styles document

Global Travel
Complete Travel Services

Introduction

Global Travel is a full-service, multi-branch travel agency, which was founded in 1970. Our specialty is corporate travel.

Global Travel has five branches: Philadelphia, Pennsylvania; San Francisco, California; Chicago, Illinois; Miami, Florida; and Houston, Texas. Each of these offices is operated by a team of qualified managers and experienced agents whose goal is to provide your company with quality service at the lowest price.

Customer Service

We at Global Travel feel that communication with our corporate accounts is essential for providing good service. Each corporate account is assigned to a specific account executive. Your account executive will be available to answer any questions and provide you with any information that you request.

The corporate travel division of Global Travel is designed to offer the best and most professional service available to your business travelers. We encourage you to tour our facility and meet our staff at your convenience.

International Travel

We offer complete international itinerary assistance. We maintain a supply of passport and visa applications so that we can provide the necessary papers to our clients with minimum delay. Our International Rate Program guarantees your fast and accurate pricing, no matter how complicated the itinerary.

Corporate Profiles

Your company profile will be stored in our computer, and individual profiles will be maintained on each frequent traveler. Each profile will contain information regarding passport information, seating preference, car rental preference, frequent-flyer membership number, and corporate discount numbers. This information ensures that we can provide frequent travelers, fast, cost-effective itineraries.

Worldwide Services

Global Travel's Reservation Center will handle all of your weekend and after-hour reservations and changes. The reservation center can be dialed toll-free 24 hours a day. The worldwide service emergency numbers will be clearly marked on your travel itineraries.

Desired Result	How to Do It
Create style	Format paragraph as desired; select formatted paragraph; select style name in Style list; type new style name; press **Enter**
Modify style	Apply formatting changes to paragraph containing desired style; select paragraph; choose **Format, Style**; click on **Modify**; to modify font, click on **Format** and choose **Font**; click on **Font** tab, if necessary; make desired modifications; click on **OK**; click on **OK**; click on **Apply**

Congratulations! You have now learned how to use many of Word's features. You are now prepared to take all that you've learned and apply it to your own documents. Remember, to master the skills that you've acquired, you must supply the most important ingredient—practice. Only through practice will you be able to get beyond the techniques themselves. Good luck!

APPENDIX A: INSTALLATION

Before You Begin
Installing

Installing Word on
Your Computer

Selecting a Printer
for Use with Word

This appendix contains instructions for installing Word 7.0 for Windows on your computer and for selecting a printer for use with Word.

BEFORE YOU BEGIN INSTALLING

Please read through the following two sections before beginning the installation procedure.

PROTECTING YOUR ORIGINAL INSTALLATION DISKS

Word comes with several floppy disks that you'll need to install the program on your computer. Before you begin, you should protect your original installation disks from accidental erasure. When a disk is protected, its data can be read, but not modified.

To protect a 3 $\frac{1}{2}$-inch disk:

• Slide the plastic locking button in the corner of the disk to its uppermost position.

To protect a 5 $\frac{1}{4}$-inch disk:

• Place a write-protect tab over the notch on the edge of the disk.

REQUIRED HARD-DISK SPACE

You need to have at least 24MB (24,000,000 bytes) of free hard-disk space to install Word 7.0 for Windows. (While this is the amount required for complete installation, not the installation we will perform, we recommend this upper limit to be safe.) If you do not have this much free space, you will have to delete enough files from your hard disk to bring the total free space up to 24MB. For help in doing this, please refer to your DOS or Windows manual.

Note: Remember to back up (copy to a floppy disk) any files that you wish to preserve before deleting them from your hard disk.

INSTALLING WORD ON YOUR COMPUTER

Follow these steps to install Word 7.0 for Windows:

1. Start Windows 95. (If you have not already installed Windows 95 on your system, please do so now; for help, see your Windows 95 reference manuals.)

2. Insert the installation disk labeled **Setup** in the appropriate drive. If you are installing Word from a network, you will be prompted for the drive and folder later in the installation process.

3. In the taskbar, click on **Start**, point to **Settings**, and choose **Control Panel**.

4. Double-click on the **Add/Remove Programs** icon, and verify that the Install/Uninstall tab is active.

5. Click on the **Install** button to begin the installation.

6. Follow the on-screen instructions to complete the installation. Here are some guidelines:

   • For help understanding the contents of an installation dialog box, click on its Help button.

   • In general, accept all installation defaults (by clicking on **Continue** or **OK**).

   • When prompted to select an installation option, choose either **Typical** or **Custom** to install Word. The *Typical* option installs the basic Word setup, which will still give you access to many features. The *Custom* option allows you to install the Word components of your choice. The hard-disk space required for each component is listed next to it. **(Note:** Do not choose the Compact option, as doing so will prevent you from completing the exercises in this book!)

   • If you discover that you don't have enough free hard-disk space to install the option of your dreams, either exit the installation procedure, free up some space on your hard disk and repeat the installation, or try life without it.

7. When the installation is complete, you are returned to Windows. To start Word, click on **Start**, point to **Programs**, and click on **Microsoft Word**. If you've installed Microsoft Office, you'll need to click on **Microsoft Office** in the Program menu, and then click on **Microsoft Word**.

SELECTING A PRINTER FOR USE WITH WORD

Before you can print from Word, you must select a printer. To do so, follow these steps:

1. Start Word 7.0 for Windows.

2. Choose **File, Print** from the menu to open the Print dialog box.

3. In the Printer section, click on the **Name** drop-down list to display a list of the printers that are currently installed on your system.

4. If your printer appears on the list (you may have to scroll), select it and click on **OK**. You can now use this printer with Word.

5. If your printer does not appear on the list (even after scrolling), install the printer on your system. (For instructions, refer to your Windows documentation.) Then repeat this printer-selection procedure from step 1.

6. Click on **OK** to close the Print dialog box.

Note: The printed examples shown in this book were all printed on a PostScript laser printer. Your printouts may differ somewhat, depending on which printer you are using. Printer choice also affects how text appears on your screen. If you are using a non-PostScript printer, your screen typestyles and sizes may differ from those shown in this book's figures.

APPENDIX B: KEYSTROKE REFERENCE

Insertion Pointer Movement

Text Selection

Text Entry and Formatting

Text Editing

Font Formatting

Paragraph Formatting

File and Window Management

Miscellaneous

This appendix lists the keystrokes that you can use to issue Word commands.

INSERTION POINTER MOVEMENT

Move	Key/Key Combination
One character to left	Left Arrow
One character to right	Right Arrow
One line up	Up Arrow
One line down	Down Arrow
One word to left	Ctrl+Left Arrow
One word to right	Ctrl+Right Arrow
To end of line	End
To start of line	Home
Down one screen	PgDn
Up one screen	PgUp
To start of document	Ctrl+Home
To end of document	Ctrl+End
To any page of document	F5
Back to last insertion point location	Shift+F5

TEXT SELECTION

Select	Key/Key Combination
Left character	Shift+Left Arrow
Right character	Shift+Right Arrow
Previous line	Shift+Up Arrow
Next line	Shift+Down Arrow
Extend selection	F8

Select	Key/Key Combination
Shrink selection	Shift+F8
Vertical block	Ctrl+Shift+F8

TEXT ENTRY AND FORMATTING

Format	Key/Key Combination
Start new paragraph	Enter
Start new line	Shift+Enter
Insert hard page break	Ctrl+Enter
Insert column break	Ctrl+Shift+Enter
Insert normal hyphen	Hyphen
Insert optional hyphen	Ctrl+Hyphen
Insert hard hyphen	Ctrl+Shift+Hyphen
Insert hard space	Ctrl+Shift+Spacebar

TEXT EDITING

Edit	Key/Key Combination
Move selected text	F2
Copy selected text	Shift+F2
Delete character to right	Del
Delete character to left	Backspace
Delete word to right	Ctrl+Del
Delete word to left	Ctrl+Backspace

FONT FORMATTING

Format	Key/Key Combination
Increase point size	Ctrl+]
Decrease point size	Ctrl+[
Change point size	Ctrl+Shift+P
Change case	Shift+F3
Remove formatting	Ctrl+Spacebar
Capitalize	Ctrl+Shift+A
Capitalize (small caps)	Ctrl+Shift+K
Bold	Ctrl+B
Underline	Ctrl+U
Underline words, but not spaces	Ctrl+Shift+W
Double underline	Ctrl+Shift+D
Enlarge font	Ctrl+Shift+>
Shrink font	Ctrl+Shift+<
Change font	Ctrl+Shift+F
Hidden text	Ctrl+Shift+H
Italic	Ctrl+I
Subscript	Ctrl+Equal sign (=)
Superscript	Ctrl+Plus sign (+)

PARAGRAPH FORMATTING

Format	Key/Key Combination
Single-space lines	Ctrl+1
Double-space lines	Ctrl+2
1$\frac{1}{2}$-space lines	Ctrl+5
Center lines	Ctrl+E
Left-align lines	Ctrl+L
Right-align lines	Ctrl+R
Justify lines	Ctrl+J
Remove paragraph formatting	Ctrl+Q

FILE AND WINDOW MANAGEMENT

Format	Key/Key Combination
Save As	F12 or Alt+F2
Save	Ctrl+S
Open	Ctrl+O
Close document window	Ctrl+F4
Restore document window	Ctrl+F5
Maximize document window	Ctrl+F10
Close Word window	Alt+F4
Restore Word window	Alt+F5
Maximize Word window	Alt+F10
Next window	Ctrl+F6

Format	Key/Key Combination
Previous window	Ctrl+Shift+F6
Next pane	F6
Previous pane	Shift+F6

MISCELLANEOUS

Function	Key/Key Combination
Help	F1
Help pointer	Shift+F1
AutoText	F3
Repeat command	F4
Repeat Find/Go To	Shift+F4
Insert bookmark	Ctrl+Shift+F5
Spelling checker	F7
Thesaurus	Shift+F7
Menu	F10
Print	Ctrl+Shift+F12
Insert date field	Alt+Shift+D
Insert time field	Alt+Shift+T
Insert page number field	Alt+Shift+P
Update fields	F9

INDEX

W

Z

The Quick and Easy Way to Learn.

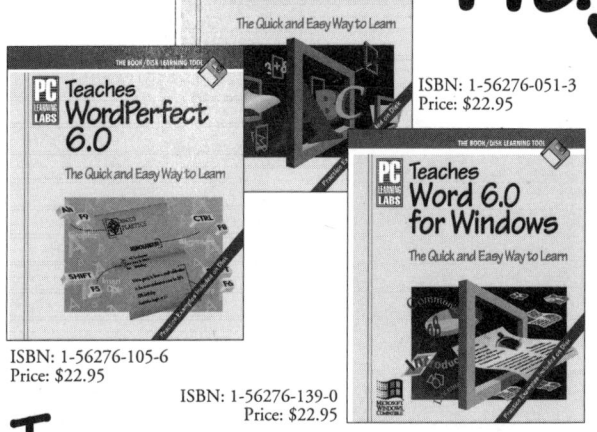

PC Teaches Windows 3.1
The Quick and Easy Way to Learn
ISBN: 1-56276-051-3
Price: $22.95

PC Teaches WordPerfect 6.0
The Quick and Easy Way to Learn
ISBN: 1-56276-105-6
Price: $22.95

PC Teaches Word 6.0 for Windows
The Quick and Easy Way to Learn
ISBN: 1-56276-139-0
Price: $22.95

We know that PC Learning Labs books are the fastest and easiest way to learn because years have been spent perfecting them. Beginners will find practice sessions that are easy to follow and reference information that is easy to find. Even the most computer-shy readers can gain confidence faster than they ever thought possible.

The time we spent designing this series translates into time saved for you. You can feel confident that the information is accurate and presented in a way that allows you to learn quickly and effectively.

ISBN: 1-56276-225-7
Price: $22.95

ISBN: 1-56276-176-5
Price: $22.95

ISBN: 1-56276-188-9
Price: $22.95

ISBN: 1-56276-272-9
Price: $22.95

ISBN: 1-56276-020-3
Price: $22.95

ISBN: 1-56276-134-X
Price: $22.95

ISBN: 1-56276-226-5
Price: $22.95

ISBN: 1-56276-141-2
Price: $22.95

ISBN: 1-56276-199-4
Price: $22.95

ISBN: 1-56276-100-5
Price: $22.95

ISBN: 1-56276-229-X
Price: $22.95

ISBN: 1-56276-253-2
Price: $22.95

Also available: Titles featuring new versions of FoxPro, 1-2-3, Ami Pro, and new applications, pending software release. Call 1-800-688-0448 for title update information.

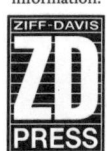

ZIFF-DAVIS ZD PRESS

Available at all fine bookstores, or by calling 1-800-688-0448, ext. 276. For Corporate/ Government programs, call (800) 488-8741 ext. 297. For Education programs, call (800) 786-6541.

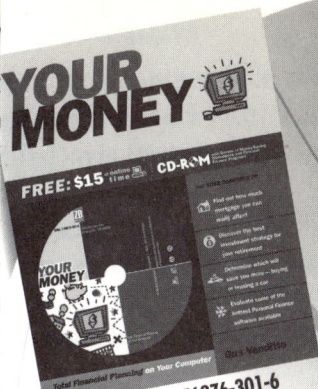

1-56276-301-6 $24.95

1-56276-307-5 ...4.95

1-56276-314-8 $24.95

-56276-326-1 $24.95

1-56276-334-2 $24.95

1-56276-327-X $24.95

1-56276-302-4 $24.95

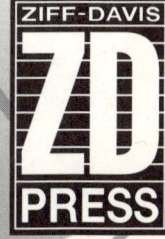

ZIFF-DAVIS
ZD
PRESS

©1995 Ziff-Davis Press

6. What is your level of experience with personal computers? With the subject of this book?

	With PCs	With subject of book
Beginner...............	☐ -1 (24)	☐ -1 (25)
Intermediate..........	☐ -2	☐ -2
Advanced.............	☐ -3	☐ -3

7. Which of the following best describes your job title?

Officer (CEO/President/VP/owner)........ ☐ -1 (26)

Director/head.......................... ☐ -2

Manager/supervisor..................... ☐ -3

Administration/staff.................... ☐ -4

Teacher/educator/trainer................ ☐ -5

Lawyer/doctor/medical professional....... ☐ -6

Engineer/technician..................... ☐ -7

Consultant............................ ☐ -8

Not employed/student/retired............ ☐ -9

Other (Please specify): _____ ☐ -0

8. What is your age?

Under 20............................... ☐ -1 (27)

21-29................................. ☐ -2

30-39................................. ☐ -3

40-49................................. ☐ -4

50-59................................. ☐ -5

60 or over............................. ☐ -6

9. Are you:

Male.................................. ☐ -1 (28)

Female................................ ☐ -2

Thank you for your assistance with this important information! Please write your address below to receive our free catalog.

Name: _____

Address: _____

City/State/Zip: _____

Fold here to mail.

03199-01-01

■ TO RECEIVE 5¼-INCH DISK(S)

The Ziff-Davis Press software contained on the $3\frac{1}{2}$-inch disk included with this book is also available in $5\frac{1}{4}$-inch format. If you would like to receive the software in the $5\frac{1}{4}$-inch format, please return the $3\frac{1}{2}$-inch disk with your name and address to:

Disk Exchange
Ziff-Davis Press
5903 Christie Avenue
Emeryville, CA 94608